ĪŚVARA PRATYABHIJÑĀ KĀRIKĀ

OF UTPALADEVA

The Muktabodha Indological Research Series

ĪŚVARA PRATYABHIJÑĀ KĀRIKĀ
OF UTPALADEVA

Verses on the Recognition of the Lord

TRANSLATION AND COMMENTARY BY
B. N. PANDIT

Edited by Lise F. Vail

Muktabodha Indological Research Institute
New Delhi

Motilal Banarsidass Publishers Pvt. Ltd.
Delhi

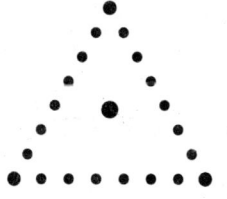

First Edition: New Delhi, 2004

Published by
Muktabodha Indological Research Institute
Sri Aurobindo Marg, M/3 Hauz Khas, New Delhi-110 016

in association with
Motilal Banarsidass Publishers Private Limited
Bungalow Road, Delhi 110 007

ISBN: 81-208-1785-0 (Cloth)
ISBN: 81-208-1786-9 (Paper)

Also available at:
MOTILAL BANARSIDASS

41 U.A. Bungalow Road, Jawahar Nagar, Delhi 110 007
8 Mahalaxmi Chamber, 22 Bhulabhai Desai Road, Mumbai 400 026
120 Royapettah High Road, Mylapore, Chennai 600 004
236, 9th Main III Block, Jayanagar, Bangalore 560 011
Sanas Plaza, 1302 Baji Rao Road, Pune 411 002
8 Camac Street, Kolkata 700 017
Ashok Rajpath, Patna 800 004
Chowk, Varanasi 221 001

Printed in India
By Jainendra Prakash Jain at Shri Jainendra Press,
A-45 Naraina, Phase-I, New Delhi 110 028

श्रीशिवार्पणमस्तु

Let this be an offering to Lord Śiva

CONTENTS

NOTE ON THE TEXT ix
FOREWORD xi
ACKNOWLEDGMENTS xv
ABBREVIATIONS xvii
INVOCATION xix

INTRODUCTION TO THE ĪŚVARA PRATYABHIJÑĀ KĀRIKĀ

Historical Context xxiii
Scriptural Tradition of Kashmir Śaivism xxvii
A Summary of the Īśvara-pratyabhijñā-kārikā . xxxviii

THE TEXT AND COMMENTARY OF THE ĪŚVARA PRATYABHIJÑĀ KĀRIKĀ

Book I: Jñānādhikāra: Divine Knowledge

Chapter 1 Introduction 5
Chapter 2 The Antagonistic View 13
Chapter 3 Refutation of Pūrva-pakṣa 27
Chapter 4 The Recollective Power 37
Chapter 5 The Cognitive Power 49
Chapter 6 The Power to Discriminate 71
Chapter 7 The Unity of the Master 81
Chapter 8 The All-Powerful Essence 93

Book II: Kriyādhikāra: Divine Creative Action

Chapter 1 The Power to Act 105
Chapter 2 Unity and Diversity 115
Chapter 3 Epistemology 121
Chapter 4 Causation 135

Book III: Āgamādhikāra: Scriptural Knowledge

Chapter 1 The Tattvas in Śaivism 155
Chapter 2 The Classification of Sentient Beings . 171

Book IV: Tattva-saṃgrahādhikāra: The Treasury of Divine Principles

Chapter 1 Conclusion 191

APPENDIX: COSMOLOGY OF KASHMIR ŚAIVISM 209
NOTES 211
GLOSSARY 219
BIBLIOGRAPHY 235
INDEX 241
NOTE ON THE MUKTABODHA INDOLOGICAL RESEARCH INSTITUTE 251

NOTE ON THE TEXT

The Sanskrit text of this edition of the *Īśvara-pratyabhijñā-kārikā* agrees with the verses in the *Īśvara-pratyabhijñā-vimarśinī* of Abhinavagupta (IPV), Kashmir Series of Texts and Studies (KSTS) vols. XXII and XXXIII, with several minor exceptions.

The verses of the *Īśvara-pratyabhijñā-kārikā* of Utpaladeva are also included in two other publications of the Kashmir Series of Texts and Studies. These are the *Īśvara-pratyabhijñā-kārikā* with *Vṛtti* of Utpaladeva (IPK) KSTS vol. XXXIV, and the *Īśvara-pratyabhijñā-vivṛti-vimarśinī* of Abhinavagupta (IPVV) KSTS vols. LX, LXII, and LXV (see bibliography for details). In addition to a few minor differences due to orthography, sandhi conventions, fallen types or printer errors, the KSTS editions of the IPK and the IPV have variation in the readings of twenty verses. Of these actual variations Dr. Pandit has agreed with the readings of the KSTS IPV in the majority of cases but has followed the readings from the KSTS IPK in four cases. In addition Dr. Pandit has used a variant reading for one verse from the KSTS IPVV. The following table lists the verses for which Dr. Pandit has used readings different from those in the KSTS IPV.

IPV verse number	Source of variant reading
1.8.9	IPVV
2.3.13	IPK
2.4.18	IPK
3.2.12	IPK
4.1.12	IPK

FOREWORD

The *Īśvara-pratyabhijñā-kārikā,* or 'Verses on the Recognition of the Lord', was composed by Utpaladeva, an influential philosopher-theologian of the Pratyabhijñā school of Śaiva thought. Written in Kashmir in the tenth century C.E., a time of intensely active theological and philosophical productivity in that region, the *Īśvara-pratyabhijñā-kārikā* is, in part, a response to the Buddhist doctrine that there is no abiding ultimate reality because of the impermanent nature of all things.

In this text, Utpaladeva responds to this doctrine of momentariness and argues cogently that there is indeed such an eternal reality he identifies as Śiva and whom he speaks of as God (*Īśvara:* the Lord). Utpaladeva knows Śiva to be pure and Absolute Consciousness that is the single, universal Self within all things. He understands Śiva to reveal himself to himself through a process of recognition *(pratyabhijñā)* of his own nature as consciousness.

Like texts from other classical philosophical schools, or *darśanas,* the *Īśvara-pratyabhijñā-kārikā* places much emphasis on the epistemological weight of *anumāna,* the logic of inference, as it goes about proving the reality of Śiva as Eternal Consciousness. Presenting his views in the form of a *kārikā,* or set of verses, Utpaladeva holds that it is through the awareness of the dynamics of one's own consciousness that one comes to recognise the abiding Self within one's experience of the otherwise constantly changing world.

This translation and commentary of the *Īśvara-pratyabhijñā-kārikā* by Dr. B. N. Pandit emerges from and is an authentic part of the Indian scholarly tradition of learned pandits. Here, the scholar understands himself to be interpreting the text at hand from within the same philosophical and theological stance as that in which the text itself stands. The approaches, assumptions, stylistic conventions, and intentions of scriptural study in the *paṇḍita* tradition sometimes differ quite markedly from those employed by scholars who are not themselves aligned with the spiritual tradition from which the texts emerge. Dr. Pandit is personally committed to the Śaiva tradition that has given rise to the texts he studies.

Consistent with the *paṇḍita* tradition in general, Dr. Pandit holds many texts in memory and offers his knowledge to individual students by means of conversation. He has honed some of his publications, such as this translation and commentary on the *Īśvara-pratyabhijñā-kārikā,* by working with his students. In such a setting, he takes relatively little recourse to dictionaries or to other scholars' interpretations of a text, but rather draws on his own experience, knowledge, and understanding of the material from within its own religious context. He recites a verse or short passage, writes a commentary on it, and then discusses both the verse and his commentary with his students, thereby sharing with them the riches and depth of his study. He does this with erudition, humour, and affection. The present volume presents an edited version of his verbal discourses on this text as given over many months of daily study with a group of Western students.

Dr. Pandit is a contemporary of the renowned traditional scholar of Kashmir Śaivism and spiritual teacher, Lakshman Joo, who conveyed his respect for Dr. Pandit by saying, 'He is not only a living authority on the Pratyabhijñā school of Kashmir Śaivism, but he is also well informed in the Spanda, Krama, and Kula schools which together with the Pratyabhijñā school comprise the whole of Kashmir Śaivism.'

By publishing Dr. Pandit's comments on Utpaladeva's *Īśvara-pratyabhijñā,* the Muktabodha Indological Research Institute continues its commitment to help preserve and make known to the larger world this mode of scriptural study and learning based on the *paṇḍita* tradition.

William K. Mahony

Professor of Religion, Davidson College
President, Muktabodha Indological Research Institute

ACKNOWLEDGMENTS

I would like to offer heartfelt thanks to the many people who helped with this publication. In particular I would like to express my deep appreciation to Dr. Lise F. Vail of Montclair State University (USA) for her thoughtful editing of the manuscript—her tireless dedication to this project has been instrumental in the shaping of the manuscript.

I wish to offer special thanks to Harry Spier who offered invaluable assistance in the preparing of the manuscript for publication: checking the Sanskrit text, assisting in copyediting and typesetting throughout and creating the index. Special thanks also to both Swami Sushilananda, who oversaw the copyediting and book production, and Theresa Norris, who designed the cover and text.

And thank you to the following people for their dedication and meticulous care in each stage of the project: Nadine Berardi, Jude Berman, Marcy Braverman, Cynthia Briggs, Dr. Douglas R. Brooks, Jennie Boyd Bull, Priscilla Campbell, Stephane Dehais, Laura Duggan, Martin Epstein, Dr. Katherine Freeman, Joan Gordon, Dr. Elizabeth Grimbergen, David Kempton, Dr. Jeffrey Lidke, Dr. William K. Mahony, Rebecca Nako, John Nemec, Dr. Paul Muller-Ortega, Carlos Pomeda, Christina Richardson, Javier Ruiz, Ron Suresha, and Erik Weibel.

Finally, I would like to thank the Muktabodha Indological Research Institute for sponsoring this project, offering its resources, and bringing this book to publication.

ABBREVIATIONS

IPK	=	*Īśvara-pratyabhijñā-kārikā*
IPV	=	*Īśvara-pratyabhijñā-vimarśinī*
IPVV	=	*Īśvara-pratyabhijñā-vivṛti-vimarśinī*
KSTS	=	Kashmir Series of Texts and Studies
MCV	=	*Mātṛkā-cakra-viveka*
MVV	=	*Mālinī-vijaya-vārtika*
SDr	=	*Śiva-dṛṣṭi*
SDVr	=	*Śiva-dṛṣṭi-vṛtti*
SvT	=	*Svacchanda-tantra*
TA	=	*Tantrāloka*
TAV	=	*Tantrāloka-viveka*
TS	=	*Tattva-saṃgraha*
YS	=	*Yoga Sūtras* of Patañjali

INVOCATION

परिचिनुत तदेनामीश्वरप्रत्यभिज्ञां
दहत हृदि निविष्टं वासनाचक्रवालं ।
ज्वलदनलशिखान्तर्लेलिहानारणेय-
स्थिरपरिचयभाक् किं सूतये बीजपुञ्जः ॥

paricinuta tadenām īśvara-pratyabhijñām
dahata hṛdi niviṣṭam vāsanā-cakra-vālam /
jvalad-anala-śikhāntar lelihānāraṇeya-
sthira-paricaya-bhāk kiṃ sūtaye bīja-puñjaḥ //

Take up the recognition of your divine essence (offered here in the *Īśvara-pratyabhijñā*) and reduce to ashes the whole circle of passions lying in your unconscious mind. Can any heap of seeds sprout while lying firmly inside an all-devouring burning fire, surrounded by the circle of its flames?

—Abhinavagupta (IPVV III.407)

INTRODUCTION TO THE ĪŚVARA PRATYABHIJÑĀ KĀRIKĀ

Historical Context

The ancient masters of Kashmir Śaivism were among the most advanced yogins of the highest calibre. These *Siddhas,* or enlightened teachers, developed a philosophy of life remarkable in both its theory and practice. The theoretical principles they developed withstood the minute tests of the subtle logic of non-existentialism and atheism that had reached its apex in Kashmir through the philosophies of the great masters of Vijñānavāda Buddhism like Dharmakīrti and Dharmottara. The subtle logic exploring the workings of the mind with regard to the finer mental consciousness (which was ignored or overlooked even by great monistic thinkers such as Śaṅkarācārya)[1] was given full scope by the ancient masters of Kashmir Śaivism, from Somānanda (ninth century C.E.) to Abhinavagupta (tenth to eleventh century C.E.). They refuted the correctness of the atheistic perspective on all points of common discussion. For this they used not only subtle logic aided by psychological observation, but also the extensive intuitive wisdom gleaned from their own spiritual experiences.

One can argue that the *Īśvara-pratyabhijñā-kārikā* is the most important philosophical work of Kashmir Śaivism. Composed by the sage Utpaladeva in the tenth century C.E., its intent was mainly to present the important principles of the monistic Śaivism of Kashmir and secondarily to discuss and refute the arguments of the antagonist theories of philosophy prevalent in that age.

The *Īśvara-pratyabhijñā-kārikā* enjoys the same position among the philosophical works on Kashmir Śaivism as is enjoyed by the *Brahma-sūtra* in Vedānta. Although not the first work on the subject, it has attained the first place in popularity. For this reason the fourteenth-century philosopher Mādhavācārya named Kashmir Śaivism the *Pratyabhijñā-darśanam,* 'The Philosophy of Self-Recognition'.

Generally speaking, one can beneficially compare and contrast it with the well-known text of Śaivism, the *Śiva-dṛṣṭi* of Somānanda, composed in the early ninth century C.E. Although presenting an all-round comparative study of the subject at hand through a highly developed method of subtle logic—silencing the arguments of the contemporary schools of thought—the *Śiva-dṛṣṭi* did not become as popular with scholars as did the *Īśvara-pratyabhijñā* of Utpaladeva. In the *Śiva-dṛṣṭi,* considerable time is spent refuting the validity of the argumentation of Vijñānavāda Buddhism that was based on minutely subtle logic and aimed to establish the principle of non-existentialism, and especially to deny the existence of *Ātman* as the basis of the flux of momentary mental consciousness. Yet, unlike the *Īśvara-pratyabhijñā-kārikā,* in the *Śiva-dṛṣṭi* just a little attention is given to a detailed presentation of the principles of Śaiva monism.

In addition, the major portion of the last chapter of the *Śiva-dṛṣṭi* is devoted to the presentation of many esoteric practices of Śaiva yoga through a mystic method and in a style such that only some expert practitioners of the methods of Trika theology can understand its worth. Scholarly readers in general, perhaps, would not take sufficient interest in its study. The *Īśvara-pratyabhijñā-kārikā,* on the other hand, provides only a few tantalizingly vague hints about the highest practices of Trika yoga, including detailed discussions of many items of philosophical theory in which common scholars have sufficient interest. These two important works on the philosophy of Kashmir Śaivism can be compared to the river Ganga flowing rapidly between the narrow Himalayan valleys and that same river flowing more slowly in the North Indian plains. While one cannot even dive into the Ganga in the mountainous area (the esoteric), the boats of philosophical discourse can traverse the river of the *Īśvara-pratyabhijñā* more easily in the plains.

Abhinavagupta composed a commentary on the *Īśvara-pratyabhijñā-kārikā* in which he says that this scripture is highly useful in testing the validity of philosophical points in several important *śāstras,* notably Mīmāṃsā, Nyāya, Vyākaraṇa, Sāṃkhya, and Āgama. It therefore provides the highest means for achieving the optimum utility from these works. As for the immense depth of the philosophical thought contained in the *Īśvara-pratyabhijñā,* he goes on to say:

> It is possible that someone may pick up enough courage to plunge into a situation even much more dangerous than the heart of a surging ocean at the time of the universal dissolution. [This ocean] has been made highly fearful by the scattered flames of that [mythical] *Aurva* fire, which has been highly amplified by fearful gales of wind. Consequently, at the time of the final dissolution, [this fiery ocean] swallows all the great mountain ranges and the whole of material existence. None other than Śiva [that is, a yogin having recognised his Śivahood] can fathom the depth of the [awe-inspiring] truth discussed in the *Īśvara-pratyabhijñā.* (IPVV III.406)

From a structural point of view, the particular merits of this work are many. It is sufficiently brief and to the point in matters of discussion about other schools of philosophy, avoiding lengthy repetitions of arguments already dealt with in other important works. Its logical discussions, too, are brief. Logic is generally dry in character, and the master avoids it except where it is essential. For instance, the *Īśvara-pratyabhijñā* does not indulge in mutual differences in the logical approaches put forth by the masters of materialistic and idealistic Buddhism, but accepts partly the view of the latter and adds just a little to point out its main lacunae. It adopts the same policy with respect to differences between Buddhist Vijñānavāda and Sāṃkhya theories about knowledge. Examining briefly some central points of the theories of some antagonistic schools, it proceeds to present extensively the basic principles of Kashmir Śaivism. Logical discussions concerning Śaivism are again present, but are presented with clarity and brevity.

Since the *Īśvara-pratyabhijñā* deals mainly with purely philosophical topics and theories, it does not present lengthy delineations of practical aspects of subjects. It deals agreeably and artistically with the *jñāna,* or knowledge, aspect of Śaivism and presents only a brief hint of its *kriyā* aspect, or practice. Most felicitously, Utpaladeva correlates many of his logical arguments with psychological findings. His presentation of philosophy is thus based on experiences attainable through both one's head and heart, a highly rich combination that is beautifully presented toward the close of his work. There, an adept aspirant's Self-realisation is metaphorically compared with the sudden recognition by a loving maiden of her loved one. She is burning in the fire of separation from him; even though he has been sitting by her side all the while, she has not yet recognised him. Utpaladeva here says that he has composed the *Īśvara-pratyabhijñā* so that all people can recognise and taste the ineffable joy of the supreme Lord, the great Lover. For all of these reasons, this scripture is rightly taken as the most valuable philosophical work on the monistic Śaivism of Kashmir.

Scriptural Tradition of Kashmir Śaivism

The Āgamas are a primary scriptural source of Kashmir Śaivism. They have been classified into three categories: the dualistic, the mono-dualistic (i.e., dualistic cum non-dualistic),[2] and the monistic Āgamas; and all of them have been recognised as authorities on Śaivism. 'Āgama' is the basic name given to the truth revealed to yogins in an intuitional manner. The transmission of such truth through long lines of descendants and disciples was given the name 'Tantra', meaning 'long extension', the word being derived from the root *tanu-vistāre*. Therefore, such scriptures are known as Āgamas as well as Tantras.

Kashmir Śaivism depends much more on another group of Āgamas known as *Trika,* 'the group of three': specifically the scriptures called (1) the *Siddha-tantra,* (2) the *Mālinī-vijayottara-tantra,* and (3) the *Vāmaka-tantra* (or the *Nāmaka-tantra*), as printed in the *Tantrāloka-viveka.*[3] These three Tantras were voluminous works composed as dialogues between Lord Śiva and Śakti. Such Āgamic works do not deal either with philosophical principles or with the doctrines of practice in a systematic way. One must search out these principles and doctrines, compile them in a proper order, and present them to seekers of Truth in a palatable manner.

Most copies of these Kashmiri Āgamas were destroyed in the fifteenth century by a Muslim fundamentalist ruler of Kashmir named Sikandar Butshikan, 'the idol-breaker'. Quotations from many of these Āgamas are available in Jayaratha's commentary on the *Tantrāloka,* but the Āgamas themselves have been lost. The pandits of Kashmir in this time of tyranny could not carry the very heavy Tantric volumes on their backs, and consequently only the

Svacchanda-tantra and the final portion of the *Mālinī-vijayottara-tantra* are available at present. In addition we have a secondary *Āgama* known as the *Netra-tantra.*

Early Works. Two works on Kashmir Śaivism of notable importance are the above-mentioned (1) the *Śiva Sūtras* of Vasugupta and (2) the *Spanda-kārikā* of Bhaṭṭa Kallaṭa. As has been said, the *Śiva Sūtras,* although a work of highly refined and artistic technique, is an Āgama and not a philosophical treatise. It deals with highly esoteric yoga practices and their results, not discussing in detail principles of philosophy through logical method. The *Spanda-kārikā* reflects the same knowledge as is dealt with in the *Śiva Sūtras,* although it is a philosophical treatise and not an Āgama. It also does not deal directly with such philosophical topics as metaphysics, ontology, and cosmology. Information about such topics of pure philosophy can be minutely searched out in it, as can also be done in the proper Āgamas, and then arranged in a philosophical format and order and expressed through logical method and style. Both works are so highly mystical in character that they cannot be used successfully as a medium in an ordinary teacher-pupil relationship. Their verbal expression, although outwardly very simplistic, suggests some of the highly esoteric principles and mysterious doctrines of Śaiva monism; they employ such a mystical method that their essence cannot be grasped easily through academic study unaided by the practice of yoga. Both the works are devoted mainly to the development of *spanda-tattva-vivikti,* a direct realisation of the divine vibratory character of divine Consciousness in one's day-to-day life activities, and thus they do not deal at length with the main theoretical principles of philosophy.

Somānanda, the fourth-degree descendant of Saṅgamāditya, was the earliest author who collected and compiled the main principles of theory and doctrines of practice of Kashmir Śaiva monism out of some extensive Āgamic texts and the two above-mentioned brief works. He composed the *Śiva-dṛṣṭi,* the first philosophical treatise on Kashmir Śaivism, which is written in a clear, logical method and style. This work deals briefly with the fundamental principles of Kashmir Śaivism in its first chapter, proceeding with an extensive presentation and refutation of the principles of some other schools of thought, such as those of the Śaktism of Bhaṭṭa Pradyumna and Śabda-brahman of Bhartṛhari. A full chapter is devoted to establishing absolute monism as the correct principle of spiritual philosophy. One lengthy chapter is devoted to the refutation of the principles of all the other schools of Indian thought prevalent in that age, some of which are now unknown. Somananda's logical discussions with the Vijñānavādins are so extensive and so tersely written that one cannot understand them correctly in the absence of an elucidative commentary. Understanding the arguments it contains also requires mastery over the *Pramāṇa-vārtika* of Dharmakīrti, whose views have been presented at length and refuted in the *Śiva-dṛṣṭi*.[4] The last chapter of the work starts with the presentation of many esoteric methods of Śaiva sādhana, yet such methods have not been fully clarified. The greatest tragedy concerning the *Śiva-dṛṣṭi* is the partial loss of a paraphrase written on it by Utpaladeva and the total loss of the *Śiva-dṛṣty-ālocana* written on it by Abhinavagupta. These limitations stand in the way of its becoming a popular textbook of Kashmir Śaivism, in spite of its being the first comprehensive logical treatise written on the subject. These lacunae were properly filled by the works of Utpaladeva, the worthy disciple of Somānanda, who succeeded him in the chain of masters of the Tryambaka school of Kashmir Śaivism.

Utpaladeva. The reign of King Lalitāditya, an eighth-century monarch of Kashmir, was the golden age in the history of the valley. The luxurious prosperity of Kashmir during his reign, his love for learning, and his respect for the learned, as well as his highly generous nature, attracted great scholars from several regions of

India to Kashmir. Two famous examples of this migration are Saṅgamāditya, the fourth-degree ancestor of Somānanda, and Atrigupta, the ancestor of Abhinavagupta. It is probable that some ancestors of Utpaladeva also migrated to Kashmir from Gujarat during this period, since Abhinavagupta, while commenting on the *Vivṛti* on the *Īśvara-pratyabhijñā,* refers to the word *lāṭa* used by Utpaladeva for his father, Udayākara (IPVV III.404). *Lāṭa* was the name given to scholars who belonged to the Gujarat area, and *lāṭī-rīti* was the name of a poetic technique popular in that region.

Utpaladeva himself does not say much about his personal history, except that he was the son of Udayākara, a *lāṭa* scholar, and that his mother's name was Vagiśvarī. In his paraphrase *(vṛtti)* on the *Śiva-dṛṣṭi,* he mentions Vibhramākara as his son and Padmānanda as his class-fellow (SDVr 2). In addition, he mentions the author of the *Śiva-dṛṣṭi* (Somānanda) as his preceptor. Pandit Madhusudan Kaul, the editor of the first edition of the *Īśvara-pratyabhijñā-kārikā,* says. that the exact name of the author may have been Utpalākara, the son of Udayākara and the father of Vibhramākara, and that, out of people's immense respect for him, he may have become known as Utpaladeva, 'the divine Utpala'.

A tradition prevalent among some old pandits of Srinagar says that Utpaladeva lived in the northern area of the city of Srinagar, on the other side of the Sarika hillock, known at present as Gotapur. It is probable that an ancestor of Abhinavagupta at some time shifted to that locality from the bank of the Vitasta River, and the locality may afterwards have become famous as Gotapur (Gupta-pura), the residence of Guptas. It is also possible that King Lalitāditya may have established Atrigupta, the ancestor of Abhinavagupta, in the same locality. There is a stream with its source in Dal Lake that still flows through Gotapur; it is a slow-moving stream, flowing toward the northwest from the corner of Dal Lake. Its bank may have been indicated by Abhinavagupta in his *Tantrāloka,* as *Vaitasta-rodhasi,* which is a term meaning 'the bank of the Vitasta'. However, the word *vitastā* (*veth* in modern Kashmiri) was used to refer to all such slow-moving streams that were fit for boating.

But neither Utpaladeva, nor anyone in his line, has said anything about his exact place of residence. He has been referred to as a *rājānaka,* a worthy Brahmin scholar who was religiously authorised to consecrate a person as king on the royal throne of Kashmir. These *rājānakas* were very often members of the council of ministers. The descendants of an influential and famous *rājānaka* were usually given such surnames in common usage. It is thus probable that Utpaladeva was a descendant of some important minister of Kashmir.

Utpaladeva's Contribution to Kashmir Śaivism. Utpaladeva is famous as the author of the important and popular philosophical treatise the *Īśvara-pratyabhijñā-kārikā*. In addition, he composed three smaller philosophical works, bound together under the common title the *Siddhitrayī,* 'The Three Indisputable Conclusions', that is, philosophical works proving the correctness of three important and powerful principles. (1) The *Ajaḍa-pramātṛ-siddhi* aims to refute the theory of non-existentialism, propounded by Vijñānavāda Buddhism, and establishes the existence of *Ātman* as the Master of the chains of the momentary flux of human mental consciousness. (2) The *Īśvara-siddhi* refutes the validity of the atheism of classical Sāṃkhya philosophy and lays emphasis on the existence of God as the guide and Master of the unconscious *mūla-prakṛti* (the cosmic material energy) in the field of its transformations, which aim at some definite results such as pleasure or physical well-being, and the spiritual liberation of beings. (3) The *Sambandha-siddhi* text explores the origin of the emergence of the principle of relativity, explaining its nature and character in all phenomenal dealings.

These books are considered three supplementary works because they deal with topics that could not be given full justice in the *Īśvara-pratyabhijñā-kārikā*. In addition, Utpaladeva composed a commentary *(vṛtti)* that is a brief paraphrase of the *Siddhitrayī* and the *Īśvara-pratyabhijñā-kārikā*. This commentary is only partly available at present. He explained his *vṛtti* on the *Īśvara-pratyabhijñā* through a detailed commentary called the *Vivṛti* or *Ṭīkā*. Although it seems to have been lost, a single manuscript of this *Vivṛti* was in the possession of the family of an employee of the Government Research Department in Srinagar. It may have been purchased by Smt. Kapila Vatsyayana for a manuscript library that was established at Delhi sometime in the 1980s, but its existence in the collection is doubtful.[5] Abhinavagupta's voluminous *Vimarśinī* commentary on this *Īśvara-pratyabhijñā-vivṛti* is available in print in three large volumes, but the loss of the original *Vivṛti,* known also as the *Ṭīkā,* stands strongly in the way of its full scholarly use.

Utpaladeva wrote a paraphrase, called simply the *Vṛtti,* on the *Śiva-dṛṣṭi* of Somānanda, but the second half of this work has been lost. Abhinavagupta had also written a detailed commentary on the *Śiva-dṛṣṭi,* which has also been lost. This is a bigger tragedy, as otherwise, that work of Somānanda would have proved to be a great storehouse of information about Kashmir Śaivism and the merits and shortcomings of all the schools of Indian philosophy. The above-mentioned *Vṛtti* of Utpaladeva helps greatly in understanding the philosophical discussions presented in the *Śiva-dṛṣṭi* in the first half of that work. Abhinavagupta quotes several passages as having been taken from the works of Utpaladeva, without mentioning the names of these works, proving that the master philosopher must have written additional works that have been lost.

Utpaladeva was not only a great philosopher, but also a master of beautiful and sweet devotional *stotra* poetry, contained in his *Śiva-stotrāvalī,* which is even now popularly sung by the pandits of Kashmir. Regarding the practical aspect of Kashmir Śaivism, Utpaladeva placed great emphasis on *bhakti,* devotional love for the Lord. The light streaming out of his lyric poetry dealing with the principles of philosophy is very often much easier to absorb than that pouring from his logical works mentioned above. Logical works have an appeal to one's mind and intellect, while such poetical utterances have a powerful effect on one's heart, and that beauty helps us greatly in our ability to digest such profound philosophical principles.

Abhinavagupta. Before introducing the text and commentary of the *Īśvara-pratyabhijñā-kārikā,* it seems important to present something of the life and works of Abhinavagupta, a brilliant scholar and saint who followed Utpaladeva in the tenth and eleventh centuries. He represents the pinnacle of the development of Kashmir Śaivism and is the most important commentator of the *Īśvara-pratyabhijñā* scripture.

Kashmir Śaivism grew to its climax in Kashmir in both theory and practice through Abhinavagupta's highly valuable literary efforts. His ancestor Atrigupta was invited to live in Kashmir by the brave and generous monarch Lalitāditya sometime in the eighth century. A feudal administrative chief governing an area of about one hundred villages was designated as a *goptā* in ancient India. Some ancient ancestor of Atrigupta may have been such an efficient and influential *goptā* that the common people gave all the members of his family the surname *Goptā.* The word may have later been abbreviated as *Gupta.* The great scholar Atrigupta was such a Gupta. Considered a *'Prāgrya-janma'*, a person born in the highest caste, he was definitely a Brahmin and not a Vaiśya (businessman), as they are called at present. Similarly, Cāṇakya, the Brahmin administrator of the great Mauryan empire and the author of Kauṭilya's *Artha-śāstra,* was called Viṣṇugupta; and Brahmagupta, the great astronomer, was also a Gupta Brahmin. It is highly probable that Vasugupta, the discoverer of the *Śiva Sūtras,* was a descendant of Atrigupta, as was Lakṣmaṇagupta, a teacher of Abhinavagupta. Narasiṃhagupta and Varāhagupta were the immediate ancestors of Abhinavagupta. The name of his mother was Vimalakalā, and he had a younger brother named Manorathagupta. Abhinavagupta did not have a wife or children, but lived in his home with family members. He did not become a wandering monk, nor did any of his predecessors in the line; all were householders living with their families.

Abhinavagupta was a perfect master of all the schools of philosophy and other subjects of study prevalent in his time. The traditional study of his works has continued through the centuries in Kashmir up to the present exodus of pandits from the valley because of political difficulties. Abhinavagupta is the most important among the ancient masters of monistic Śaivism of the Tryambaka school and the Trika system of theology prominent within it. He learned the exact essence of the practical doctrines of both the Trika and Kaula systems of theological practice from the great master Śambhunātha, alias Siddhanātha, the presiding preceptor at the Ardha-tryambaka school that flourished at that time at Kangara in Himachal Pradesh. He explained and commented upon the philosophical works composed by Somānanda and Utpaladeva. His most important work in this field is his *Īśvara-pratyabhijñā-vimarśinī,* a commentary on the *Īśvara-pratyabhijñā-kārikā*. This work has the same importance in Śaivism as the *Śaṅkara-bhāṣya* has in Vedānta, the *Śābara-bhāṣya* in Mīmāṃsā, and the *Mahābhāṣya* of Patañjali in Sanskrit grammar. Abhinavagupta also wrote commentaries on the *Śiva-dṛṣṭi* and the *Siddhitrayī,* but these works have unfortunately been lost. His detailed commentary on the *Vivṛti* of Utpaladeva (on his own *Īśvara-pratyabhijñā*) is available in three volumes, though the *Vivṛti* is not available.

Regarding the practical sādhana of the Trika system of Kashmir Śaivism, he collected the essences of all the available scriptures, arranged them in proper order, and expressed them in detail in his voluminous *Tantrāloka,* a treatise on theological practice whose greatness can have no comparison in this world. It starts with the fundamental philosophical principles of Kashmir Śaivism, explains the different methods of Śaiva yoga as contained in the scriptural works of the Trika system, and commences to throw light upon the methods of practical theology and elaborate ritual of this system, all in great detail. One of the chapters of the *Tantrāloka* is devoted to the presentation of the secret practices of the Kaula system, employing a mystic method of expression. Abhinavagupta's *Tantrasāra* is simply a prose summary of his *Tantrāloka*.

The *Mālinī-vijayottara-tantra* is said to be the most important scriptural work on practical sādhana of the Trika system. Abhinavagupta wrote a voluminous work on the practical and theoretical teachings contained in this Tantra, under the title, the *Mālinī-vijaya-vārtika*. *Mālinī* is the name given to one of the highest esoteric topics in the practical aspect of Śaiva monism, and its essence has been explained at length in his *Vivaraṇa* on the *Parātrīśikā* (incorrectly known as the *Parātriṃśikā*). He wrote several smaller works for the benefit of beginners in the study of Kashmir Śaivism; the most important among them are the *Bodha-pañcadaśikā*, the *Anuttarāṣṭikā*, and the *Paramārthasāra*.

Like Utpaladeva, Abhinavagupta was also a poet of high merit and composed several sweet hymns to Lord Śiva and the Mother-goddess Śakti. Some of his hymns are sung popularly by the pandits of Kashmir even today. He was a master of fine arts and artistic literature. He wrote a work of unique worth on dramaturgy *(Nāṭya-śāstra)* under the title *Abhinava-bhāratī*. His *Locana* commentary on the *Dhvanyāloka* of Anandavardhana is still being studied in Sanskrit institutes of learning.

Abhinavagupta is the final authority on the interpretation of both the theory and practice of Kashmir Śaivism. Having digested well the correct knowledge of the highly esoteric topics of the Trika and Kaula systems of practical Śaivism that he learned at the feet of the great master Śambhunātha of the Ardha-tryambaka school at the *Jālandhara-pītha* (present day Kāngra) in Himachal Pradesh, he carried the monistic Śaivism of Kashmir to the climax of its academic development.

The highly fruitful ability to accomplish such a task requires several essential mental qualities and practical abilities. These include: (1) a direct intuitional experience of the exact truth about the Self and non-Self; (2) a particularly sharp intelligence to impress this truth on one's understanding; (3) an ability to conceptualise such truth correctly; (4) a marvellous ability to express such truth to others; (5) a deep study of all the concerned scriptural works; (6) a correct understanding of the principles of other schools of thought; and (7) a highly developed, rich language to be used for the correct and appropriate expression of this truth realised through intuition.

Kashmir Śaivism has been highly fortunate to have a chain of such scholar-saints who possessed the above-mentioned seven qualities required for its correct academic development. All the ancient masters, from Bhaṭṭa Kallaṭa to Abhinavagupta, possessed the first six qualities of a true philosopher; and the Sanskrit language in their hands served as the seventh essential requirement mentioned above, because it is particularly well-suited to express the most subtle principles and doctrines of the profound philosophy of Śaivism. It was because of this richness of the Sanskrit language that the great Buddhist philosophers, who had been utilizing Pali and Prakrit (as did the Buddha and his immediate followers), began to compose in Sanskrit by the first century B.C.E. Abhinavagupta, having devoted all his marvellous qualities to the academic development of Kashmir Śaivism, carried it to its climax.

Someone might ask why it is that Kashmir Śaivism, being among the finest (and perhaps constituting the very finest) of all the schools of Indian philosophy, did not spread outside of the valley of Kashmir and did not attain a popular position in any of the other important Indian centres of learning, such as Varanasi, Sringeri, Kanchi or Vijayanagaram. This has not been the case with other subjects of study, such as the grammatical work of Kaiyaṭa and works on literary criticism and dramaturgy by masters such as Anandavardhana, Mammaṭa, and Abhinavagupta. Although such a question must be addressed by historians as well as philosopher-theologians, an appropriate spiritual answer to this query has already been suggested by Abhinavagupta in his *Tantrāloka*. He says:

केतकीकुसुमसौरभे भृशं
भृन्ऽग एव रसिको न मक्षिका ।
भैरवीयपरमाद्वयार्चने
कोऽपि रज्यति महेशचोदितः ॥

Ketakī-kusuma-saurabhe bhṛśaṃ
Bhṛn 'ga eva rasiko na makṣikā /
Bhairavīya-paramādvayārcane
Ko 'pi rajyati maheśa-coditaḥ //

A black bee alone becomes intensely fond of the sweet fragrance of the *ketaki* flower *(kevra* or *pandanus),* but not the honeybee; only some exceptional aspirant, having been set in such motion by Almighty God (through the bestowal of His highly powerful grace), develops interest in the utterly non-dualistic worship of His all-inclusive aspect, known as Bhairavahood. (TA IV.276)

A Summary of the Īśvara-pratyabhijñā-kārikā

The Īśvara-pratyabhijñā-kārikā of Utpaladeva is written in couplets of *kārikā* style. Abhinavagupta referred to such couplets as *sūtras,* a highly condensed form of expression extensively delineating a topic. The author has analysed the work into four books, called *adhikāras*. The first one, the *Jñānādhikāra,* deals with the nature of Consciousness. It has been analysed further by Abhinavagupta into eight chapters called *āhnikas,* or daily lessons. The second book, dealing with the nature and the results of the divine creative aspect of the Absolute Consciousness, is called the *Kriyādhikāra*. It is subdivided in the *Vimarśinī* commentary into four *āhnikas*. The third book, named the *Āgamādhikāra,* deals with scriptural knowledge. It is subdivided in the commentary into two chapters. The fourth and concluding book is called the *Tattva-saṃgrahādhikāra,* and aims to recapitulate briefly the main principles. It is also a complementary part of the work, concerned with the topics not covered by the previous three books. It contains only one chapter, although in the *Vivṛti-vimarśinī* it has been analysed in two chapters. The paraphrase or commentary *(Vṛtti)* written by Utpaladeva on the work is available only up to the seventh couplet of *āhnika* two of the third book and, as already noted, his *Vivṛti* is, so far, not available at all.

Book I: Jñānādhikāra. The first chapter of the *Jñānādhikāra,* the introductory chapter of the *Īśvara-pratyabhijñā,* begins with a salutation to Lord Śiva. It suggests the fundamental principles of metaphysics and ontology of Kashmir Śaivism, then moves ahead to lay logical emphasis on the ever-evident existence of *Ātman,* the real

Self of each and every being. This Self shines as pure I-Consciousness and serves as the Master of the flux of the conscious mind while lying beyond it as its essential base. Hinting thus at the incorrectness of the non-existential views of Vijñānavāda Buddhism, it proceeds to emphasise the powers of knowing and doing, considered part of the very essential character of *Ātman*.

The third couplet of the chapter mentions the effect of delusions that do not allow a person to realise the correct character of his real Self, and it introduces the topic of Self-recognition to be attained by the aspirant, considering this to be the main purpose of the work at hand. The next two couplets refer to the powers of knowing and doing that belong to each and every being. They serve as proofs of the existence of *Ātman,* the real Self of every being, the One who shines as I-Consciousness and witnesses all the activities of the flux of a person's mental consciousness.

The second chapter outlines the antagonistic theory proposed by the Vijñānavāda Buddhists concerning the subject of *Ātman* and its existence. Utpaladeva presents these theories in order to eventually refute them. He begins by presenting the objections raised by the Vijñānavādins against the principle of the existence of *Ātman* as the director and controller of the momentary flux of human mental consciousness, and then proceeds to disprove them. The Vijñānavādins argue that the feeling of I-ness relates, in fact, either to the flux of the physical body or to that of mind, and that it does not, therefore, refer to anything beyond mind called *Ātman*. Likewise, they claim that the phenomenon of recollection or memory, being explainable on the basis of faulty mental impressions alone, is of no avail in inferring the existence of *Ātman*. Such an *Ātman,* they say, would be no more substantial than ether. Śaiva scriptural thinkers, by contrast, argue that the ever-existent *Ātman* bears the impressions of previous experiential knowledge, and thus it becomes capable of recollecting the objects known previously.[6] For the Vijñānavādin, the phenomenon of action is merely the sequential position of closely following different active entities and is nothing substantial that can be utilised as a ground for proving the existence of *Ātman*. They mention several additional objections against the proposed character of the Self as it has been depicted by Hindu scriptural thinkers. The Buddhists claim, therefore, that all of these elements are utterly useless in proving the existence of *Ātman*. The very existence of *Ātman* as the Master of knowing and doing is thus brought into question.

Chapter 3 of Book I aims to establish the existence of *Ātman* as the basis of memory. Utpaladeva refutes the complicated arguments put forth by Vijñānavādins to prove that the momentary flickers of mental consciousness alone are sufficient to explain the activities of knowing, recollecting, and so forth.

The Vijñānavādins believed that no physical phenomena exist in reality; these are just the manifestations of one's mental ideas that appear (wrongly) as outwardly existent phenomena, just as in a dream world. Yet even the mind is not accepted as a permanently existent entity; it is just a constantly moving flux of momentary mental awareness. This is like the brilliant flickers of a burning lamp, all of which are momentary in character and are collectively and erroneously taken as one single shining light although they are accountably many in number, following one another and becoming extinct in the next moment.

Utpaladeva utilises subtle logical arguments aimed at establishing the existence of *Ātman* as the basic recollector. He forcefully attacks the Vijñānavāda perspective that both ideation (thought, conceptualisation) and recollection (memory) are mistaken cognitions. He establishes the eternal existence of *Ātman* as the real Master of perception, conception, ideation, and recollection through a subtler logical argumentation, and his perspective is aided with evidence provided by psychology and illustrations of common experiences in mundane life. For instance, he says that although memory results from the waking up of impressions of past experience, by itself it cannot take up any previous experiential knowledge as its object. Thus, memory cannot throw any light on past experience or its objects because, as has been accepted by all the main schools of Indian philosophy, each act of knowing is self-evident and self-luminous. No knowledge can be taken as an object by any other form of knowledge, although objects known can be assumed and known by another. Knowing is subjective, never objective, since it is self-luminous. Memory is only possible, therefore, if the underlying source or controlling authority is the self-luminous *Ātman* and not the dependent mind or mental flux. Utpaladeva does agree with the Buddhists' theory of the non-existence of material phenomena lying outside the field of Consciousness, but not with their theory of the non-existence of the knowing Subject who directs and controls the flux of mental activity.

Ātman is the necessary foundation on which all such mental activities rest. The existence of the single universal Subject, the Supreme Self, appearing as all subjective and objective phenomena in the universe, is emphatically stated toward the close of the chapter. The systematic flow of mundane transactions, based on mutual understandings between human beings' thought processes, would abruptly come to an end if the eternal existence of a single Master were not accepted. It is He who contains in Himself all the vividly different mental phenomena and who Himself consists of pure Consciousness, able to appear as He wills. *Ātman* processes His own divine power of perception, recollection, ideation, and so on. He runs the whole orderly universe without engendering any chaos.

The fourth chapter of Book I is meant to justify further the existence of *Ātman* as the real recollector of previously known objects, remembering them in various ways and analysing and synthesising their data quite independently, in accordance with objectives of various types, at His free will. All such principles are discussed through a highly refined and subtle logical method.

Ātman, the Master of both perception and recollection, continues to exist throughout the whole span of time in between these two mental activities. He continues to bear the impressions of the past experiences, their objective data, circumstances, aims, objects, and so on, throughout the whole span of time. Besides that, He is independent and free to analyse and/or synthesise the data of His previous experiences and to recollect them wholly or only partly, in accordance with His present situation. The author proves that various types of both subjective and objective manifestations are nothing other than different forms of the single infinite I-Consciousness, the *Ātman* praised in various scriptural schools of Indian philosophy.

The fifth chapter of Book I aims to establish that *jñāna-śakti,* the power of gnosis, belongs to *Ātman*; it throws light on the character of the special type of spiritual realism maintained in Kashmir Śaivism. Śaivism agrees partly with Vijñānavāda in refuting the existence of any objective phenomena lying outside subjective gnostic reality. Therefore, Utpaladeva expresses and subsequently refutes the arguments of the Sautrāntika school of Buddhism, which is in favour of the real existence of objective phenomena outside the subjective reality. Actual illustrations of phenomena lying outside the field of Consciousness can never be proved through any type of inference.

The Vijñānavāda theory of the awakening of impressions in various ways has been expressed and accepted, but any effort to explain the basis of this variety has been shown by the Śaiva philosopher to be absolutely unsatisfactory in the absence of *Ātman* as the Master who analyses and synthesises the data of the past experiences.

The theory of spiritual realism, maintaining the real existence of everything appearing as phenomenal existence inside the *Ātman* in the forms of His divine power, has been established in the chapter. Just as the many utilitarian qualities of electricity are accepted today to be existent in electric power in an unmanifest form, so the whole universe exists basically in pure and infinite Consciousness in the form of its latent divine powers. The divine will of Consciousness manifests all phenomena outwardly as both unconscious matter and finite conscious beings, living in unconscious bodies. Just as a poet's entire poetic creation basically exists inside his poetic talent, so all phenomena lie in the Absolute in the form of His divine potency. When these phenomena manifest, we have world creation.

This chapter points out that Absolute Consciousness is ever aware of itself, its nature, and its activities, even at the level of the initial stir of a perception. Such realisation within the individual requires a highly refined introspective vigilance that can be developed through the practice of Śaiva yoga. Consciousness is fully aware of the phenomenal existence lying in it in the form of its divine potency. Awareness is the essential character of Consciousness, the essence of pure Consciousness. Ancient thinkers named it *citi* (pure Consciousness), *parāvāk* (absolute speech), *svātantrya* (absolute independence or Self-dependence), and *aiśvarya* (lordship, divine essence). It has also been called *sphurattā* (spiritual throbbing) and *mahāsattā* (absolute existence), shining beyond the limitations of time and space, and also the essence as well as the heart of the Absolute Master.

The principle of the outward vibration of the inwardly existent universe in *Ātman* is established in this chapter in detail, although without the use of the term *spanda*. The fundamental principle of the objective manifestation of all objects in the world, existing as one with the universal Subject and appearing as different from finite subjects, has been discussed at length. This is the principle of cosmogony as constructed and maintained in Kashmir Śaivism. The absolute monism of this philosophy is also established in chapter 5. The creative nature of absolute Reality, called *spanda* in other works, is explained clearly, using the terms *sphurattā* and *mahāsattā*. This divine vibration is established as the basic cause of the creation of the universe, which appears in multifarious types of subjective and objective phenomena. Herein is the fundamental principle of the absolute independence, or Self-dependence, of the Lord, established in the monistic Śaivism of Kashmir. This philosophical school of Kashmir Śaivism has evolved to express the theism and monism of the one supreme Absolute, divine Consciousness.

The sixth chapter of Book I aims to explain the essential character of ideation and the manner in which it is manifested by the Lord, who shines beyond its reach. Mental ideation is shown to be erroneous in character, since it is based on different degrees of oblivion created by the independent universal Self, through His divine creative power. All types of mundane self-awareness lie in this plane of manifest ideas, including human self-consciousness with respect to unconscious entities such as the physical form, the sense of understanding, sense of being alive, breathing, and awareness of the void. Also included are any concepts of unity or relation between some present and past remembered objects.

However, a person's self-awareness—manifesting as simple 'I', not mixed up with the body, mind, life-force, and so on—cannot be taken as an idea, because although it involves the use of speech, no mental decision is made in favour of the acceptance of only one pair of name-and-form with respect to an object of knowledge. Acceptance of such a special pair of name and form, after the rejection of all other such possible pairs, is the key point in the definition of an ideation (and it is on such account termed *apoha,* or avoidance of other options, in Vijñānavāda).

The principle of spiritual realism, as taught in the Śaivite scriptures, is thus established here again. It includes the eternal existence of all phenomena, lying within Absolute Consciousness in the form of its divine power and appearing phenomenally through the creative activity of the Absolute. Finite beings, who also are created through the vibratory activity of the Absolute, appear as well. Sometimes, in finite beings, one also sees a direct, although partial, manifestation of this creative vibration, such as in a person's spontaneous, imaginative intellect. In truth, the Lord Himself pervades and shines within all such entities as the physical body, objects, human perception, ideation, and memory.

The seventh chapter of Book I is meant to establish the constant existence of a single Master *(Ātman)* of all varieties of knowing, who serves as the base on which all sequential human mental activities rest. Although the human being appears to be a self-indulgent, conscious individual, bedecked with the trappings of a past, present, and future, he or she is none other than almighty God, the great Master of existence, who has taken up the form of a knowing subject, a person. This person's mutually unrelated flickers of momentary mental consciousness must have a common and a permanent base, without which all activities based on their supposed mutual relationships cannot become possible, since all objects are self-centred and separate from one another. This permanently existing entity is the *Ātman,* the divine soul, who, while lying beyond the scope of all ideas of sequence, bears and notices the particulars of all such momentary minds within Himself. These particulars include all mental activities such as establishing equality or generality, working out the relationship between cause and effect, and conducting recollection, refutation, inference, and all other such mental transactions of a pure or impure character. For instance, the relationship between a cause and its effect can be established only when one and the same knowing subject sees both of them as necessarily being together. Similarly, in memory, the *Ātman* bears in His own Self-experience both the past and present and their mutual relation.

This chapter also includes a long discussion exploring the truth regarding the process of refuting the correctness of a mistaken cognition on the basis of a subsequent correct one. When, for example, a gleaming shell must be proven to be different from silver, or a touch of sunlight from the presence of a ghost[7], again *Ātman*'s all-pervading presence becomes necessary to unify the false and true perceptions into one body of interrelated knowledge. All mundane activities, both worldly and spiritual, become possible only on the basis of the permanent existence of the Lord, who is said to be bedecked with the amazing variety of phenomenal entities.

Since the eternally existent, knowing, and doing Subject has already been well-established in the seventh chapter as the Master of the flux of momentary mental consciousness, chapter 8 is devoted to establishing, through correct argumentation, that the infinite divine essence is this Subject's innermost essential character.

The chapter offers a brief description of the character of several types of perceptions, explaining that—despite some objects being clearly manifest and others remaining obscure, or objects and feelings differing in character from one another—all these are only exterior differences. There is, in fact, no difference in the basic character of objects according to their interior nature. Here we see the ideas of interiority and exteriority as presented in Kashmir Śaivism. The use of such terms here is not related, in any way, to positions in space. Unity with the Self is interiority and difference and distinctness from it is exteriority. The 'outwardness' of any entities is something thrust upon them and is not their own basic character, since their eternal existence lies within pure Consciousness. This is a further illustration of Kashmir Śaivism's spiritual realism.

Only in their aspect of exteriority, manifested by *māyā* and appearing in the views of worldly beings, do phenomenal entities gain various types of 'utility'. Even mental conceptions, such as concepts of pleasure and pain, are similarly considered external and have been manifested by the Lord as outward entities even though they exist inside one's mind. All this creation is due to the divine nature of the Absolute.

All these universal activities of this world and the people living here cannot go on smoothly as long as the monistic unity of everything is not accepted. Such unity is basically the monistic, infinite I-Consciousness, the absolute Knower, who pervades all of existence and runs it as a cosmos. This is Maheśvara, the omnipotent all-knowing God, and His Self-Consciousness is itself known as His active powers of pure gnosis and action.

The single common base of different human mental activities has thus been proclaimed as Maheśvara. He has been established as the Master of the manifestation of all sorts of knowing in this *Jñānādhikāra* of the *Īśvara-pratyabhijñā-kārikā.*

Book II: Kriyādhikāra. Book II of the *Īśvara-pratyabhijñā-kārikā,* known as its *Kriyādhikāra,* establishes the power of divine activity in the Absolute. This power of divine activity *(kriyā-śakti)* is the main source and cause of the wonderfully diverse variety of knowing and doing in the world. On account of Absolute Reality's tremendous active power, He is called Maheśvara, the great Lord. This active power is said to be basic to His character. All the mundane activities of knowing and doing of various beings, as well as each and every objective phenomenon, have been shown to be basically the results of the outward manifestations of this divine nature. This book of the *Īśvara-pratyabhijñā-kārikā* has been divided into four chapters according to the *Vimarśinī* commentary on it by Abhinavagupta.

Chapter 1 reminds the reader that objections raised by some Vijñānavādins against the notion that the power of action could belong to the Absolute *Ātman* have already been discounted. Such power has been established, through logical arguments contained in the last six chapters of Book I, on the basis of the unity of the Master of action. While mundane actions appear to be conditioned by time sequence and spatial sequence, the basic active nature of God is infinite and unconditioned by time or space. However, He creates both time and space out of His own being; through the play of His own divine activity, He creates and enters into the perspective of finite beings. The active power of the Absolute has been said to be that part of His character that is responsible for the manifestation of diversity between subject and object on the plane of the phenomenal creation.

Chapter 2, Book II, deals with the scope and the actual existence of unity in diversity, as becomes manifest in the world. Kashmir Śaivism agrees with Nyāya-Vaiśeṣika philosophy in so far as mundane situations and activities in phenomenal existence are concerned. That is, it accepts sensual perceptions and mental calculations as being correct and useful with respect to all mundane dealings and the mutual relations between entities in the world, since those understandings have been intellectually calculated by worldly people and so serve as the valuable basis for their activities.

In fact, everything is one with the real Subject of knowing, and diversity is based simply on mental calculations, conducted under the conditions laid down by time, space, and so on. To explain, unity definitely shines at the moment of a direct perception as an experience without thought *(nirvikalpa-anubhava)*. An object seen shining is one with the consciousness of the perceiving person. However, it soon appears to be different from him at a certain stage of his thinking process. He thinks this way on the basis of his previous impressions about objects. Ideal conceptions or thoughts immediately arise in the mental process of the person, who proceeds to classify the experience *(savikalpa-anubhava)*[8], resulting in diversity of view-point. The ordinary mental calculations of a person are based on past impressions and constitute the bondage of a worldly being. Ordinary people are not aware of the absolute unity of the Self, existing at the moment of the beginning of a direct perception; however, yogins well-versed in the practice of Trika yoga realise and experience it.

Moreover, it is only through the common knowing Subject, the *Ātman,* that mutual relations can even be established between subjects and objects, since objects of knowing are self-centred and self-limited by their nature and thus cannot establish such connections on their own. This resorting to articles and concepts having both unity and diversity as their nature, for the purpose of the attainment of worldly aims, has been accepted in Kashmir Śaivism and is not called delusion. This is because we live in gross bodies in this mortal world. To ignore the actual problems of life by pushing them into a sphere called 'delusion' would be to deceive both one's own self and one's nation. Therefore, Utpaladeva proclaims boldly here: *Na bhrāntir īdṛśī,* 'This is not delusion'. Many philosophers after him, however, did not follow this doctrine so closely, and perhaps Kashmir would have been better protected against tyranny in her later history if they had.

The third chapter of Book II is devoted to discussions on the topic of Kashmir Śaivism's epistemology. The author does not bother about the numerous means of correct knowledge, as have been dealt with in other schools of thought. Accepting the views of Kumarila Bhaṭṭa's sub-school of Mīmāṃsā with respect to all mundane knowledge, Utpaladeva points out the truth that Absolute Reality, lying beyond the reach of all *pramāṇas* (the mundane means of correct knowledge) and shining through the light of its own Consciousness, serves as the base on which all the *pramāṇas* in the world rest. Certain situations and conditions during which *pramāṇas* serve in mundane dealings are also discussed in detail.

The existence and the character of the Absolute Truth are accepted to be self-evident. The same is said of mundane beings who themselves shine in the form of individual I-Consciousness and serve as the base on which stand all the means of knowledge (discussed with great detail and emphasis in most Indian philosophical schools of thought). The topic of epistemology is addressed employing an innovative viewpoint, avoiding the perhaps excessive argumentation worked out by Nyāya philosophy and the Vijñānavāda school of Buddhism.

Perception and inference are examples of *pramāṇas,* or means of correct knowledge about an object or its character. Utpaladeva sees these means as self-evident and ever new in character. When they shine as one's accurate interior conceptions, they are known as *pramiti,* correct knowledge. He notes that the enlightening of an object by means of a *pramāṇa* differs considerably in accordance with a person's liking and aims, as well as according to the usual denotations of speech and thought utilised by the knowing subject. The result is that everyone does not learn the particulars of an object in the same way, nor treats objects in the same way once perceived. In the same way, many objects can be perceived to be one, depending on the viewer. And objects that may appear to be different from what they are are not thereby changed from their basic nature by virtue of appearance or by the fact that their utility is not evident. The essential character of an object is ordained by the will of the Lord under the laws of destiny created by Him. Moreover, differences between substances can only be known when concepts concerning them shine in one and the same knowing subject.

Complicated argumentation—which had become a hobby for scholars, especially those enjoying patronage at royal courts in Indian states—is introduced briefly in this chapter to counter the doctrines of the other schools of philosophy. However, Kashmir Śaivism maintains that the Absolute Lord cannot be brought under the scope of *pramāṇa* at all, because He is, metaphysically, the canvas on which the wonderful paintings of the universe are painted. This canvas has an even surface, while the paintings on it appear as diverse and uneven. He is the eternal and basic Master of all correct cognitions.

The chapter concludes by saying that the work in hand has been composed in order to regenerate the cognisance of the divine essence within each person, a knowledge that has remained suspended as the result of forgetfulness or Self-oblivion. The recognition of this true nature of the Self is the ultimate aim of the *Īśvara-pratyabhijñā-kārikā.*

Chapter 4 of Book II deals with the main principle of world causation as discovered by the Śaiva philosophers of Kashmir through their intuitional revelation. According to this revelation, the basic cause of the universe is the infinite divine essence of the Absolute Lord Himself, who assumes all forms through His divine power of irresistible will. Utpaladeva rejects philosophical suggestions that principles such as atoms, cosmic energy, or mere ignorance alone are the basic source of all phenomena. To Utpaladeva these are incorrect because all such elements are themselves just effects that must have some eternally existent reality as their source and cause. He also rejects the theory of the false appearance of phenomena *(māyā),* instead insisting on the efficacy of the Śakti, or powerfully creative aspect of the Lord's will.

This is the main difference between the fundamental ontological principles of Advaita Vedānta and Kashmir Śaivism. The former attributes the universe, along with its immense variety of objects, to beginningless ignorance and takes it to be absolutely false, like a dream world. Kashmir Śaivism, however, sees the source of the universe as lying within the divine creative will power *(icchā-śakti)* of the Absolute and takes it to be phenomenally real, not totally unreal as a dream world or the son of a barren woman.

On the basis of intuitional revelation, Utpaladeva establishes the basic Kashmir Śaiva cosmogonic explanation of creation as follows: Outward manifestation (in the form of the universe) occurs out of the inwardly existent phenomenon (the universal 'I' or supreme Subject, God). Such intuitional awareness of the origin of the universe in God is brought about as a result of successful practice in Śaiva yoga. Principles such as *avidyā* (cosmic ignorance) and *māyā* (cosmic illusion) are not absolute, but instead come from God. He is accepted as the sole creator of even the mundane objects that are constructed by human craftsmen. His cosmic will is the source of all phenomenal laws such as cause and effect, the relations between an action and its agents, and the mutual inseparability of certain substances such as smoke and fire. One can speak of the materialisation of the will of God as the main cosmogonic principle. Only an entity that already contains in it some other entity can become the source of the latter's creation; thus *Ātman* alone, as the sole universal Subject, is capable of bearing within Himself and bringing into form all of the universe. No activity in the world, be it vocal or mental or actual, can stand by itself without having *Ātman,* the all-knowing Subject, as its support.

To prove this doctrine of the sole existence of the active power of the Absolute Lord is the main aim of Book II of the *Īśvara-pratyabhijñā-kārikā.* Universal creation has thus been asserted emphatically to be fundamentally due to the creative nature of God. This principle has been designated His divine power of action, *kriyā-śakti.*

Book III: Āgamādhikāra. Books I and II of the *Īśvara-pratyahijñā-kārikā* deal with the fundamental principles of the philosophy of Kashmir Śaivism through pure logical argumentation. Book III takes a different course, throwing light on some of the mystic principles mentioned in the Śaiva Āgama scriptures, including certain higher principles and doctrines of philosophy that lie beyond the scope of all mundane logic and general human experiences.

It is said that the essence of these higher principles and doctrines, such as the *tattvas,* or principles of creation, will most commonly be revealed to yogins through their practices in the Śaiva yoga of the Trika system. Their correctness can be verified even today by these yoga practices, which can result in a direct realisation of all the esoteric principles and doctrines of Śaiva philosophy.

Abhinavagupta divided Book III into two chapters in his *Vimarśinī* commentary. The first chapter is devoted to analysing the whole phenomenal existence into thirty-six *tattvas,* or cosmic principles. The second chapter deals with the nature and character of seven types of living beings. (See chart: Cosmology of Kashmir Śaivism, page 209.)

A *tattva* is a principle or category of phenomenal existence, and each *tattva* includes within it an immensely vast number of entities of similar status and position. These entities are outward reflections (or emanations) of the divine power of Paramaśiva, the divinely potent, infinite, pure, and Self-aware Absolute Consciousness. In the words of Abhinavagupta, a *tattva* is a sort of highest denominator in a group of similar items found in God's creation. The existence of thirty-six *tattvas* has been accepted by the authors and practitioners of the schools of Śaivism in southern India (Vira-śaivism and Śaiva-siddhānta), as well. But the philosophical significance of some of the most subtle and highest of these principles has only been discussed in detail in the Śaivism of Kashmir. These are the subtle *tattvas* that lie above the *puruṣa* (spirit) and *prakṛti* (material energy) of the Sāṃkhya system. Similarly, although *māyā* (illusion) as a *tattva* has been mentioned and accepted in Advaita Vedānta, its origin, development, and character are more clearly delineated in a philosophical manner by Kashmir Śaivism.

It should be noted that the *Īśvara-pratyabhijñā-kārikā,* since it is mainly aimed at the direct realisation *(pratyabhijñā)* of the true nature of the Self, does not include such elaborate discussions of the *tattvas* as Abhinavagupta presented later in chapter 9 of his *Tantrāloka*. He also did not indulge in any repetition of facts about the *tattvas* already discussed by other schools such as Sāṃkhya.

The first chapter explores the character of the thirty-six *tattvas* of world creation and the process of their phenomenal evolution out of the Absolute Lord (Paramaśiva), starting with *śiva-tattva* (the 'Śiva Principle', or the quiescent and all-knowing self-manifestation of infinity) and *śakti-tattva* (the 'Śakti Principle', or the active self-awareness of infinity). These two are also known as *prakāśa* and *vimarśa* or *jñāna* and *kriyā,* respectively. Both principles are merely two aspects of the one Lord. The Absolute is thus eternally shining as the universal and pure I-Consciousness and is ever aware of itself and its nature of infinite divine essence.

Following this discussion, the text throws light on the character of the pure principles of creation that are, in descending order, *sadāśiva, īśvara,* and *sad-vidyā* or *śuddha-vidyā*. At the first two stages, the world appears as (1) the inner idea of a painting in the head of a painter, with the focus remaining upon subjectivity ('I', or *aham*), and (2) the painter actually painting the scene outside on a canvas, making it objective ('this', or *idam*). At the third stage, (3) the painter sees both himself and the painting, but knows that the two are one. This is the viewpoint of unity in diversity and diversity in unity, the viewpoint of pure knowledge *(śuddha-vidyā)*. The text refers to three different types of beings, or yogins, whose viewpoints correspond to pure knowledge found in these stages. These are the *mantra-maheśvaras,* living in *sadāśiva-tattva,* the *mantreśvaras,* living in *īśvara-tattva,* and the *vidyeśvaras,* living at the *śuddha-vidyā* level.[9]

The text then proceeds to describe *māyā-tattva* (the principle of illusion) and the five *kañcukas,* or principles of limitation, that evolve from it. Divine Consciousness becomes limited in individual beings because of the effects of time sequence, finite capability, the law of restriction, specific interests, and imperfect knowledge. This occurs due to the illusory power of diversity in the world and the lack of recognition of one's true divine identity. Identifications with the body, mind, or even *śūnya* (emptiness)[10] are all given as examples of the lack of genuine Self-recognition.

Then the two principles of *puruṣa* and *prakṛti* and the manner of their creation are described. The supreme *puruṣa* (spirit) of Sāṃkhya is here declared to be divinity limited in conception, confined by the five *kañcukas* mentioned above. This discussion is followed by a brief mention of the remaining twenty-three *tattvas* of phenomenal creation already dealt with in the Sāṃkhya system of philosophy. They include (1) the thirteen instrumental principles (consisting of three interior senses, five exterior senses, and five organs of action), and (2) the ten objective principles (consisting of five subtle objective elements and five gross objective elements). According to Sāṃkhya, these twenty-three *tattvas* have their basic origin in *prakṛti,* but Kashmir Śaivism attributes their ultimate origin to

Paramaśiva, the Absolute Lord. Thus, it does not agree with the Sāṃkhya principle of an independent propensity of *prakṛti* towards its own transformation into these inanimate *tattvas*. Such a thing, in the view of Śaivism, requires direction from some fully conscious, omniscient, and all-powerful authority, who controls the causes and results of such transformations of the inanimate *prakṛti*. Otherwise, the transformations of *prakṛti* would not be orderly events at all, aimed at any certain and definite results and related to past actions of being. Instead, transformation of *prakṛti* would have been chaotic in character.

The second chapter of Book III includes a discussion of the variety of beings, or knowing and doing subjects, on different planes of understanding in the universe. These are the seven categories of living beings. First is a description of the famous trinity of Hindu gods named Śiva or Rudra, Viṣṇu, and Brahmā. Then the text throws light on the general character of pure and impure beings, or rather, liberated and bound ones, also called, respectively, *pati* beings and *paśu* beings. The character of beings known as the *mantra-maheśvaras* and the *mantreśvaras,* who are included among the *pati* beings, is not discussed in detail since the previous discussion about the *sadāśiva-* and *īsvara-tattvas* covers the topic sufficiently.

The *paśus,* or bound beings, are bound by the three impurities known as the *āṇava-, māyīya-,* and *kārma-malas,* as dealt with mystically in the Āgamas. Utpaladeva throws light on their basic character and proceeds to explain the manner in which these two types of beings are bound, mentioning the causes of their bondage. The *vijñānākalas* are bound by both the *āṇava-mala,* the impurity of finitude, and the *māyīya-mala,* the impurity of diversity. Although they do understand that they are divine Consciousness, these beings are limited because they do not have access to their active divine power, and they also continue to see themselves as separate from other individuals and from God. At times, these *Vijñānākalas* are associated by Kashmir Śaivas with the liberated beings of Advaita Vedānta.

The *pralayākala*-beings are bound by the misunderstanding of their basic nature; they identify themselves with other elements besides supreme Consciousness. They are affected by both the *āṇava-* (finitude) and the *kārma-malas* (the impurity of past actions). These beings take eternal rest in *suṣupti;* they are influenced by their limited knowledge, yet they are able to remain free from bodies, senses, organs, and so on, up to the time of the *pralaya* (the next dissolution) of all items of existence back into *prakṛti.*

A third type of pure, yet partially bound, being is called the *vidyeśvara.* These beings, also called the *mantra*-beings, are described as basically pure, yet nevertheless tainted by the impurity of diversity. Such beings correctly take the infinite, potent, and omniscient pure Consciousness as their Self, and so they are ever free from the impurity of any past actions.

The text says that all beings—from the gods in heaven down to worms, insects, and plants—are beset with all the three types of impurity, although their greatest misery is due to the impurity of past actions *(kārma-mala),* which is the direct cause of their transmigratory existence. Such beings do not feel themselves to be pure Consciousness, but instead see it shining as just a quality of some unconscious entity such as the breath or the intellect or the body.

This chapter also briefly deals with the nature of *samāveśa,* a flash of divine Self-realisation in which one becomes, for a time, one with the Almighty Lord who creates, destroys, protects, conceals, and bestows grace in the universe. All yogic methods of the Trika system utilise practices involving focus on *samāveśa* and expanding its presence in the yogi's awareness.

The three states of deep sleep *(suṣupti),* dreaming sleep *(svapna),* and wakefulness *(jāgrat)* are discussed as well. In deep, dreamless sleep a person is tainted primarily by the *āṇava-mala,* the impurity of finitude, or sense of a limited self. In dreaming sleep, he is bound by all three *malas* inside his mental universe. While in the waking state, a person is bound by all three impurities in the physical body and its actions. The text advises an aspirant to withdraw himself from these three states in order to become fixed in the fourth state of spontaneous Self-revelation, known as *turyā* (or *turīya*). This is because the previous three states are plagued with the misery of momentary pleasure and pain and their prominence pushes awareness of the true Self into the background.

Utpaladeva's presentation of the five *prāṇas* (or vital airs) is unique among the other schools of thought that deal with them, such as the Nyāya. The *prāṇas* are the life-force, or the five activities of animation or vivification of the body and mind. All physical and mental activities of a person, consisting of assimilation and elimination of gross and subtle objects in the waking and dreaming states, are called in the scriptures of Kashmir Śaivism *apāna* and *prāṇa*. *Samāna* is a third vital air that is a state of rest between the processes of assimilation and elimination, and is often associated with the state of sleep.

The special character of *udāna* and *vyāna,* the two final vital airs, is presented here in a way unknown in Vedānta philosophy. *Udāna* is experienced as a fiery sensation moving upward through one's spinal cord, reducing all ideas and feelings to ashes. Its movement is spontaneous and intuitively revealing of a person's true divinity, termed *vyāna,* the universal life-force. Its upward activity serves as a step toward Self-realisation, and it vibrates with the brilliance of the light of such realisation. This *vyāna* shines with increasingly greater brilliance in higher beings such as the *vijñānākalas,* the *mantras,* the *mantreśvaras,* and the *mantra-maheśvaras*—the higher their awareness, the more it shines forth in splendour.[11]

The still more pure and transcendental activity of vivification is called *vyāna*. With this vital air prominent, the yogi actually scintillates as one complete whole of the pure and potent infinite Consciousness, Paramaśiva. He or she sees the Self and nothing other than it.[12] The state produced by *vyāna* can be experienced in brief moments of Self-realisation during *samāveśa*. These analyses of *udāna* and *vyāna* are to be found in Kashmir Śaivism alone. What are commonly known as the five vital airs (for instance, as they are discussed in Nyāya-Vaiśeṣika) can more properly be understood merely as a physical analysis of the activities of bodily and mental vivification, rather than a vaulting up into a higher form of yogic experience, as is illustrated here.[13]

Book IV: Tattva-saṃgrahādhikāra. The single chapter of the fourth book concludes the discussion given in the *Īśvara-pratyabhijñā-kārikā* and throws light on a few topics not discussed in its previous chapters. It is thus both a supplementary addition and a conclusion.

Utpaladeva recapitulates the previously discussed principle that the Absolute Lord alone is, in His universal aspect, appearing variously as the Self of each and every being. He is thus manifesting Himself as subjects and objects in an immense variety of particular forms; yet most finite individuals do not realise their true nature, and thus are bound. They persist, in a deep-rooted way, in identifying themselves with small 'I-ness' related to the mind, physical form, or other insentient entities, and in regarding other objects and people as objective entities different from themselves and the Lord. Thus, they are bound by ignorance and continue to conduct finite activities of knowing and doing that result in their tasting many experiences of pleasure and pain.

This book explores the essential character of the three *guṇas,* or qualities of nature, and how they condition the life of a bound being *(paśu),* as opposed to one who is free or liberated *(pati)*. This is a topic not explained in previous chapters. While Sāṃkhya philosophy has discussed the character and effect of the three *guṇas,* one can argue that this school has neither fully explored their origin, nor the source of their character, nor the process of their manifestation. Kashmir Śaivism attempts to present a more complete elucidation of the subject.

The infinite knowledge and Self-bliss of a free *pati* being has become constricted in a bound *paśu* being, leaving him only the *sattva-guṇa* that can be characterised by limited knowledge and limited happiness or pleasure *(sukha)*.

The infinite capacity for action of a free *pati* being also becomes constricted in a bound being, leaving him only the *rajo-guṇa* which can be characterised by pain and turbulence in action. This is because *rajas* is a mixture of the pleasure of *sattva* and the absence of pleasure in *tamas*—thus producing turbulent actions and reactions. The bound being is thus severely limited in his capacity for action by this admixture of pleasure and pain. An example given is the combined experience of both happiness and pain felt by a father upon seeing his long-separated and well-loved son, yet finding that his son is dying of an incurable disease.

A free *pati* being has the wonderful power of creating illusion, called *māyā,* at his command, yet a bound being experiences that he or she is bound by this very power. This is the *guṇa* called *tamas,* and it is the experience of *moha* or ignorance, as well as an experience of the lack of Self-bliss. *Tamas* has the quality of no Self-awareness and non-existence found in conditions such as deep sleep or fainting. In a bound being, the text says, each of the three *guṇas* creates all sorts of misery.

The text continues to throw light on the manner in which the world appears to bound beings, on the one hand, and to liberated, pure beings, on the other. For a liberated being, the world appears as a simple objectivity not denoted by any word-image with conventional meaning. It is objectivity in what might be called its 'sprouting' stage; objects thus appear as partly different and partly one with the viewer. But to a bound being, the world seems to have a separate existence totally outside him and separate from him. He denotes objects by conventional words and meanings and uses ordinary perceptions, conceptions, recollections, imaginings, and so on, to express his confused notions about the diverse world. In fact, a *paśu* being even creates a world of his own through his imagination, believing it to be real for the time being. However, it must be understood that even his power of fanciful conception depends on, and emerges from, the Lord's own creative power.

In this way, a secret path of easy salvation is provided for the bound individual as a means for the attainment of the Godhead. He must concentrate on his individually created worlds with the (non-ideational) awareness of their origin in the playful divine essence of God. He must do this with the understanding: 'My creative power is the Lord's creative power'. Such contemplative meditation gradually leads the aspirant to expand his awareness until it becomes one with the infinite nature of the Lord. He then sees the whole world as his own divine exuberance, and can eventually remain steadily in this exalted position of the Absolute Lord even while outwardly engaged in the flow of mundane thoughts and activities. A person who fixes his awareness upon the awareness of his true Self, the divine 'I-Consciousness', in moments of *samāveśa* in spiritual practice, thus opens himself to the perfection of divine unity, identity, and experience. The whole universe exists in the Absolute Lord. Realising this in full is *pratyabhijñā,* Self-recognition.

In the next to last couplet of this work, the philosopher Utpaladeva discloses another side of his personality. He is also the master of an excellent poetic art, as evident in his *Śiva-stotrāvalī* collection of poems to Lord Śiva. Couplet 17 is a poetic end-note to the text, for it compares an aspirant, proceeding on the path of Self-recognition, to a love-torn damsel. The young woman is deeply in love, but experiencing the dreadful pain of separation from her lover. Even though he is standing by her side and talking to her, she is not able to ease this pain of separation from her desired and loved youth because she does not yet recognise him as her beloved. This reminds the reader of the last verses of the fifth canto of the

Kumāra-śāmbhava, in which Parvati is described as not recognising Śiva, even in His presence, because He has come to her in the guise of a youthful and beautiful ascetic *brahmacārin*. Just so, the aspirant must clearly and finally recognise the Lord's presence in his or her own heart in order to be filled with undying happiness.

In conclusion, Utpaladeva states that his purpose in writing this scriptural text is to help aspirants attain the most desirable absolute perfection, which is the *Īśvara-pratyabhijñā,* Self-recognition of the Lord.

TEXT AND COMMENTARY OF THE ĪŚVARA PRATYABHIJÑĀ KĀRIKĀ

Book I

JÑĀNĀDHIKĀRA

Divine Knowledge

Chapter 1

INTRODUCTION

The chapter begins with a salutation to Almighty God and hints at the general philosophical view of Kashmir Śaivism.

Verse 1

कथंचिदासाद्य महेश्वरस्य
दास्यं जनस्याप्युपकारमिच्छन् ।
समस्तसंपत्समवाप्तिहेतुं
तत्प्रत्यभिज्ञामुपपादयामि ॥ १ ॥

kathaṃcid āsādya maheśvarasya
dāsyaṃ janasyāpy upakāram icchan /
samasta-saṃpat-samavāpti-hetuṃ
tat-pratyabhijñām upapādayāmi //

Having somehow attained the position of a servant of the great Almighty Lord Maheśvara, and being now desirous to do [the greatest] good to other people as well, I am presently expounding the doctrine of His recognition; that is, on one hand, the source of the attainment of all affluence of divine powers (literally riches) and that can, on the other hand, be achieved through the attainment of such divine affluence.

Commentary

The word *kathaṃcid* (literally "somehow or other") signifies here an indescribable and mysterious process. This process of the divine gracious activity of God is mysterious in character, because the cause and conditions of its bestowal cannot be located exactly. All that depends on the free will of the Lord, with regard to the playful manifestation of His divine essence. God's will is independent in all respects, as it does not always take into consideration the merits and demerits of the person on whom He bestows His grace. God can, if He likes, become highly gracious in His divine play even to an unworthy person and can sometimes ignore a person appearing to be worthy, although both such actions are generally rare. Besides, God Himself appears as each and every being, worthy or unworthy. Therefore, there cannot be any grounds for an objection based on His partiality. The grace and wrath of the Lord are just two stages of His divine sport being played out with none other than His own Self, who appears in the form of all kinds of living beings. This wondrous character of His grace is suggested by the word *kathaṃcid.*

Maheśvara is the supreme authority, Almighty God, ruling over the great gods such as Brahmā, Viṣṇu, Rudra, Īśvara, and Sadāśiva. *Dāsyam* is the position of the servant for whom each and every thing is provided by the master, who takes care of him in all situations. *Jana* is a person involved in, and bound by, the cycles of rebirth. *Pratyabhijñā* signifies recognition; that is, the recollection of the particulars of someone who had been forgotten. An aspirant must recollect his forgotten divine essence and recognise himself as none other than Almighty God. Such recognition happens through a sudden direct realisation of his authentic nature. It becomes the means of the attainment of everything that is, in fact, really desirable *(samasta-sampat). Sampat* means here the richness, the exuberance of all divinity. It suggests that what is worthy to be desired is mastery over the riches of divine powers.[14] Self-recognition is the source of the attainment of this exuberant richness, and it is this splendour through which an aspirant recognises himself as none other than Almighty God, the great Master of all exuberant divine powers. This mutual benefit of the two has been mentioned by Abhinavagupta in his commentary.

Verse 2

कर्तरि ज्ञातरि स्वात्मन्यादिसिद्धे महेश्वरे ।
अजडात्मा निषेधं वा सिद्धिं वा विदधीत कः ॥ २॥

kartari jñātari svātmany ādi-siddhe maheśvare /
ajaḍātmā niṣedhaṃ vā siddhiṃ vā vidadhīta kaḥ //

Other than the person taking some insentient entity as his Self, who would try to either deny or establish the existence of the eternally existent Almighty God, who has the independent power of doing and knowing, and is, in fact, one's own [real] Self?

Commentary

The perfectly independent authority in all doing and knowing is the Godhead. Authority rests in that infinite and pure Consciousness that shines as the Self of each and every being and possesses the capacity to do and to know. The real Self of every being is therefore none other than God. No wise person, taking pure Consciousness as his Self, would therefore deny at all the existence of God, because Consciousness is eternally established by itself. The seeming limitations imposed on a human being by his gross and subtle bodies—that is, by his finite physical form and mind—vanish as soon as he realises the real nature of his basic Self through a keen and firm inward observation, aided by a sharp and super-vigilant awareness.

Thinkers who take any insentient substances such as the physical body or the system of animation and breathing or the inner sense of understanding or even the void of dreamless sleep or anything else that may resemble any of these entities as their real Self may try either to disprove or to prove the existence of God. But those who experience pure Consciousness alone as their essentially real Self would never indulge in either of these two intellectual exercises.

Thinkers who are completely atheistic in their views and deny the existence of both God and *Ātman,* the Self, take only the physical body as their Self. Semi-atheistic thinkers, including many Buddhists and Sāṃkhyas, also deny the existence of God as the supreme controller of phenomenal existence. Thinkers such as the Nyāya-Vaiśeṣikas consider God to be an authority working under the laws of destiny and restriction *(niyati),* whose action depends on the movement of atoms in accordance with the laws of causation. They do not accept God as an absolutely independent authority and the sole Master of all phenomena. They also proclaim the highest state of attainment to be an absolutely tranquil and inactive I-Consciousness, devoid of all mental activities and functions, and take this condition as the highest state of the Self. Advaita Vedāntins likewise do not admit activity or the power 'to do' as the nature of *Ātman,* the conscious Self. Such thinkers often try in various ways, through philosophical method, to establish the existence of God.

The propounders of Śaiva monism, however, stressing intuitional realisation as well as philosophic thinking, neither attempt to deny nor to establish the existence of God. Taking the finer, more pure, and potent Consciousness as their Self and experiencing it as the all-powerful Reality, they cannot deny its eternal existence. Seeing it already established eternally, by virtue of its being the ever Self-aware and infinite Consciousness, they do not feel any necessity to re-establish God's existence through the use of logical arguments.

What, then, remains to be propounded through this new philosophical treatise on Śaivism? This query is answered in the following verse.

Verse 3

किंतु मोहवशादस्मिन्दृष्टेऽप्यनुपलक्षिते ।
शक्त्याविष्करणेनेयं प्रत्यभिज्ञोपदर्श्यते ॥ ३ ॥

kiṃtu moha-vaśād asmin dṛṣṭe 'py anupalakṣite /
śakty-āviṣ-karaṇeneyaṃ pratyabhijñopadarśyate // [15]

But since the real significance of the Self is not usually grasped because of delusion *(moha),* even though [the Self] is actually seen [or felt], its recognition, through the process of illuminating its divine powers, is now being propounded [by means of the work at hand].

Commentary

Everyone knows himself as 'I', but does not know the truth of his real nature and character. In fact, pure, infinite, and divinely potent Consciousness is the Self of each and every being. But while we are in our waking state, we feel our gross material body to be our Self. In the dream state, our mind constructs a mental Self, and therefore we feel that only that is our Self. In the state of absolutely dreamless sleep, we feel as if that vacuum-like individual consciousness is our Self, and so also do not take the pure and infinite divine Consciousness as our 'I'. The real truth thus lies hidden from our inner sight on account of the delusion *(moha)* caused by *māyā,* the Lord's power of illusion. Paradoxically, we do see our true Self, but are not able to realise its real significance on account of this delusion.

The work at hand, the *Īśvara-pratyabhijñā-kārikā,* is meant to show and to teach the method through which recollection and the consequent recognition of the real nature of the Self can be attained. This happens only when an aspirant's hidden divine powers are illuminated and brought clearly to his notice. As soon as a person's divine powers start to shine with full brilliance and the aspirant feels he is in possession of such divine powers, he at once recognises himself as none other than God, who has been appearing playfully as a finite individual being. This discovery of one's hidden divine powers is thus the means of recognising our true nature. The path to attain such Self-recognition is established, both logically and psychologically, in this work, the *Īśvara-pratyabhijñā-kārikā,* which explores the Self as the basis of nature and all existence.

Verse 4

तथाहि जडभूतानां प्रतिष्ठा जीवदाश्रया ।
ज्ञानं क्रिया च भूतानां जीवतां जीवनं मतम् ॥ ४ ॥

tathā hi jaḍa-bhūtānāṃ pratiṣṭhā jīvad-āśrayā /
jñānaṃ kriyā ca bhūtānāṃ jīvatāṃ jīvanaṃ matam //

One may argue thus: All insentient beings depend on the support of sentient ones for the purpose of establishing their existence, and it is 'knowing' plus 'doing' that is accepted as the sentience of living beings.

Commentary

Insentient objects are never aware of themselves and cannot therefore establish their existence. Living beings are aware of themselves, and of insentient objects as well, because these objects are reflected in them through the pathways of their senses and minds. Such beings thus serve as an essential support on which the insentient entities can rely for the purpose of establishing their existence. The sentient entities can do so by virtue of their basic powers to know and to do, because sentience is knowing and doing.

The next couplet proves knowing and doing to be the nature of each living being.

Verse 5

तत्र ज्ञानं स्वतः सिद्धं क्रिया कायाश्रिता सती ।
परैरप्युपलक्ष्येत तयान्यज्ञानमूह्यते ॥ ५ ॥

tatra jñānaṃ svataḥ siddhaṃ kriyā kāyāśritā satī /
parair apy upalakṣyeta tayānya-jñānam ūhyate //

Of these two, knowing is self-evident [only to the knowing person]; but doing, when appearing in someone's body, becomes known to others as well, and that gives them a means to infer the existence of knowing in the concerned person.

Commentary

Only a person himself is aware of his own knowing. No one else can be directly aware of it because it cannot become an object of another person's perception. But one person's doing can also be perceived by another person; the physical form of the doer naturally becomes visible to others. Since such doing is known by others, it can serve as a logical means for the viewer to infer the existence of knowing in the doer, because no doing is possible without first knowing. All sentient beings possess powers to know and to do. God, the ultimate knower and doer, is thus self-evident in each and every being.

Chapter 2

AN ANTAGONISTIC VIEW

Chapter 2 of this *adhikāra* is devoted to the presentation of the theory of Vijñānavāda Buddhism, which opposes the metaphysics of Kashmir Śaivism. The Vijñānavāda school aimed at a logical refutation of the principle of *Ātman* as an existent reality that witnesses and directs the whole internal apparatus of being. Not only does this school try to refute the existence of the individual spirit of living beings, but it also does not accept the existence of God, the universal spirit and the authority ruling over and operating the whole universe. Other schools of divergent thought have rather been ignored in this context, because the Buddhist Vijñānavāda alone is highly rich in subtle logic.[16] It alone can therefore be seen as a powerful rival school of thought. Besides, most of the other schools of Indian philosophy accept the existence of *Ātman* lying beyond the domain of the mind. They also propound the theory of the supreme authority of God—thus coming closer to Kashmir Śaivism.

The *Vijñānavādin* now begins his arguments aimed at the refutation of the existence of (1) *Ātman,* the individual soul; (2) God; and (3) His divine powers.

Verses 1-2

ननु स्वलक्षणाभासं ज्ञानमेकं परं पुनः ।
साभिलापं विकल्पाख्यं बहुधा नापि तद्द्वयम् ॥ १ ॥
नित्यस्य कस्यचिद्द्रष्टुस्तस्यात्रानवभासतः ।
अहंप्रतीतिरप्येषा शरीराद्यवसायिनी ॥ २ ॥

nanu sva-lakṣaṇābhāsaṃ jñānam ekaṃ paraṃ punaḥ /
sābhilāpaṃ vikalpākhyaṃ bahudhā nāpi tad-dvayam //
nityasya kasyacid draṣṭus tasyātrānavabhāsataḥ /
ahaṃ-pratītir apy eṣā śarīrādy avasāyinī //

[The Vijñānavādin says:]
Just see. There is one variety of perceptual knowledge that brings to light the basic thing as it is in itself [without the imposition of any name or form on it]. The other [variety of knowing] is that which is variously accompanied by word-images and is known as knowledge with definite or indefinite ideation [that is, conceptual knowledge]. Neither of these two is related [or belongs] to any permanently existing knowing subject, because he is apparently absent in both of them. Even the idea of 'I-ness' rests only on the physical body, etc.

Commentary

Sva-lakṣaṇa means 'a thing in itself', without any imposition of the concept of name and form. *Sva-lakṣaṇābhāsam* means the knowledge in which only the thing in itself becomes evident. It is called *nirvikalpa* knowledge, knowing beyond thought. *Abhilāpa* is the word-image imposed over this higher, thought-free knowledge. *Vikalpa* is a definite idea, accompanied by a definite word-image, which is imposed on the thing in itself. Knowledge at the *nirvikalpa* stage of perception is always self-limited and centred in itself since it has no relation with any definite idea or word-image. Such knowledge is without ideation and so has no relation with any other knowledge, similar or dissimilar in character. *Draṣṭā* denotes a subject of some action of knowing. He is a person who knows, or to whom some knowledge belongs. The domain of *vikalpa,* therefore, is determinative knowing, which is called the stage of *savikalpa* knowledge. By contrast, *nirvikalpa* knowledge is found in initial, intuitive perception. It is that as it appears at first sight. It can only be experienced and not expressed or even understood at the level of the intellect.

The Vijñānavāda maintains that *vijñāna,* mental consciousness, is the only existent reality. It is momentary in character. Each momentary state of mind gives rise to another similarly temporary mental state, with each becoming extinct just after having arisen. Each fleeting state of mind, while giving rise to a similar one, transfers to it its past impressions. Such currents of conscious minds, along with their multitude of past impressions, go on moving ahead like streams of momentary consciousness.

Vijñānavāda Buddhism accepts the existence of such streams of conscious mental states flowing ahead in countless forms; that is, as countless living beings moving in the world. The exterior phenomenon of a person is, in the view of Vijñānavāda, nothing but an outward manifestation of mind, brought about on the basis of its past impressions. The existence of *citta,* or mind, cannot be denied in their view. It is self-evident. It shines itself and illuminates the objects and thoughts reflected in it in accordance with its own past impressions.

At the stage of initial perception *(nirvikalpa),* the object perceived shines in itself. But at the stage of conception *(savikalpa),* the name and the form of the thing, imposed on it by the mind in accordance with its inherited past impressions, also shine. These are the two varieties of knowledge, known variously as (1) *nirvikalpa* or *sva-lakṣaṇa* and (2) *savikalpa, sābhilāpa,* or *vikalpātmā.*

The Vijñānavādin, aiming at the negation of the existence of *Ātman* as the Master of all knowing and as the controlling director of mind regulating both the varieties of knowledge, says that there is no doubt that these two types of knowledge exist. Further, it is argued that mind alone exists in reality and appears in the forms of both a subject and an object. This philosophy thus denies the existence of the knowing Subject, *Ātman,* and God or the Supreme Self, Paramātman, as established by the thinkers of many Hindu rooted philosophies.

The next couplet puts forth the argument of Kashmir Śaivism's scriptural thinkers in favour of the existence of *Ātman* as the Master of all knowing. The question being asked is: How could the recollection of a previously experienced object become possible if there were no permanently existent entity, working as both the knower and the recollector?

Verse 3

अथानुभवविध्वंसे स्मृतिस्तदनुरोधिनी ।
कथं भवेन्न नित्यः स्यादात्मा यद्यनुभावकः ॥ ३ ॥

athānubhava-vidhvaṃse smṛtis tad-anurodhinī /
kathaṃ bhaven na nityaḥ syād ātmā yady anubhāvakaḥ //

[The Śaiva philosopher replies:]
How could memory, agreeing essentially with previous direct perception, become at all possible after such [direct] knowing comes to its end, if the *Ātman,* the experiencer, were not accepted as a constantly existing entity?

Commentary

Both an objective past experience and a consequent present recollection of that event belong to one and the same person, in whom both psychological functions occur. Only then can a particular recollection agree with that particular past experience. Something experienced by *x* can never be recollected by *y*. What is known by experience also comes to its end just after the moment of its shining in one's intellect. It does not last beyond the moment, not even at the time of consequent recollection, because each and every knowing is a phenomenon that is momentary in character. But it leaves its impression on something that must be a permanently existent entity. That entity, or reality, serves as the base of all the momentary activities of perception, conception, recollection, and so on.

Such a permanently existing reality is *Ātman,* the Subject or doer of all mental activities. It is thus *Ātman* who perceives an object, forms a conception of it, and later recollects it with the help of its mental apparatus. The phenomenon of recollection, of memory, thus proves the permanent existence of *Ātman,* the single Master of perception, conception, and recollection of any object.

A logical objection raised by the Vijñānavādins against the above argument, put forth by scriptural thinkers, is presented in the next two couplets.

Verses 4-5

सत्यप्यात्मनि दृङ्नाशात्तद्द्वारा दृष्टवस्तुषु ।
स्मृतिः केनाथ यत्रैवानुभवस्तत्पदैव सा ॥ ४ ॥
यतो हि पूर्वानुभवसंस्कारात्स्मृतिसंभवः ।
यद्येवमन्तर्गडुना कोऽर्थः स्यात्स्थायिनात्मना ॥ ५ ॥

saty apy ātmani dṛṅ-nāśāt tad-dvārā dṛṣṭa-vastuṣu /
smṛtiḥ kenātha yatraivānubhavas tat-padaiva sā //
yato hi pūrvānubhava-saṃskārāt smṛti-saṃbhavaḥ /
yady evam antar-gaḍunā ko 'rthaḥ syāt sthāyinātmanā //

[The Buddhist objects:]
Even if the existence of *Ātman* is accepted, how can the recollection of an object, known through mental experience, become possible long after such experience has already come to its end? If, however, it is argued that a particular memory

takes the same object as the object of the concerned previous experience—since it has risen according to the impressions laid [on *Ātman*] by the [previous] experience—then it can be asked: What would be the advantage of a permanently existent *Ātman*, lying there uselessly, like a lump, in between?

Commentary

To accept the permanent existence of *Ātman* would not be of any practical use. It is a fact that an experience, having come to its end just after the moment of its existence, cannot be helpful afterward in bringing about a recollection of the object illumined by it. But what can be the use of *Ātman*, an ineffective and un-affective Consciousness, in bringing about a wanted recollection?

It may be argued that each experience creates its impression, and such an impression helps the *Ātman* to recollect its previously experienced object. But, the Buddhist says, such an argument can be set aside by pointing out that, since the impression is the actual and sufficient cause of recollection, one can do away with the unnecessary supposition of *Ātman*. *Ātman*, then, could be assigned the position of a useless lump, lying in between an experience and its consequent recollection. As for the base on which such an impression rests, the flow of mental consciousness can serve such purpose well. The supposition of the existence of an additional entity called *Ātman* is of no avail. It is thus proved, the Buddhist argues, that no permanent entity or reality exists beyond the flux of mind. The existence of mental impressions is acceptable to both sides and that is sufficient to explain all the varieties of psychological activities prevalent in the world. Impression alone can cause recollection and can supply it with all the data to be recollected, without the help of the so-called *Ātman*.[17]

The next couplet is meant to wind up the argument of Vijñānavāda and to express the consequent undesirable conclusion.

Verse 6

ततो भिन्नेषु धर्मेषु तत्स्वरूपाविशेषतः ।
संस्कारात्स्मृतिसिद्धौ स्यात्स्मर्ता द्रष्टेव कल्पितः ॥ ६ ॥

tato bhinneṣu dharmeṣu tat-sva-rūpāviśeṣataḥ /
saṃskārāt smṛti-siddhau syāt smartā draṣṭeva kalpitaḥ //

[The Buddhist further states:]
Since the character of the *Ātman* does not change at all during its different functional activities [such as perception, conception, and so on], and since memory can occur [solely] with the help of impressions, the recollector [the *Ātman*] is also an imaginary entity like the experiencer.

Commentary

If perception, conception, memory, and other mental activities are taken as different functional attributes of *Ātman,* the Master of knowing and doing, then *Ātman* should develop certain modifications at the times when these different functions occur. But, since it has been proclaimed a constantly changeless reality, unaffected by the development of any such functions, *Ātman* must be simply an imaginary and useless entity that can very conveniently be done away with, leaving no disadvantage with respect to explaining the character of all mental functions. As for the problem about how recollection occurs, it is already solved: it can be brought about by impressions. This last supposition, that mental impressions make memory possible, is accepted by both theistic scriptural thinkers and the atheistic monks following Buddhism.

In the next couplet, the Vijñānavādin attempts to refute the subordination of knowledge to *Ātman,* accepted by Śaiva scholars to be self-evident.

Verse 7

ज्ञानं च चित्स्वरूपं चेत्तदनित्यं किमात्मवत् ।
अथापि जडमेतस्य कथमर्थप्रकाशता ॥ ७ ॥

jñānaṃ ca cit-sva-rūpaṃ cet tad anityaṃ kim ātmavat /
athāpi jaḍam etasya katham artha-prakāśatā //

[It is argued further:]
If knowledge has the nature of Consciousness, one can ask if, like the *Ātman,* it is eternal, or if it is non-eternal in character. [That is,] one self-dependent entity cannot be taken as dependent on another such entity. Otherwise, if it [knowledge] is taken as unconscious by nature, then how can it illuminate anything?

Commentary

If cognition, or knowing, were taken to be conscious in nature, then it would turn out to be equally eternal, like *Ātman,* and could not be considered subordinate to it. Besides, since objections have been raised against the existence of *Ātman* on the basis of its presumed eternality or non-eternality, so one can also question the existence of 'conscious cognition'. Disproving conscious cognition would result in disproving knowledge's essential eternal nature. Otherwise, if knowing were accepted as unconscious in nature, then it could not be of any use in throwing light on objects.[18]

The eighth couplet is aimed by the Vijñānavādin toward refuting the explanation worked out by Sāṃkhya philosophy on this same point.

Verse 8

अथार्थस्य यथा रूपं धत्ते बुद्धिस्तथात्मनः ।
चैतन्यमजडा सैवं जाड्ये नार्थप्रकाशता ॥ ८॥

athārthasya yathā rūpaṃ dhatte buddhis tathātmanaḥ /
caitanyam ajaḍā saivaṃ jāḍye nārtha-prakāśatā //

If it is then argued that *buddhi* (the understanding sense or intellect) bears in it the consciousness of the *Ātman,* just as it bears the reflection of an object, then it may either become sentient itself or continue to remain insentient, in which case it cannot illuminate anything.

Commentary

According to Sāṃkhya theory, *buddhi,* the intellect, is relatively pure in character because of the predominance of *sattva-guṇa* in it. Consequently it can hold the reflection of objective entities, on one hand, and on the other hand, it bears the reflection of *Ātman* or *puruṣa,* Consciousness, and thus functions like a sentient entity. In doing so, it conducts all the necessary psychic activities and thus makes all mundane functions of life possible. The Vijñānavādin objects to such a theory in this way: Does *buddhi,* while bearing the reflection of *puruṣa,* become itself sentient, or does it still remain insentient as before? If it becomes sentient, then the existence of *Ātman* becomes unnecessary. The conscious *buddhi* can itself conduct all functions related to knowing. But if it remains unconscious, which is highly probable, then it cannot become capable of conducting any activities of knowing because an unconscious entity cannot know anything. The intellect cannot manifest even its own self, much less throw light on any objective entity.

Many scriptural thinkers have declared the power of action to be another definition of the sentience of living beings. The Vijñānavādin raises objection to this definition as well. He refutes the very existence of *kriyā,* or action, as a single unified process and raises objection to its definition as put forth by theistic scriptural thinkers, as follows:

Verse 9

क्रियाप्यर्थस्य कायादेस्तत्तद्देशादिजातता ।
नान्याऽदृष्टेर्न साप्येका क्रमिकैकस्य चोचिता ॥ ९ ॥

kriyāpy arthasya kāyādes tat-tad-deśādi-jātatā /
nānyādṛṣṭer na sāpy ekā kramikaikasya cocitā //

Even an action of the body, etc., is simply its contact with different places, etc., in space. [The action] is not any special entity different from [the body, etc.] because it is not seen as such. Besides, it is not a single sequential entity and cannot suitably be an attribute of a single substance.

Commentary

According to Indian scriptural philosophy, action is a series of successive movements residing in a single process. One intended action pervades all such successive movements, from beginning to end. A person goes from Srinagar to Delhi. All his successive movements, from his first step toward Delhi to his reaching his final destination, including all his secondary actions during the long journey, are counted as parts of his intended main action of going to Delhi.

Action is thus a series of multifarious and sequential movements, aimed at a single goal. It is one in its ultimate and comprehensive character and consists of a series of movements, happening one after another, all belonging to the one person who conducts it. It is therefore said to be one single process, pervaded by a long series of movements, following one another in a definite order of succession. An action is thus an exertion of energy incorporating a series of successive movements, physical or mental.

The Vijñānavādins refute this scriptural view by raising several logical objections against it in the following manner: (1) one single entity cannot be sequential in its character; (2) it cannot be many at the same time; (3) any sequential entity cannot be one entity at the same time; and (4) a sequential entity of manifold character cannot reside in a single substance at one and the same time. On the basis of such logical objections, they conclude that action is a mere concept. It is not anything substantive in character and it adds nothing to the person or substance in which it is said to be residing.

The series of successive contacts of a substance with different points in space is only imagined to be supposed, conceived, and expressed as one single action, residing in its respective substance. In reality, there is only the person or substance, along with his/its successive contacts with different points in space. Nothing beyond the substance, points in space, and contacts of the substance with them is revealed in the phenomenon known as action. It is thus a mere concept based on the imagination of unwise worldly beings, moving in the field of ignorance. The Vijñānavādin suggests that action, being thus nothing in itself, cannot at all serve in establishing the existence of *Ātman* as its Master.

The next couplet aims to refute the existence of relativity, which could be used as a help in establishing the existence of *Ātman* on the basis of its relation with knowing and doing.

Verse 10

तत्र तत्र स्थिते तत्तद्भवतीत्येव दृश्यते ।
नान्यन्नान्योऽस्ति संबन्धः कार्यकारणभावतः ॥ १० ॥

tatra tatra sthite tat-tad bhavatīty eva dṛśyate /
nānyan nānyo 'sti saṃbandhaḥ kārya-kāraṇa-bhāvataḥ //

[The Vijñānavādin says:]
What is seen [when elements appear to be in relation to each other] is the rise of some particular objects preceded by some other [similar] ones, and nothing beyond that. Only such [succession] is the relation between cause and effect.

Commentary

The phenomenon known as 'relation' is not a substantive reality. It is a mere concept based on imagination. There are only two things preceding and succeeding each other; one is taken, in mundane dealings, as the cause and the other as the effect. Causation is thus a regular type of succession, and there is nothing else beyond the two concerned things and their own position. It is, in fact, such causation that is called 'relation'. But, in reality, there is nothing substantive in character that can be accepted as some third entity called 'relation' in addition to the two sequential objects. Relation is thus a mere concept, a false and imaginary phenomenon. It thus cannot prove that the phenomena of knowing and doing are related to something else and cannot at all help in establishing the existence of that something as *Ātman,* the doer and knower.

In the next couplet, the *Vijñānavādin* intends to refute the existence of *Ātman* as the supreme doer, the Master of action, by pointing out some logical defects with regard to the concept of relativity in action.

Verse 11

द्विष्ठस्यानेकरूपत्वात्सिद्धस्यान्यानपेक्षणात् ।
पारतन्त्र्याद्ययोगाच्च तेन कर्तापि कल्पितः ॥ ११ ।

dviṣṭhasyāneka-rūpatvāt siddhasyānyānapekṣaṇāt /
pāratantryādy ayogāc ca tena kartāpi kalpitaḥ //

[The Vijñānavādin continues:]
The concept of a doer is also based on imagination because: (1) a connection between two [substances] must involve more than one form; (2) an established entity does not require dependence on anything other than itself; and (3) mutual dependence [between two established objects or facts] is not an appropriate [concept] at all.

Commentary

Scriptural philosophies based on the Vedas and Āgamas maintain that the phenomenon of relation is a single real fact, residing always in more than one entity. The Vijñānavādin raises objection to such a principle through the arguments listed below.

A single entity, residing simultaneously in more than one substance, cannot be essentially one in its character because it must exist in such substances in different forms in accordance with their particular character. Take the example of a swan and its egg. Had there been anything additional to the two of them that could be taken as their 'mutual relation', it should have existed in the egg as the egg and in the swan as the swan, disproving its own existence as a single entity residing in more than one entity. Therefore 'relation' cannot be established as a single phenomenon that resides both in an action and its master.

We speak of the mutual dependence between actor and action, but that also cannot be accepted because two independent entities, their identities well-established by perception, do not require such mutual dependence. Both are already independently established by their own merits, and so any supposed mutual dependence cannot be taken as their mutual relation. Both sentient and insentient entities have their respective independent existences, and the latter do not therefore depend on the former. When nothing can be taken as 'relation' between an action and its acting master, the existence of the former cannot depend on the latter, nor can the existence of the acting master be proved through its relation with the action.

Thus the existence of a Self *(Ātman),* in addition to the momentary currents of mind and body, cannot be proved either on the basis of direct knowing or on that of recollection. It cannot be proved even through inference based on its active relation with knowing and doing. Memories rest in the currents of conscious minds and are based on the impressions of past experiences that reside in the constantly flowing mental currents.

Knowing is self-evident and independent. Doing is nothing but a mere concept based on imagination. Relativity is also only a concept and cannot prove knowing and doing as resting in a third element, the so-called *Ātman*. Only the currents of momentary bodies and minds are flowing constantly, and these are taken as something of enormous import, something very different from fleeting occurrences. So argues the Vijñānavādin.

Chapter 3

REFUTATION OF PŪRVA-PAKṢA

This chapter as a whole is aimed at the refutation of the previously discussed theory of Vijñānavāda Buddhism and also at establishing the Self as the permanently existent base of the psychic activities of perception, conception, recollection, recognition, and so on. A few points discussed in Vijñānavāda may, no doubt, be accepted. The very first couplet, hinting at such a fact, begins to examine the phenomenon of recollection.

Verse 1

सत्यं किंतु स्मृतिज्ञानं पूर्वानुभवसंस्कृतेः ।
जातमप्यात्मनिष्ठं तन्नाद्यानुभववेदकम् ॥ १ ॥

satyaṃ kiṃtu smṛti-jñānaṃ pūrvānubhava-saṃskṛteḥ /
jātam apy ātma-niṣṭhaṃ tan nādyānubhava-vedakam //

True, but a memory, although risen out of the impression of a past experience, is [essentially] limited to its own self. It is [therefore] not the knower of that previous experience.

Commentary

Each and every experience of knowing is, in accordance with the principle of Vijñānavāda, self-luminous and momentary in its character. No knowing can be understood by any other form of knowing. Put another way, each understanding is limited to itself and cannot become mixed up with the details of any other understanding. Experiential knowledge, obtained through perception, does not continue up to the rise of the recollection of that experience. This is because of the characteristic momentariness of experiential knowledge. Therefore a memory can neither throw light on the concerned past experience, which does not continue to shine in its psychic lustre, nor reproduce the object or objects experienced by it. How then can a memory bring to light the object known by the concerned previous experience? How can it assert that such-and-such an object came to light in some particular previous experience, when this experience does not still shine in it as its object?

A recollection like 'that park' expresses a particular park as having been an object of some past experience, which also is recollected in one's memory. Such continuity of experience and memory, says the Śaiva philosopher, can become justifiably possible only on the basis of the existence of *Ātman*. The Self is the Master of the psychic elements—like past experience, its impression, and all present recollections of it—since the *Ātman* alone can be a justifiable foundation for the active functioning of these three psychic entities, allowing them to come to one's help in all mundane dealings. The eternal *Ātman* alone is the ultimate source and Master of all such faculties. That is one of the main arguments of Śaivism in favour of the principle of the eternal existence of *Ātman*.

The next couplet presents the fact that one action of knowing cannot take any other knowing as its object and thus cannot bring it to light, since each and every knowing is self-luminous. This truth further proves the inability of a recollective cognition to bring to light any prior experiential cognition as its object.

Verse 2

दृक्स्वाभासैव नान्येन वेद्या रूपदृशेव दृक् ।
रसे संस्कारजत्वं तु तत्तुल्यत्वं न तद्गतिः ॥ २ ॥

dṛk svābhāsaiva nānyena vedyā rūpa-dṛśeva dṛk /
rase saṃskāra-jatvaṃ tu tat-tulyatvaṃ na tad-gatiḥ //

[The Śaiva thinker argues further:]
Experiential knowing is always self-luminous. It can never be known by any other [knowing], just as the knowing of taste cannot be known by the knowing of colour. [Memory], being a result of past impressions, provides just a resemblance to that. It does not mean any actual knowing [of the past knowledge by the present one].

Commentary

Just as the knowing of taste cannot become an object of the knowing of colour, so experiential knowledge cannot become an object of memory, or recollective knowledge. This is because memory has risen only out of its psychic impressions and also because one knowing cannot be known objectively by any other knowing; each and every knowing shines through its own psychic lustre. Recollection of something resembles, no doubt, the concerned previous experience, but that happens just because the past impression is based on the latter. Such an impression can, at most, provide only some resemblance and nothing beyond that. The impressions on which that memory is based cannot enable the present recollection to bring the past experience objectively to light, nor can they illuminate it as its own object.

The Vijñānavādins argue that any experiential knowing, consisting of a definite idea, although not brought to light by a subsequent recollection, appears erroneously as its object in mundane psychic activities. The validity of such an argument is refuted in the next couplet.

Verse 3

अथातद्विषयत्वेऽपि स्मृतेस्तदवसायतः ।
दृष्टालम्बनता भ्रान्त्या तदेतदसमञ्जसम् ॥ ३ ॥

athātad-viṣayatve 'pi smṛtes tad-avasāyataḥ /
dṛṣṭālambanatā bhrāntyā tad etad asamañjasam //

[The argument of the Śaiva goes thus:]
It is quite absurd to argue that a memory, forming a conception of a past experience, is seen erroneously to depend upon it. [This is] just on account of a misunderstanding [that knowledge can take another form of knowledge as its object].

Commentary

The Vijñānavādins put forth a subtle argument in order to prove that one form of knowing can mistakenly become the formidable object of another knowing on some occasion, brought about by ideations, and they say that such a thing does happen in the case of recollection. They mean to say: All conceptual knowing, accompanied by powerful definite ideas and word-images is, in fact, incorrect; this is because it rises out of the imagination of ignorant worldly beings, who impose the ideas of names and forms on some unrelated objects, which are, in fact, all that they are. No name and no form, they argue, is ever an integral part of any object that we perceive. Only the thing in itself is perceived, and everything else is imposed on it according to the conventional usage begun by primitive man, through employing his imagination. That is the basic error in all conceptual knowing.

Recollection, or memory, is like this 'knowing'. Therefore it is mistaken knowledge and so is incorrect. Memory falsely appears to take both the past experience and its object as its own objects, and thus it falsely appears to bring both to light. And so, among the numerous mundane transactions of knowledge in life, none is actually correct. Correct knowledge is only non-conceptual perception, free from name, form, ideation, and word-image. This basic perception brings to light the object as it is, in itself, and it is therefore indescribable. Such knowledge is the basic *nirvikalpa,* or thought-free, knowing. All other types of knowing, based on human imagination, are incorrect, including recollection. Memory thus attributes great weight and power to what it recalls of the past experience and its object, and takes them as its own objects.

Śaivism puts forth further objections to these arguments of Vijñānavāda Buddhism in the next couplet.

Verse 4

स्मृतितैव कथं तावद् भ्रान्तेश्चार्थस्थितिः कथम् ।
पूर्वानुभवसंस्कारापेक्षा च किमितीष्यते ॥ ४ ॥

smṛtitaiva katham tāvad bhrānteś cārtha-sthitiḥ katham /
pūrvānubhava-saṃskārāpekṣā ca kim itīṣyate //

[The Śaiva philosopher further responds:]
How is it then a recollection? How can erroneous knowledge serve as the basis of the orderliness of world affairs? So why then are past impressions necessarily required? A false conception can arise without the help of such impressions.

Commentary

If a memory does not really touch the experienced object, how can it be accepted as 'a recollection that does not allow the experienced object to be diverted away': *anubhūta-viṣayāsampramoṣaḥ smṛtiḥ* (YS I.11), as such a definition of memory is universally accepted? This is one objection. The next objection is this: if recollection is erroneous knowledge, how can it serve as the basis of the established rules governing all mundane activities?

Thirdly, if recollection is a delusion and an incorrect mode of knowing, why does it require the presence of the impressions of past experiences? Why should a false knowing bother about a proper source? That is the last great objection mentioned in the couplet. Besides, how can memory judge anything at all about past experience and the objects experienced through it, if it does not take them into consideration?

Vijñānavāda's theory of the erroneous nature of all conceptual cognitions, accompanied by the ideas of names and forms, and denoted by certain word-images, is objected to in the fifth couplet.

Verse 5

भ्रान्तित्वे चावसायस्य न जडाद्विषयस्थितिः ।
ततोऽजाड्ये निजोल्लेखनिष्ठान्नार्थस्थितिस्ततः ॥ ५ ॥

bhrāntitve cāvasāyasya na jaḍād viṣaya-sthitiḥ /
tato 'jāḍye nijollekha-niṣṭhān nārtha-sthitis tataḥ //

If all mental conception is mistaken knowledge, then it, being insentient, cannot serve as the base of the orderliness in the world. If, otherwise, it is sentient, even then, being limited to itself alone, it cannot serve like that.

Commentary

Having examined thus the Vijñānavāda views, maintaining ideational knowing as an insentient creation of the mind and thus mistaken knowledge, the Śaiva points out that such a Vijñānavāda view is absurd in character, even if recollection is accepted as being sentient. If definite conceptual knowledge is an error, then mundane orderliness cannot stand on it because of its being insentient. Otherwise, if it is taken as being sentient in nature, even then it cannot serve as the base of such orderliness, because it remains limited only to itself and ideas about it.

Conceptual knowledge is made of two elements: (1) momentary conscious awareness and (2) the creation of mental ideas. The first one is sentient and the second, Vijñānavāda argues, is insentient because its knowledge is flawed, arising as it does from human imagination. Human beings accept both momentary consciousness and conceptual knowledge together as the basis of the order of all mundane activities in the world. But worldly orderliness cannot have this momentary, ever-changing consciousness as its basis, because it remains self-centred, bringing to light only its own existence and notions about itself. It does not accurately portray any objective element in the world. Thus argues the Śaiva.

The second element, the human thought process that generates ideas, is insentient and therefore cannot in any way assist the world's mundane order. But it is true that the world's orderly patterns have been well-established during countless past aeons, and they will continue to be like that in the future as well. Therefore it must have some powerful element, other than the momentary flux of the conscious mind, as its basis. Śaivism says such an element can be none other than the constantly existing, eternal Consciousness, known as *Ātman,* that pervades and holds within it the entire flux of momentary knowing and that bears in it the impression of such knowing

The next two couplets point out the insufficiency of the non-existentialist views of Vijñānavāda and conclude the whole discussion in favour of the Śaivite principle of the effectiveness of *Ātman* (the higher Self) as the eternally existent, pure, infinite, and single Consciousness endowed with all divine potency.

Verses 6-7

एवमन्योन्यभिन्नानामपरस्परवेदिनाम् ।
ज्ञानानामनुसंधानजन्मा नश्येज्जनस्थितिः ॥ ६ ॥
न चेदन्तःकृतानन्तविश्वरूपो महेश्वरः ।
स्यादेकश्चिद्वपुर्ज्ञानस्मृत्यपोहनशक्तिमान् ॥ ७ ॥

evam anyonya-bhinnānām aparaspara-vedinām /
jñānānām anusaṃdhāna-janmā naśyej jana-sthitiḥ //
na ced antaḥ-kṛtānanta-viśva-rūpo maheśvaraḥ /
syād ekaś cid-vapur jñāna-smṛty-apohana-śaktimān //

[The Śaiva says:]
The orderliness of the world, based on the unified assumptions of mutually ignorant [unacquainted] and different mundane cognitions, would thus vanish if the existence of the one Almighty God, having pure Consciousness as His form, bearing in Him the numerous universal phenomena and possessing divine powers to know, to recollect, and to differentiate, were not an undeniable fact.

Commentary

All cognitions, all instances of knowing, are by themselves different and unrelated to each other, as well as ignorant about one another. No thought can have any other thought as an object of its knowing. Since each and every thought is always a self-luminous entity, none of them can be brought to light by anything other than itself. All cognitions are thus absolute strangers, knowing nothing about one another. The orderliness of all worldly affairs can only be the result of some broader consideration of these different cognitions. Unified human understanding cannot be conducted by self-centred and disparate thoughts alone. This broader understanding of human affairs requires some additional entity that can contain disparate cognitions within itself and can bring about human understanding in an overarching, collective fashion. Such an additional entity is the infinite, all-pervading, and pure universal Consciousness, which can bear within itself all phenomena in the form of reflections. Such higher Consciousness is the universal Self, known as Almighty God. He is divinely potent, able to bring about differentiation between (1) a subject and an object; (2) one subject and another subject; and (3) one object and another object; as well as (4) between Himself and the entire phenomenal existence consisting of numerous finite subjects, objects, and mental processes possessed by the subjects.

It is thus the Lord who differentiates all thoughts and causes any collective consideration about them. It is He who is competent to manifest different experiential and recollective thoughts in so great a variety. He is powerful enough to synthesise and to differentiate all cognitions and their contents. He is, in fact, the one single Reality that is actually and eternally existent. But He is always inclined by His essential nature to manifest a multifarious diversity and is potent enough to do so. This power of differentiation is called here *apohana-śakti*. The Lord also has the power to make some particular entities appear as knowing subjects and others as objects of knowing. This is His cognitive power, called *jñāna-śakti*. Thirdly, He is capable of manifesting memory, the recollection in a subject of some previously experienced objects, in wonderfully various ways. That is His *smṛti-śakti,* His power of memory. While recollecting, He is efficient and potent enough to synthesise and to analyse the data of past experiences in fantastically different ways. Thus He causes the drama of the whole universe to unfold.

These three powers of the Lord—differentiation, knowledge, and memory—account for the world's amazing variety of different knowing subjects, objects, and means of these subjects knowing the objects. Such a variety of manifestations accounts for this complex, incredible phenomenal existence. One sees multitudes of 'triangular' situations among subjects (called *pramātṛ*), objects *(prameya),* and the means of knowing *(pramāṇa)*. If there were no such supreme authority, possessing this regulating capacity and causing all phenomena to be operated through the three divine powers *(apohana, jñāna,* and *smṛti),* the orderliness of the phenomenal world could not exist at all. The universe would not be a perfect cosmos, but an utter chaos. Therefore the existence of such a divinely potent universal authority must be accepted by each correctly oriented, wise thinker. This authority is Almighty God, appearing Himself in the form of the Self of each and every being, as well as in that of all objective phenomena.

That is the main argument put forth by the masters of Śaiva monism against the atheism and non-existentialism of the thinkers in the line of Vijñānavāda. This argument continues to be discussed in ample detail throughout the entire *Jñānādhikāra* of the *Īśvara-pratyabhijñā-kārikā* and is further explained by Abhinavagupta in his *Īśvara-pratyabhijñā-vimarśinī,* continuing all the way to its eighth and final chapter.

Chapter 4

THE RECOLLECTIVE POWER

Utpaladeva explains the principles of the phenomenon of recollection, or memory, according to Śaiva monism and presents it in the first couplet of the fourth chapter.

Verse 1

स हि पूर्वानुभूतार्थोपलब्धा परतोऽपि सन् ।
विमृशन्स इति स्वैरी स्मरतीत्यपदिश्यते ॥ १ ॥

sa hi pūrvānubhūtārthopalabdhā parato 'pi san /
vimṛśan sa iti svairī smaratīty apadiśyate //

The experiencer of a previously experienced object continues to exist afterward as well [at the time of recollection]. Deliberating on [the object] as 'that', in accordance with his free will, he is said to be remembering it.

Commentary

Experience is a momentary phenomenon. It vanishes just after its emergence. But the experiencer is, without a doubt, a constantly existent entity, continuing to exist even at the time he recollects the previously experienced object. Besides, he is free to analyse the contents of his experience and to recollect parts of it or the entire event in as many various ways as he likes. He has the freedom to synthesise the contents of his many experiences, whether in parts or as a whole, and also to recollect the experienced objects in various imaginative ways.

This freedom of the knower proves that he is in possession of divine powers and disproves the atheism of Vijñānavāda Buddhism as well. It also disproves its theory of the non-existence of the Self, *Ātman,* as the Subject of knowing; He is the one who wields His power over our entire psychic apparatus.

A person who knows something experiences the object known in the moment as 'this'. But since he is sufficiently free and independent in matters of thinking, he can recollect it later as 'that'. The word 'this' denotes a thing experienced in the present, while the word 'that' denotes it as having been experienced in the past and remembered in the present. Combining the past and present, memory can throw new light on the concerned object of experience and reassess its significance.

The next couplet emphasises the fact that recollection cannot be erroneous knowledge in essence, as maintained by the Vijñānavādins, because it is definitely capable of bringing to light the previously experienced object in our present awareness.

Verse 2

भासयेच्च स्वकालेऽर्थात्पूर्वाभासितमामृशन् ।
स्वलक्षण घटाभासमात्रेणाथाखिलात्मना ॥ २ ॥

bhāsayec ca sva-kāle 'rthāt pūrvābhāsitam āmṛśan /
sva-lakṣaṇaṃ ghaṭābhāsa-mātreṇāthākhilātmanā //

[A memory is] a deliberation upon something in itself, something previously brought to light [by perception]. [The recollection] must illuminate it at the same time; either simply, as in the case of a particular object like a pitcher, or along with all its characteristics, because [recollection always] has an object that is illumined by it.

Commentary

Recollection always involves a core of objective knowing. Generally one remembers some object helpful to some purpose. While a recollection, being a cognition, shines through the light of the Consciousness of the concerned recollector, its object, being part and parcel of that memory, must also shine with it. But this memory does not shine as something present and new, because, in that case, it would not be a recollection, rather a fresh experience. Therefore, the object that shines in memory is the same past object that came to light in the previous perceptual experience.

An object, coming to light in a perception, is always the thing in itself, without any name or form. These features are imposed on it by means of mental ideation, or conception, which is the next step. Such a phenomenon, appearing in both its aspects of perception and conception, is deliberated upon in a recollection. A recollector is free enough to analyse any experience and to synthesize his different experientially based perceptions and conceptions. He recollects them variously in accordance with his aim and will and abilities. He can recollect a thing either as a simple object or remember it in more detail. For instance, he can recollect an object simply as a *ghaṭa,* a round, pitcher-shaped earthen water pot. Or he can remember it more elaborately, as a beautiful, shining, and costly golden pitcher, worthy to be used in a Śiva temple, bearing water from the river Gaṇga that constantly drips from the pitcher onto the head of the *śiva-liṅga,* thus worshipping the Lord.

A recollecting person may also remember only a part of the object of an experience. For instance, having perceived the entire panorama of a large battle, he may recollect, once out of it, only some particular exploit of a brave fighter.

On the other hand, he can combine the data of parts of several experiences, recollecting the whole thing as one single objective cognition. That is due to his freedom in such activity.

The next couplet emphasises the unity underlying all our experiences, both past perceptions and conceptions and also later recollections; all are to be embraced as one's own Self. This couplet pronounces disagreement with certain doctrines held by Vijñānavāda.

Verse 3

न च युक्तं स्मृतेर्भेदे स्मर्यमाणस्य भासनम् ।
तेनैक्यं भिन्नकालानां संविदां वेदितैष सः ॥ ३ ॥

na ca yuktaṃ smṛter bhede smaryamāṇasya bhāsanam /
tenaikyaṃ bhinna-kālānāṃ saṃvidāṃ veditaiṣa saḥ //

If a remembered object were different and separate from the memory of it, its coming to light as a thing remembered would be an absurdity. This proves the fact that several cognitions, [although] arising at different times, do have a mutual unity. Their unity is actually the single cogniser [the Self], shining as both 'this' and 'that' [that is, as the present and the past].

Commentary

In the doctrine of the momentariness of *vijñāna* (the conscious thought process), experience and later recollection are two mutually unrelated and different forms of knowing. The object that is brought to light by perception and the name and form imposed on it by subsequent mental creation are both different from recollection, because neither of these two psychic activities, nor their contents, exists at the time of recollection. Since memory, according to Buddhism, is erroneous knowledge, it cannot bring to light anything real.

But if Vijñānavāda's doctrines are accepted, then an object of recollection cannot be taken as itself. One can newly experience an object, rather than remembering one, because it appears as a new thing in *vijñāna,* the mind. In this case it is brought to light at the present moment and has no relation to any past momentary thought or event. It is thus freshly experienced and not anything recollected, for memory brings to light only some past object that shone in a past experience. So, logically speaking, only new experiences are possible in life and there can be no memories at all; unless of course there is a permanently existing entity, the higher Self, that can embrace both past experience and present memories of it.

Recollection of past objects of knowledge is definitely a fact of human experience, and this proves a sort of unity between past and present cognition. The fundamental basis of such unity is, in fact, that eternally existent entity that we call *Ātman,* the Subject and the Master of all psychic activities, whether they happen in the past or present, or shine as 'this' (current experiences) or 'that' (recollections).

The *Ātman* is the pure and self-luminous I-Consciousness that pervades the entire succession of momentary mental states and conducts all mental activities, including perception, conception, recollection, recognition, and imagination. This pure I-Consciousness is not different from all its cognitions. These simply consist of its own psychic flutter and are thus nothing different from it. The *Ātman* with its present recollective thoughts is the same as the *Ātman* with some past experienced perceptions. Only the existence of such an overarching and all-inclusive Reality, bearing both past and present psychic activities within itself, can make possible all the sensible cognitions and collective deliberations that comprise mundane human thought. *Ātman* is thus the basis of all the orderliness and credibility of the human mind.

The next couplet is devoted to proving that, although the object of a previous experience can appear as an object of a present memory, the previous experience itself does not.

Verse 4

नैव ह्यनुभवो भाति स्मृतौ पूर्वोऽर्थवत्पृथक् ।
प्रागन्वभूवमहमित्यात्मारोहणभासनात् ॥ ४ ॥

naiva hy anubhavo bhāti smṛtau pūrvo 'rthavat pṛthak /
prāg anvabhūvam aham ity ātmārohaṇa-bhāsanāt //

A past experience, unlike its object, does not shine as a [separate] object in a recollection because there it shines resting within the Self [of the recollecting subject] and appears as 'I experienced it previously'.

Commentary

Objectivity, treating something as an object, attributes 'this-ness' or 'that-ness' to the object. Such an object is thus separated from and non-identical with the knower, the subject of the action of knowing. Subjectivity, however, shining as part and parcel of 'I-ness', means identity with the knower. The past content of some previous experience can shine once again as an object of knowing in the psychic light of recollection. It becomes 'that particular object', different from the one who knows it, the subject. But the previous experience, which had enlightened that object, does not shine there as well as an 'object'; it does not, in fact, become 'that particular experience'. Such a thing can, no doubt, be the case with someone's calculated guesses and consequent deliberations about another's experiences; however, genuine experiential knowledge, shining in its essential and basic psychological aspect, can never appear as an object of any other experiential cognition. Instead, it shines in the psyche as a peculiarity of a person's own experience, a faculty of the knowing subject. It comes to light in awareness not as 'that', but as 'I experienced'. Thus, within the person of the knowing subject, experience shines in him as part and parcel of his own being and not as anything different from him.

An opponent may raise an objection here by saying that one experience of knowing can surely appear as an object of another knowing. He may cite the example of the telepathic experience of a yogin who has knowledge of the thoughts of other people. The next couplet answers this objection.

Verse 5

योगिनामपि भासन्ते न दृशो दर्शनान्तरे ।
स्वसंविदेकमानास्ता भान्ति मेयपदेऽपि वा ॥ ५ ॥

yogināṃ api bhāsante na dṛśo darśanāntare /
sva-saṃvid eka-mānās tā bhānti meya-pade 'pi vā //

No cognitions can shine as objects in another's thoughts, even if the latter be the telepathic experiences of yogins. Even these shine there validly only by virtue of their own Self-awareness; or, even if the argument [about a yogin's knowledge] is accepted as right, [knowledge] can shine there as an object [only as the cognition of others and not as any cognitive particulars of one's own Self shining as 'I'].

Commentary

The author means to say that such an example, if accepted as valid, can prove only that a yogin may be capable of experiencing objectively someone else's knowledge; but he cannot at all justify that he can cognise objectively his own knowledge, just as he cognises an object. This is because, laying emphasis on his own Self, he merely feels that he has experienced himself. For this reason, he does not see his perception objectively as 'this', but only as 'I'. The example of the yogin's telepathy is thus not apropos to the point at hand: *meya-pade* 'in the position of an object' *api vā* 'even if it is accepted'.

In fact, a yogin with supernormal powers does not see the mental activities of others as objective elements of his telepathic knowledge. By becoming one with others, entering their mental apparatus and pervading their minds and senses, he witnesses the contents of their mental activities as if they were his own. Such activities shine in him as 'I' and not as 'this'. Such a yogin can enter any number of minds and perceive through all of them simultaneously, just as a person can put into action more than one of his senses and limbs at the same time. But even a yogin does not thereby comprehend his own knowledge as an object, as 'this'. He rather experiences it as a subject, as 'I'.

If, however, the contrary argument, that experiential knowledge can be comprehended as an object, is accepted for the time being as an *abhyupagama-siddhānta,* an admitted axiom of Indian logic, even then the argument is not valid at all. This is because the example of the yogin's power to read minds does not correspond with the point in question and cannot therefore serve as an example. A yogin may know the perception shining in other beings as 'this', while a recollector remembers his own experiences as 'I'. A yogin may observe that such-and-such person thinks of an object, while a recollector sees that he himself experienced an object. The two cases are not similar,[19] and the example of a yogin cannot prove that one's past experience is recollected by him objectively.[20]

The disputant might argue again based on the possibility of someone's recollection appearing as 'I had such an experience'. Since a past experience appears here objectively in the recollection, one cognition can be known objectively by another cognition. Śaivism's answer to such an argument is contained in the next couplet.

Verse 6

स्मर्यते यद्दृगासीन्मे सैवमित्यपि भेदतः ।
तद्व्याकरणमेवास्या मया दृष्टमिति स्मृतेः ॥ ६ ॥

smaryate yad dṛg āsīn me saivam ity api bhedataḥ /
tad vyākaraṇam evāsyā mayā dṛṣṭam iti smṛteḥ //

It is possible that sometimes a recollection may occur as, 'Such-and-such an experience arose in me like this'. [This might verbally give an objective colour to the past experience and make the memory appear to be something different from it.] Yet it is just a different sort of verbal expression or explanation of the recollection, which is shining as 'I experienced like this'.

Commentary

Utpaladeva means to say that a different type of verbal expression about a cognition cannot change the cognition's basic character. Just as a sentence in active voice can be explained through another sentence in passive voice, without causing any change in its content or difference in meaning, so differences in verbal expression of recollections will not prove any difference in their basic character. They are still non-different from the recollecting subject.

This fact is elucidated further in the next couplet, which quotes another example from experiential knowledge.

Verse 7

या च पश्याम्यहमिमं घटोऽयमिति वाऽवसा ।
मन्यते समवेतं साप्यवसातरि दर्शनम् ॥ ७॥

yā ca paśyāmy aham imaṃ ghaṭo 'yam iti vāvasā/
manyate samavetaṃ sāpy avasātari darśanam //

Conceptual knowledge, appearing either as 'I see this pitcher' or as 'This is a pitcher', also presupposes cognition being inseparably related to its subject, the cogniser.

Commentary

Even though in verbal expression some conceptualisations may show an apparent predominance of either the subject or the object, in both cases experiential knowing remains continuously inseparable and non-different from its subject. In fact, this experiential knowing is the subject himself taking a particular stance. Besides, not only is recollection inseparable and non-differentiable from its recollector, but such is the case with all conceptual knowing. All knowing is thus, in fact, an inseparable quality of the inner divine Knower who alone shines as Himself in the form of such activities as perception, conception, recollection, imagination, contemplation, recognition, realisation, and so on.[21]

The fundamental principle of the basic unity of all psychic activities with the divine Self, the Subject of all types of knowing, is expressed in the next couplet as the conclusion of the chapter.

Verse 8

तन्मया दृश्यते दृष्टोऽयं स इत्यामृशत्यपि ।
ग्राह्यग्राहकताभिन्नावर्थौ भातः प्रमातरि ॥ ८॥

tan mayā dṛśyate dṛṣṭo 'yaṃ sa ity āmṛśaty api /
grāhya grāhakatā bhinnāv arthau bhātaḥ pramātari //

It is thus established that two types of phenomena, the relative finite subject and the object, appear [in conceptual manifestation] within one basic subject while [he is] considering: 'This is' and 'This is being seen by me', or 'That was' and 'That was seen by me'.

Commentary

Conceptual knowing takes two forms in its verbal expression, showing either the existence of an object or an object being conceived by a subject. The forms of this expression are either 'This is' or 'I see this'. An apparent verbal emphasis on the object shines in the former and on the subject in the latter. Each of these conceptions corresponds with two types of future recollection. Memory will take one of these forms of verbal expression, either 'That was' or 'I saw that'.

Conceptions and recollections of all types involve two elements, a relative subject and a finite object. But both of them shine in the light of pure Consciousness, which has the character of the basic Subject, who is infinite, eternal, divinely potent, ever blissful, and playful in nature. Such pure Consciousness alone appears as all finite subjects, phenomenal objects, and all types of perception, conception, recollection, imagination, and so forth, taking all these different forms like a mirror in which reflections shine. Thus, everything shines within the Absolute Subject, Supreme Śiva, who has all divine potency as His character and a blissful propensity to manifest the divine phenomenal play as part of His essentially powerful nature. This blissful potency and manifestation, in fact, illustrate the fundamental philosophical principle of Kashmir Śaivism—the nature of supreme Śiva as both subject and object and as both essence and activity.

Chapter 5

THE COGNITIVE POWER

The fifth chapter of Book I is aimed at establishing the existence of the monistic and theistic Absolute of Kashmir Śaivism through its principle of cosmogony, based on the theory of spiritual realism. The first couplet points toward such a theory.

Verse 1

वर्तमानावभासानां भावानामवभासनम् ।
अन्तःस्थितवतामेव घटते बहिरात्मना ॥ १॥

vartamānāvabhāsānāṃ bhāvānām avabhāsanam /
antaḥ-sthitavatām eva ghaṭate bahir ātmanā //

The external manifestation of entities (objects) currently appearing [in one's perception] actually becomes possible just because they are already present internally [as 'I'].

Commentary

Only objects that are already shining within the light of pure Consciousness, and which are identical with it, can appear as 'this thing' or 'that thing' in our perception. For how could they otherwise shine or appear at all? It is only Consciousness that can shine by itself. Assuming the form of any phenomenon, it can shine in that form as well, appearing as 'this object' or 'that object'. Otherwise such phenomena, not being conscious, could not shine by themselves and consequently could not appear at all as objects. This power of the Lord that manifests outwardly as objects, as the multifarious types of phenomena, shines inwardly as 'I' and is known as *jñāna-śakti*. It is the power of knowledge and it belongs to Him.

If an object of knowing had not been identical with the light of the knower's consciousness at the time of its perception, it would have remained totally unknown. An object of knowing cannot be an entity different from the light of Consciousness because the lustre of Consciousness is the very soul of any object of knowing.

The next couplet explains that an object is not different from the psychic light of divine Consciousness and shines by virtue of its identity with it.

Verse 2

प्रागिवार्थोऽप्रकाशः स्यात्प्रकाशात्मतया विना ।
न च प्रकाशो भिन्नः स्यादात्मार्थस्य प्रकाशता ॥ २ ॥

prāg ivārtho 'prakāśaḥ syāt prakāśāt matayā vinā /
na ca prakāśo bhinnaḥ syād ātmārthasya prakāśatā //

Had the light of Consciousness not been the essence of an object, the latter would have remained unmanifest as [it was] before [its contact with the former]. Such light cannot be different from it, as the object has Consciousness as its very soul.

Commentary

If the light of Consciousness manifests an object, it is because this psychic light is capable of pervading the known object, assuming its form for the time being and shining in the form of the object. Had it not been so, the object concerned, lying outside the field of the individual I-Consciousness, would not have become manifest at all.

It is Consciousness alone, shining as an 'I', that manifests all objects in the world as 'this' or 'that'; and doing so, Consciousness itself assumes their objective forms. This is the *ābhāsa-vāda,* or the doctrine of idealist world creation, as accepted in Kashmir Śaivism.[22]

There are logical defects in any attempt to present objective entities as having independent existence and a different nature from Consciousness. These are pointed out here in the third *kārikā*.

Verse 3

भिन्ने प्रकाशे चाभिन्ने संकरो विषयस्य तत् ।
प्रकाशात्मा प्रकाश्योऽर्थो नाप्रकाशश्च सिद्ध्यति ॥ ३ ॥

bhinne prakāśe cābhinne saṃkaro viṣayasya tat /
prakāśātmā prakāśyo 'rtho nāprakāśaś ca siddhyati //

Non-identity of a manifest object with *prakāśa,* the light of Consciousness [which makes it manifest and] which has a constant uniformity in its essential character, would result in an intermixture *(saṃkara)* of objects [in mundane activities]. Therefore, a manifest object has this spiritual light as its very soul; otherwise even its very existence cannot be proved.

Commentary

Manifestation of objects by the light of Consciousness becomes possible only when the light of awareness *(prakāśa),* pervading the concerned objects and assuming their forms for the time being, itself shines. Had this not been the case, an object, lying outside the field of Consciousness, could not have become manifest at all, because it is only Consciousness that shines by itself and brings to light all manifest objects, while assuming itself their particular forms. If different objects were accepted as being non-identical with *prakāśa,* a confusing intermixture *(saṅkara)* of objects would be the result in all mundane activities. In other words, if *prakāśa* were accepted as a reality quite different from its objects—like something black and something white, two mutually different entities—then, if both of them were shining in *prakāśa,* being one with it, they would invite the logical defect known as *saṃkara,* an intermixture, because the two different substances would appear as one. But *prakāśa,* being pure Consciousness and capable of bearing both white and black as reflections identical with it, does not involve Śaivism in such a defect. Like a mirror, it can shine while appearing identical with both these mutually different entities.

Therefore, it must be accepted that a manifest object has *prakāśa* as its very soul and essence. Its existence cannot otherwise be proved, because it is *prakāśa* which is independent and powerful and assumes both black and white forms, to manifest them as such. If Consciousness were taken as being always of a uniform character, as an entity different from manifest objects, it would involve us in the logical defect of their intermixture. How could one and the same Consciousness be both black and white? Both of them would, in such a case, become identical. When $a = b$ and $a = c$, then $b = c$ would be the result. Non-difference between the objects of different character would be the result and that would mean an end to the harmony of mundane dealings, based as they are on the different characters of phenomenal entities.

Therefore, it must be accepted that a manifest object has *prakāśa* as its real nature and becomes manifest by virtue of this. Just as the light of the sun, assuming the form of both black and white, shines itself upon different forms, so does the spiritual light of Consciousness. Besides, the very existence of a manifest object becomes an impossibility if it were taken as an entity quite different from *prakāśa,* the psycho-spiritual luminosity undergirding everything in existence. As will be discussed later, Consciousness is divinely potent and has the propensity to assume different forms and shine through them.

In the next couplet the differing view of the Sautrāntika school of Buddhism is presented by Utpaladeva.

Verse 4

तत्तदाकस्मिकाभासो बाह्यं चेदनुमापयेत् ।
नह्यभिन्नस्य बोधस्य विचित्राभासहेतुता ॥ ४ ॥

tat-tad-ākasmikābhāso bāhyaṃ ced anumāpayet /
na hy abhinnasya bodhasya vicitrābhāsa-hetutā //

If it is argued that *prakāśa,* being always of a uniform character, cannot become the source [or cause] of the wonderfully different [world] manifestations, then this would prove, through inference, the existence of some [objective, causative] elements lying outside the plane of Consciousness.

Commentary

The Sautrāntika teachers argue that if the wonderfully varied world manifestations appear within *prakāśa,* which has always a 'uniformity' in its character, this suggests the existence of objects lying outside Consciousness, objects that cast their reflections into it. How can unchanging Consciousness, always having a uniform character, by itself produce different manifestations? Just as outward objects, casting their reflection into a uniformly existent mirror, show it as having wonderfully different hues and appearances, such is also the case with Consciousness, which maintains uniformity in its basic character and yet appears to bear shades and appearances of varied character. These Buddhists thus try to prove the existence of matter and material objects as entities independent of mind and mental appearances. This argument will be nullified in *kārikā* 6. *Kārikā* 5, in the meantime, refers to and refutes the views of the Vijñānavāda school of Buddhist idealism.

Verse 5

न वासनाप्रबोधोऽत्र विचित्रो हेतुतामियात् ।
तस्यापि तत्प्रबोधस्य वैचित्र्ये किं निबन्धनम् ॥ ५ ॥

na vāsanā-prabodho 'tra vicitro hetutām iyāt /
tasyāpi tat-prabodhasya vaicitrye kiṃ nibandhanam //

[Even] the variegated types of awakened past impressions *(vāsanās)* cannot serve as the source [of the world], because the cause of their awakened diversity can be questioned.

Commentary

Vijñānavādins, the philosophers of Buddhist idealism, argue that the impressions of past experiences *(vāsanās),* lying in the mind, wake up in myriad ways and consequently cause the manifestation of the wide variety of objects in the world, just as impressions are awakened and manifested in so much variety in our dreams. In this way they deny the real existence of two entities, namely: *bhūta,* matter, and *bhauta,* material objects; and accept only two varieties of phenomena: *citta,* mind, and *caitta,* mental ideas. But the Sautrāntikas, refuting these views of the Vijñānavāda, argue that mind, which consists of a uniform type of Consciousness, cannot appear as a diversity of phenomena. Therefore, they suppose the existence of matter and material entities lying outside the plane of mind, casting their reflections into it, and becoming thus the cause of the mundane experiences of diversity in life.

But the Vijñānavādins also deny that we can experience the independent existence of material phenomena apart from mind. Śaivism accepts their view on this matter, though it finds the basic origin of phenomena and phenomenal activities not in mind but in infinite, pure, and divinely potent Consciousness. Idealism is thus more akin to Śaivism than materialism is, at least to some extent. Such a statement is made by the author in the next couplet.

Verse 6

स्यादेतदवभासेषु तेष्वेवावसिते सति ।
व्यवहारे किमन्येन बाह्येनानुपपत्तिना ॥ ६ ॥

syād etad avabhāseṣu teṣv evāvasite sati /
vyavahāre kim anyena bāhyenānupapattinā //

That may be the case; of what use would be the unjustifiable theory of a material existence lying outside the field of Consciousness, when all mundane activities can satisfactorily be explained simply on the basis of [divine Consciousness' own Self-] manifestations?

Commentary

The master philosopher Utpaladeva argues here that all objective manifestations in the world can be explained satisfactorily by the theory that pure Consciousness appears itself as such. He therefore disagrees with the theory of the Sautrāntikas, which attempts to establish that matter and mind are independent of one another. He also disagrees with the theory of Vijñānavāda, which denies the existence of *Ātman* at the root of the mind.

The Śaivite principle regarding the phenomenal manifestation of the world is precisely laid out here.

Verse 7

चिदात्मैव हि देवोऽन्तःस्थितमिच्छावशाद्बहिः ।
योगीव निरुपादानमर्थजातं प्रकाशयेत् ॥ ७ ॥

cidātmaiva hi devo 'ntaḥ-sthitam icchā-vaśād bahiḥ /
yogīva nirupādānam artha-jātaṃ prakāśayet //

None other than the Lord, who is pure Consciousness, can manifest outwardly the whole phenomenal existence that lies within Him. [He does so] through the power of His will, just as a yogin does, without using any substantive material for this purpose.

Commentary

The master Utpaladeva presents the example of a yogin who can create things like a mango tree laden with ripe fruit only by exercising his will power. He needs no material causes, such as seeds, soil, moisture, or warmth, nor any time process for his purpose. Utpaladeva deduces the principle that all of phenomenonal creation exists always in the Lord in the form of the divine potency of His pure Consciousness, and it is at times manifested objectively by Him through the exercise of His irresistible divine will. He does not need to make use of any material other than Himself, such as atoms, cosmic energy, or *avidyā* (the power of ignorance) for this purpose. All such entities (like *avidyā*) owe their very origin and existence to the divine will of the Lord.

The master Utpaladeva continues, examining the possible scope of logical inference in deducing the existence of matter as something different from Consciousness.

Verse 8

अनुमानमनाभातपूर्वे नैवेष्टम् . . .

anumānam anābhāta-pūrve naiveṣṭam . . .

Inference is never meant to be used to prove the existence of an object that has not previously become manifest anywhere . . .

Commentary

Logicians see a phenomenon becoming manifest in some special environment. Using this phenomenon as an example, they deduce the existence of similar 'causes' elsewhere when they see similar phenomena. But an entity that has not already become known somewhere cannot thus become the target of inference. The existence of objective phenomena, lying outside the field of Consciousness, has so far never been ascertained. Therefore, for want of a proper example, the existence of matter lying outside the field of Consciousness cannot be deduced even with the help of inference.

The senses of a person are in fact his psychic powers to see, to hear, and so on. These powers do not have any perceptible forms and cannot therefore be perceived. What we perceive is the seat of a sense and not the sense itself. The ears of a deaf person can be perceived, but his hearing capacity, the actual sense as such, does not exist therein. Both its existence or non-existence have to be guessed at and are not perceived.

The plausibility of inference in proving the existence of the senses, for example, which have never become known to anyone through perception, is established by the remaining portion of the couplet.

Verse 8 continued

. . . इन्द्रियम् ।
आभातमेव बीजादेराभासाद्धेतुवस्तुनः ॥ ८ ॥

. . . indriyam /
ābhātam eva bījāder ābhāsād dhetu-vastunaḥ //

. . . The existence of the senses, as some special cause [of perception] has already been revealed, [as] in the case of a seed being the cause of a sprout.

Commentary

An antagonist would raise an objection against the above argument about the incapability of inference in deducing the independent existence of matter outside Consciousness by quoting the example of the senses. The existence of the senses is never directly known to anyone through perception, but may be deduced. A Śaiva answer to this objection is given.

Logicians do not actually try to infer the existence of the senses as such, but simply locate some special cause of perception. The object of inference is actually this unknown special cause. The existence of some special cause is already perceived as, for instance, a seed is seen as the cause of a sprout. Such particular causes of perception are called 'senses' for the purpose of mundane usage.

The next verses are aimed at pointing out the impossibility of an entity manifesting outside its underlying field of conscious awareness and the consequent inability of proving its existence through logical inference.

Verse 9

आभासः पुनराभासाद्बाह्यस्यासीत्कथंचन ।
अर्थस्य नैव तेनास्य सिद्धिर्नाप्यनुमानतः ॥ ९ ॥

ābhāsaḥ punar ābhāsād bāhyasyāsīt kathaṃ-cana /
arthasya naiva tenāsya siddhir nāpy anumānataḥ //

Matter has never been experienced as in any way lying outside one's perception of it. Therefore its [independent] existence cannot be proved even through inference.

Commentary

Matter, wherever or whenever it is perceived, is essentially not a thing different or separate from one's perceptual knowing of it. Therefore its existence outside knowing cannot be proved. Knowing is a state of Consciousness. Therefore, matter and all material phenomena have Consciousness as their essence and cannot be proved, even by inference, to be anything outside Consciousness.

The next couplet states the principle of spiritual realism with regard to phenomenal existence and its manifestation, as seen by the masters of Kashmir Śaivism.

Verse 10

स्वामिनश्चात्मसंस्थस्य भावजातस्य भासनम् ।
अस्त्येव न विना तस्मादिच्छामर्शः प्रवर्तते॥ १०॥

svāminaś cātma-saṃsthasya bhāva-jātasya bhāsanam /
asty eva na vinā tasmād icchāmarśaḥ pravartate //

The divine Master surely has the knowledge of the entire phenomenal existence contained within Himself [in the form of His divine potency]; otherwise the throb of His will [to manifest it outwardly] could not proceed.

Commentary

The entire phenomenal existence is always present in the infinite and absolute Consciousness, called Paramaśiva, the Supreme Lord. It shines in Him as the pure and infinite I-Consciousness and lies in Him in the form of His divine potency, which has the capability to act or not to act, to act one way or to act any other way it chooses. Such potency is His divine essence and is the source of His five divine phenomenal activities of cosmic creation, preservation, absorption, self-oblivion, and self-revelation. Had He not been aware of the existence of the whole phenomenon lying in potential form within Him, He could not have exercised His divine will to create it outwardly. Such creation is merely an outward manifestation of the inwardly existent entities shining there as potencies of the pure and infinite I-Consciousness. This objective manifestation of the subjective divine powers is precisely the theory of divine realism, or *sat-kārya-vāda,* on one hand, and *ābhāsa-vāda* on the other hand, the theory of creation by the divine display of emanation, as seen by the masters of Kashmir Śaivism through their yogic revelation.

The next couplet establishes awareness as the essential nature of Consciousness.

Verse 11

स्वभावमवभासस्य विमर्शं विदुरन्यथा ।
प्रकाशोऽर्थोपरक्तोऽपि स्फटिकादिजडोपमः ॥ ११ ॥

sva-bhāvam avabhāsasya vimarśaṃ vidur anyathā /
prakāśo 'rthoparakto 'pi sphaṭikādi-jaḍopamaḥ //

Awareness is the essential character of Consciousness [as each conscious being is aware of himself and his nature and character]; otherwise *prakāśa* (the light of Consciousness), even though bearing the appearance of an object, could at most be compared to some insentient [reflective] elements like crystal.

Commentary

Crystal, put before an object, no doubt bears the object's colour and appearance. It shines itself as the object but does not, or rather cannot, prove or assert the existence of the object. How can it do so when it is not ever aware of the object? Nor is it aware even of its own self. Had *prakāśa* been ordinary luminosity, devoid of *vimarśa* (awareness), it would have not been anything better than crystal, which reflects but is insentient in nature. Therefore it must be accepted that (1) *prakāśa* is always aware of itself, and (2) it becomes aware of the object appearing in it. Consciousness thus has two aspects: one is its nature of shining and being ever manifest in itself *(prakāśa),* and the other is its self-awareness (*vimarśa*). Consciousness shines always as 'I' and is always aware of itself and its essential character. When it assumes the form of some object, it brings to light the object concerned and becomes aware of its existence as well.

Thus, the infinite and absolute Consciousness shines constantly and at the same time is always aware of itself and its nature of divine potency and playfulness. This awareness of its divine essence, vibrating outwardly, manifests the five divine activities of creation, preservation, and so forth. It thus becomes the source and foundation of the dramatic show of the entire universe, which appears within the light of pure Consciousness in the manner of multiple reflections. The divine power of God, shining in Him as Himself and becoming reflected outwardly within the light of His Consciousness, appears as all phenomena and the divine activities that involve them. This is precisely the basic theory of cosmogony, as discovered in their inner experience by the ancient masters of Kashmir Śaivism.

The twelfth *kārikā* also deals with the subject of awareness.

Verse 12

आत्मात एव चैतन्यं चित्क्रिया चितिकर्तृता ।
तात्पर्येणोदितस्तेन जडात्स हि विलक्षणः ॥ १२ ॥

ātmāta eva caitanyaṃ cit-kriyā citikartṛtā /
tāt paryeṇoditas tena jaḍāt sa hi vilakṣaṇaḥ //

For this very reason the Self has been defined [in the *Śiva Sūtras*] as Consciousness and [in the *Yoga-bhāṣya*] as the activity of awareness, in order to express its independent authority with respect to the activity of becoming conscious. This character accounts for its being different from an insentient entity.

Commentary

The definition of the Self beyond mind, as given in the *Śiva Sūtras* and the *Yoga-bhāṣya,* suggests that its essential character is its shining constantly in its phenomenal and noumenal aspects and its independent power, which includes the propensity to promote active conscious awareness of itself. This independent nature of the Absolute Self is its divine essence and, on account of it, the Self is accepted as Almighty God.

Supreme awareness is described in the next couplet as the highest divine essence of the Absolute Lord.

Verse 13

चितिः प्रत्यवमर्शात्मा परावाक्स्वरसोदिता ।
स्वातन्त्र्यमेतन्मुख्यं तदैश्वर्यं परमात्मनः ॥ १३ ॥

citiḥ pratyavamarśātmā parāvāk sva-rasoditā /
svātantryam etan mukhyaṃ tad aiśvaryaṃ paramātmanaḥ //

To be Self-aware is the very essence of Consciousness. It is the supreme speech, rising out of its own ecstasy, and is itself the special [and absolute] Self-sufficiency of God as well as His extraordinary divine essence.

Commentary

Consciousness is always aware of itself. Such Self-awareness is its essential character. The Self-awareness of Infinite Consciousness has been described by Bhartṛhari as supreme speech, *parāvāk*. Absolute Reality is always aware of itself and its divine character through this subtle speech of Self-awareness. *Parāvāk* rises out of the supreme Self-ecstasy of the Absolute Reality and has infinite bliss as its essential character. The Absolute Lord, being constantly aware of His divine potency and divine propensity, is always, by means of *parāvāk,* playing the infinite drama of creation, preservation, and so on.

One may ask why *parāvāk* is called 'speech'. We normally only speak of objects about which we have already formed some idea in our intellect. The speech of ideation is thus the finer form of articulated speech. Ideation, in turn, is based on awareness, because we can form ideas only about objects of which we are already aware. Objective awareness thus has the subjective Self-awareness of a speaker as its basis. Such Self-awareness in its purest form is thus called *parāvāk,* supreme speech. Being the awareness of the divine essence of the Absolute, it is pronounced here to be the divine and supreme authority, the *aiśvarya,* of Almighty God.

The wonderful character of such awareness is expressed in the next couplet.

Verse 14

सा स्फुरत्ता महासत्ता देशकालाविशेषिणी ।
सैषा सारतया प्रोक्ता हृदयं परमेष्ठिनः ॥ १४ ॥

sā sphurattā mahāsattā deśa-kālāviśeṣiṇī /
saiṣā sāratayā proktā hṛdayaṃ parameṣṭhinaḥ //

[Pure Self-awareness] has been described as a [shining] pulsation, as supreme existence not conditioned by time and space, and as the very heart of the Supreme, because it is the real essence [of all existence].

Commentary

The divine essence of the Lord manifests the dramatic performance of the constantly expanding and contracting universe. This subtle movement is described poetically as a sort of throbbing activity, or *spanda,* which means the pulsating, vibratory activity of manifestation. This divine essence has therefore been described as the Supreme Existence, the basis of all existence and non-existence. Time, space, causation, and so forth, are themselves mere manifestations of the pulsating activity of Absolute Reality; therefore it can never be conditioned by them. Being the reality underlying all existence, *spanda* has been described as the very essence of the Supreme Lord.

The next couplet throws light on the results of the Absolute Lord's divine Self-awareness.

Verse 15

आत्मानमत एवायं ज्ञेयीकुर्यात्पृथक्स्थिति ।
ज्ञेयं न तु तदौन्मुख्यात्खण्ड्येतास्य स्वतन्त्रता ॥ १५ ॥

ātmānam ata evāyaṃ jñeyīkuryāt pṛthak sthiti /
jñeyaṃ na tu tad-aunmukhyāt khaṇḍyetāsya sva-tantratā //

It is because of this that the Lord manifests His own Self objectively. Objective existence (the world) is not a thing existing separately from Him. His looking for such a thing would disprove His absolute independence.

Commentary

All of phenomenal existence shines in God as His own divine power. His power is never different from Him. Thus the world exists in Him as His own Self. By virtue of the playful and blissful activity of His spiritual vibration, He manifests the world objectively as an existence seeming to be different from His subjective Self, the pure and infinite I-Consciousness. But if objective existence were truly different from God, and if He were to depend on it, as is said of Īśvara (the Lord) in Nyāya-Vaiśeṣika philosophy, His supreme independence would be disproved.

Kārikā 16 throws light on the cosmogonic principles of Kashmir Śaivism.

Verse 16

स्वातन्त्र्यामुक्तमात्मानं स्वातन्त्र्यादद्वयात्मनः ।
प्रभुरीशादिसंकल्पैर्निर्माय व्यवहारयेत् ॥ १६ ॥

svātantryām uktam ātmānaṃ svātantryād advayātmanaḥ /
prabhur īśādi-saṃkalpair nirmāya vyavahārayet //

The Master, using the perfect freedom of His monistic Self, can and does create and bring into existence [all] phenomenal activities. His own Self is never devoid of independence throughout the process of the fanciful conceiving of the elements [right from *sadāśiva-tattva* down to earth].

Commentary

The Lord, being perfectly independent and playful, manifests creation by fancying His own Self to be all the cosmic principles *(tattvas)* from the first *(sadāśiva)* to the last (earth), and then He instantly appears as them. This objective manifestation of His monistic, subjective Self is known in philosophy as the created phenomenal world. While appearing thus as all phenomena, the Lord does not diverge from His transcendental, infinite, and pure I-Consciousness since all such manifestations happen in the manner of reflections. All *tattvas* already exist in Him as His subjective I-Consciousness and become objectively reflected in Him through His playful divine will. So, this reflectional manifestation does not involve His pure Consciousness in any limiting transformation.

The next *kārikā* suggests that the use of different names for the Absolute Lord does not at all signify any differences in His nature.

Verse 17

नाहन्तादिपरामर्शभेदादस्यान्यतात्मनः ।
अहंमृश्यतयैवास्य सृष्टेस्तिङ्वाच्यकर्मवत् ॥ १७ ॥

nāhantādi-parāmarśa-bhedād asyānyatātmanaḥ /
ahaṃ-mṛśyatayaivāsya sṛṣṭes tiṅ-vācya-karmavat //

Just as an action denoted by a verbal form or a verbal suffix does not thereby become different, so the *Ātman* coming into the process of creation does not become enmeshed in any sort of diversity, although it is called different names (such as Paramaśiva, God, or Paramātman). This is because these [words all] point toward one and the same end, [infinite] I-Consciousness.

Commentary

Just as the words *pākaḥ, paktiḥ, paca.i,* and so on, are meant to denote only one and the same action of cooking, though they are spoken differently and are different parts of speech, so words like *ātman, īśvara, paramātman,* and others aim to denote one and the same Absolute Reality. These examples point to the fact that the divine manifestation of diversity in the world does not at all compromise the unity and absolute purity of the Creator. In reality, all the diverse forms of creation continue to be the absolute and perfect I-Consciousness, who alone is called by names such as Śiva-bhaṭṭāraka, Maheśvara, Bhagavān, and Paramātman.

Verse 18

मायाशक्त्या विभोः सैव भिन्नसंवेद्यगोचरा ।
कथिता ज्ञानसंकल्पाध्यवसायादिनामभिः ॥ १८ ॥

māyā-śaktyā vibhoḥ saiva bhinna-saṃvedya-gocarā /
kathitā jñāna-saṃkalpādhyavasāyādi-nāmabhiḥ //

That [Consciousness] comes under the effect of *māyā-śakti,* the Lord's differentiating power, and consequently focuses on diverse objects and directs itself toward becoming the objects of senses and the sense organs. [In these forms, *citi*] is referred to by different names, such as *jñāna* (perceptual knowledge), *saṅkalpa* (imagination), and *adhyavasāya* (mental apprehension), and so on.

Commentary

Māyā, the delusive power of the Absolute, imposes a viewpoint of diversity on all created beings, and for this reason they see objects as different from their subjective selves. Besides, they perceive objects with the help of the senses and sense organs, which they also take as entities different from themselves. Thus *citi,* infinite Consciousness, having come under the effects of *māyā,* is called by different names such as *jñāna, saṅkalpa,* and *adhyavasāya* whenever humans engage in different activities. It is called *jñāna,* or perceptual knowledge, while coming in contact with an object. It is called *saṅkalpa* while one is thinking about the name and form of an object. It is called *adhyavasāya* when one comes to a conviction with regard to the definite name and form of the object concerned. Many such mental activities go on in our daily mundane transactions.

The next couplet lays stress on the fact that awareness has an important place even at the perceptual stage of knowing.

Verse 19

साक्षात्कारक्षणेऽप्यस्ति विमर्शः कथमन्यथा ।
धावनाद्युपपद्येत प्रतिसंधानवर्जितम् ॥ १९ ॥

sākṣāt-kāra-kṣaṇe 'py asti vimarśaḥ katham anyathā /
dhāvanādy upapadyeta pratisaṃdhāna-varjitam //

Awareness is present even in an instant of perception. Otherwise, how could actions such as running become possible or explicable, when deliberation about one's steps is not possible?

Commentary

Cognition of the name and form of an object is preceded by simple perceptual awareness, known as *nirvikalpa,* or non-conceptual, knowledge. A person running very fast or reciting scriptures at a high speed does not form any clear ideas of the succession of steps or syllables. How does he then perform these activities correctly? This fact suggests that there must be some awareness of the steps and syllables even in the *nirvikalpa,* or thought-free, state of knowing.

The next couplet says that even conceptual knowledge shines as the Supreme Lord if it is freed from the name and form imposed on it, since it then becomes again the direct power of the great Lord.

Verse 20

घटोऽयमित्यध्यवसा नामरूपातिरेकिणी ।
परेशशक्तिरात्मेव भासते न त्विदन्तया ॥ २० ॥

ghaṭo 'yam ity adhyavasā nāma-rūpāti-rekiṇī /
pareśa-śaktir ātmeva bhāsate na tv idantayā //

When the name and form are taken out of the concept 'This is a pitcher', then the remaining [pure subjective knowledge] shines, like the Self of [each] being, as the divine power of the Supreme Lord, not in the form of 'this-ness' or objectivity.

Commentary

Conceptual knowledge of an object contains two elements. One of them is the Self-aware, pure Consciousness, and the other one consists of the name and form of the object, as given to it by the viewpoint of *māyā*. If the second element is eliminated from such knowledge, the remaining pure Consciousness will shine as the *Ātman* (Self) of a being, the divine power of the Absolute Lord. The object will not appear as an object having 'this-ness' as its character.

The next *kārikā* shows the effects of time and space on all types ot cognitions.

Verse 21

केवलं भिन्नसंवेद्यदेशकालानुरोधतः ।
ज्ञानस्मृत्यवसायादि सक्रमं प्रतिभासते ॥ २१ ॥

kevalaṃ bhinna-saṃvedya-deśa-kālānurodhataḥ /
jñāna-smṛty-avasāyādi sa-kramaṃ pratibhāsate //

It is just because of considerations of time and space, both of which are experienced as having variety in them, that cognition, recollection, ideation, and so forth appear to be successive [actions].

Commentary

Time and space are the characteristics of objective phenomena, and both have sufficient variety in them. Pure Consciousness is never bound by such limitations; but since it assumes the forms of all concerned objects, it appears erroneously to be conditioned by time and space. Since such limitations also become manifest in the viewpoints of beings residing in the plane of diversity, the resultant objects are named as different, phenomenally existent elements, according to Kashmir Śaivism's *ābhāsa-vāda* theory of manifestation. In other words, perception, recollection, conception, and so on appear to be successive in their character, just because of the consideration of time and space, which have diversity or variety in them, and also because of their being taken as such by the knowing subjects, who themselves belong to the plane of diversity.

Chapter 6

THE POWER TO DISCRIMINATE

The purpose of this chapter is to focus on the philosophical understanding of the *apohana-śakti* of the Lord. The term *apohana* means the discrimination that makes a thing appear distinct from other similar things. Through His divine power, the Lord manifests a distinction between subjects and objects with regard to knowing and doing; they appear respectively as 'I' and 'this', myself and this other thing. But the all-pervading, basic 'I-ness' of the Absolute Lord is not apparent within these concepts. This subject-object duality is manifested through His power, which is the basic seed of the manifestation of all ideas. The first couplet points this out.

Verse 1

अहं प्रत्यवमर्शो यः प्रकाशात्मापि वाग्वपुः ।
नासौ विकल्पः स ह्युक्तो द्वयाक्षेपी विनिश्चयः ॥ १ ॥

ahaṃ pratyavamarśo yaḥ prakāśātmāpi vāg-vapuḥ /
nāsau vikalpaḥ sa hy ukto dvayākṣepī viniścayaḥ //

The inner Self-awareness shining as 'I', though being conscious light *(prakāśa)* in its essence and having [subtle] speech as its form, is not any definite mental idea *(vikalpa)*. This is because an idea, being decisive in its character, rejects all possible similar ideas, inviting duality [of 'that' and 'not that'].

Commentary

Perception consists of the reflection of an object into an inner sense centre. The mind imagines several possible pairs of names and forms for this reflected object, and the intellect *(buddhi)* proceeds to accept only one particular pair, rejecting all other possible ones. It thus forms a definite idea regarding the identity of what is perceived. Such a definite idea, formulated by the intellect, is known as a *vikalpa*. The mind, or *manas,* the thinking capacity, and the intellect, or *buddhi,* the capacity to form ideas, are taken as two different interior senses in Indian philosophy, although both are called 'mind' in the West. A *vikalpa,* therefore, being just a definite idea of some particular name and form, cannot have full control over the thought process. The conscious light of *prakāśa,* however, does have such control, because it is the source of thought. It can become manifest as the counterpart of any thought.

Take the example of a person seeing a red object. The mind entertains the question of whether the object is red or not. So both the concepts of red and non-red shine in the mind in the process of ideation. Similarly, both *prakāśa* and non-*prakāśa* would shine simultaneously as ideas if *prakāśa* were simply a thought and if ideation had control of it. But *prakāśa* and non-*prakāśa* do not shine together as counterparts of each other; they are not mere thoughts. The process of ideation can thus have no influence on the conscious light of the Self, as expressed below.

Verse 2

भिन्नयोरवभासो हि स्याद्घटाघटयोर्द्वयोः ।
प्रकाशस्येव नान्यस्य भेदिनस्त्ववभासनम् ॥ २ ॥

bhinnayor avabhāso hi syād ghaṭāghaṭayor dvayoḥ /
prakāśasyeva nānyasya bhedinas tv avabhāsanam //

It can actually be possible that the concepts of two mutually contradictory phenomena, for example a pitcher and a non-pitcher, may both rise [in the mind of a knowing subject], but it cannot be possible in the case of *prakāśa* and anything else which may be [like it and yet] different from it, [as non-*prakāśa* cannot appear].

Commentary

If *prakāśa,* the Self-aware Consciousness, were a kind of ideational knowing, it would have been preceded by the ideas of both *prakāśa* and non-*prakāśa*. But this can never be possible, because *prakāśa* (the spiritual luminosity of pure Consciousness) cannot allow non-*prakāśa* to appear before it as its rival. Thus a *dvayākṣepī viniścayaḥ,* a conceptual decision preceded by the manifestation of multiplicity of ideas, cannot happen in the case of *prakāśa,* which is thus not any *vikalpa,* or form of thought.

The next *kārikā* presents the definition, along with an example, of ideational knowledge.

Verse 3

तदतत्प्रतिभाभाजा मात्रैवातद्व्यपोहनात् ।
तन्निश्चयनमुक्तो हि विकल्पो घट इत्ययम् ॥ ३ ॥

tad-atat-pratibhābhā-jā mātraivātad-vyapohanāt /
tan-niścayanam ukto hi vikalpo ghaṭa ity ayam //

It is the knowing subject alone who, having the glimpse of both 'that' and 'non-that', and rejecting instantly everything 'non-that', concludes in favour of the existence of 'that' and announces the object to be, for example, a water pot. Such psychic activity is known as ideation, or *vikalpa*.

Commentary

When a person sees a white object, both 'white' and everything similar to it become simultaneously manifest in the mind of a person perceiving 'white'. His intellect *(buddhi)* rejects everything 'non-white' and concludes in favour of white. The person thinking, 'It is white', announces the existence of a white object, because white is the object of his or her perceptual cognition. This is the psychic process involved in the formation of ideas; both the object and its opposites or counterparts must thus shine in the initial glimpse. *Prakāśa* allows such a shining of mutually opposite ideas to occur.

However, since *prakāśa* does not have non-*prakāśa* as its counterpart, it cannot become an object of ideation itself. It shines independently, only as *prakāśa,* without even a faint glimpse of non-*prakāśa,* because non-*prakāśa* (non-light) could not shine and thus could never become manifest. *Prakāśa* alone might be able to assume the form of some so-called 'non-*prakāśa*', and shine itself as that.

The next two couplets are intended to point out that finite 'I-ness', the limited sense of self or ego, when woven around inanimate substances, such as the physical body, the mind, and so forth, does belong to the field of the discriminating, separating *(apohana)* thought process, even though it is the infinite Self that often appears in the garb of such finite 'I-ness'.

Verse 4-5

चित्तत्त्वं मायया हित्वा भिन्न एवावभाति यः ।
देहे बुद्धावथ प्राणे कल्पिते नभसीव वा ॥ ४ ॥
प्रमातृत्वेनाहमिति विमर्शोऽन्यव्यपोहनात् ।
विकल्प एव स परप्रतियोग्यवभासजः ॥ ५ ॥

cit-tattvaṃ māyayā hitvā bhinna evāvabhāti yaḥ /
dehe buddhāvatha prāṇe kalpite nabhasīva vā //
pramātṛtvenāham iti vimarśo 'nya-vyapohanāt /
vikalpa eva sa parapratiyogy-avabhāsa-jaḥ //

Infinite I-Consciousness, having pushed into oblivion its real nature under the effect of *māyā,* appears to be identical with *deha* (the physical body) or with *prāṇa* (the animating life-force) or with the vacuous individual Consciousness (termed *śūnya* elsewhere); and it is taken as the [individual knowing and acting] subject, who is no doubt [merely] a *vikalpa* (an idea), because it shines as an entity cut off from all others taken to be different from it.

Commentary

The egoistic, finite I-Consciousness lies beyond the mind and shines as in the animated state of awareness beyond dreams. This is the deep sleep state, and it is called *śūnya* (empty) because it is devoid of all mental activities and the mental apparatus. It is this *śūnya* that is known as *jīva,* the individual I-Consciousness. This *śūnya* is, like objective existence, a *vikalpa,* a definite mental idea, because it stands cut off and distinct from other similar entities that could serve as its counterparts. It is on this account that one *jīva* is different from all other *jīvas,* or individual beings, moving within the field of *vikalpa.* Thus, it is only the infinite I-Consciousness (not the limited ego), shining beyond the domain of ideation, that is not a *vikalpa.*

The purpose of the next couplet is to show that when two ideas are brought together with the help of mental impressions, they are not truly unified. This is because the unity was brought about only within the field of discriminatory ideas, based on the imagination of a finite being.

Verse 6

कादाचित्कावभासे या पूर्वाभासादियोजना ।
संस्कारात्कल्पना प्रोक्ता सापि भिन्नावभासिनि ॥ ६ ॥

kādācit kāvabhāse yā pūrvābhāsādi-yojanā /
saṃskārāt kalpanā proktā sāpi bhinnāvabhāsini //

Unification of an object that appears at a certain time [such as a physical body] with a past or future object, brought about by mental impressions, has also been accepted as imagination, because the only objects to which it applies are those that appear in the plane of manifest diversity.

Commentary

Imagined unity between limited entities, for instance a present-day physical body with all past or future bodies, is just a *vikalpa,* an idea. This unity is not real; it does not involve actual Self-recognition because it happens within the viewpoint of diversity and limitation. However, it can serve to illuminate the pure nature of the Self if utilised in accordance with a yogic method of the Trika system.[23]

The next couplet places emphasis on the fact that the world of objective phenomena, being manifested outwardly by the Lord, is in fact that which always shines inwardly in Him as His Self.

Verse 7

तदेवं व्यवहारेऽपि प्रभुर्देहादिमाविशन् ।
भान्तमेवान्तरर्थौघमिच्छया भासयेद्बहिः ॥ ७ ॥

tad evaṃ vyavahāre 'pi prabhur dehādim āviśan /
bhāntam evāntar-arthaugham icchayā bhāsayed bahiḥ //

Thus the Lord, pervading physical bodies and so forth in worldly dealings, can and does go on manifesting objectively, through His divine will, only the phenomena that are already shining inwardly in Him as His Self.

Commentary

All the activities of all sorts of beings in the world are, in fact, being performed only by the Lord, appearing in all these forms. Whatever is manifested objectively in this divine dramatic performance of the Master is, in fact, already present in Him and shines in Him as His 'I'. The whole universe shines in Him as pure Consciousness and also appears outwardly through His playful divine will in a multitude of objective forms, as the Lord acts out His divine universal drama. Each living being is, in fact, the Lord and is conducting all his or her objective activities with other phenomenal entities who are also the Lord. All beings are, in fact, non-different from His subjective person. However, a person does not usually realise this fact because of the effect of *māyā,* the Self-oblivion caused by the same playful activity of God.

The next couplet concludes that the divine inner potency to create is always present in all types of idea-creating mental activities of beings.

Verse 8

एवं स्मृतौ विकल्पे वाप्यपोहनपरायणे ।
ज्ञाने वाप्यन्तराभासः स्थित एवेति निश्चितम् ॥ ८ ॥

evaṃ smṛtau vikalpe vāpy apòhana-parāyaṇe /
jñāne vāpy antar-ābhāsaḥ sthita eveti niścitam //

It is thus a fact that an internal manifestation is surely present in the [human] memory and ideation that leads to the mutual distinction of objects, as also in perceptual cognition.

Commentary

Since the entire universe exists in the Absolute Consciousness of the Lord in the form of its divine potency, it also shows its presence even in finite human consciousness as well, shining there faintly during occasions when a person is perceiving, conceiving ideas, remembering, and so forth. A Trika yogin, catching hold of this fact through the power of his superattentive awareness, can enter into infinite Consciousness, which possesses all divine powers.

The ninth couplet throws light on the difference between the conceptions the mind forms during direct experiential knowing and those that are formed due to recollection and other secondary mental activities.

Verse 9

किन्तु नैसर्गिको ज्ञाने बहिराभासनात्मनि ।
पूर्वानुभवरूपस्तु स्थितः स स्मरणादिषु ॥ ९ ॥

kintu naisargiko jñāne bahir-ābhāsanātmani /
pūrvānubhava-rūpas tu sthitaḥ sa smaraṇādiṣu //

However, in the case of the direct perception of outer manifest objects, [their mental presence] is natural or direct; while in the case of recollection and so forth, they remain present in the form of the [impressions of] past experiences.

Commentary

The formation of ideas about objects is direct in the case of a person who has just directly perceived something in the world, but this is not so in the case of recollection, memory, and other secondary forms of knowing. The latter appear through the revival of past impressions rather than direct experience. Nonetheless, it is the same divine manifestation *(ābhāsa)* that exists in both of them.

The tenth couplet throws light on the status of the inner mental creation of objects that occurs in the exercise of a person's imagination.

Verse 10

स नैसर्गिक एवास्ति विकल्पे स्वैरचारिणि ।
यथाभिमतसंस्थानाभासनाद्बुद्धिगोचरे॥ १०॥

sa naisargika evāsti vikalpe svaira-cāriṇi /
yathābhimata-saṃsthānābhāsanād buddhi-gocare //

[Inner mental creation] is but natural in the case of fanciful imagination, rising in the field of one's intellect as it manifests images quite in accordance with one's liking.

Fanciful imagination manifests only those objects that already exist as ideas in the intellect of the fancying person. Such independent creation hints at the independent creation conducted by God.

The next couplet concludes that every living being possesses the two powers to know and to do, because each being retains a portion of the powers of his or her true Self, the Absolute Lord.

Verse 11

अत एव यथाभीष्टसमुल्लेखावभासनात् ।
ज्ञानक्रिये स्फुटे एव सिद्धे सर्वस्य जीवतः ॥ ११ ॥

ata eva yathābhīṣṭa-samullekhāvabhāsanāt /
jñāna-kriye sphuṭe eva siddhe sarvasya jīvataḥ //

Therefore it stands clearly proved that every living being has the powers to know and to do, because he [or she] is capable of manifesting his [or her] imaginary creation in accordance with his [or her] own will.

Commentary

God, appearing in the form of bound beings, does not totally lose all of His divine powers. While embodied, He retains a fraction of these powers. It is on this account that even a bound person is capable of creating the world of his or her imagination in accordance with his or her own free will.

Chapter 7

THE UNITY OF THE MASTER

In this chapter Utpaladeva aims to establish that different mental operations can have a mutual interrelation only when they occur in one and the same knowing subject. The first couplet states that Absolute God alone acts as each individual knowing subject, appearing in the forms of all the wonderfully different types of finite beings. The Lord is thus the basis on which all sentient activities, such as perception, conception, discrimination, recollection, and recognition, stand and function.

Verse 1

या चैषा प्रतिभा तत्तत्पदार्थक्रमरूषिता ।
अक्रमानन्तचिद्रूपः प्रमाता स महेश्वरः ॥ १॥

yā caiṣā pratibhā tat-tat-padārtha-krama-rūṣitā /
akramānanta-cid-rūpaḥ pramātā sa maheśvaraḥ //

Then this mental illumination, [although] devoid of [time] sequence, bears the impression of the sequence of different objects, and is [in fact] the great God. He [alone], being devoid of sequence and having infinite Consciousness as His Self, is the true knowing Subject.

Commentary

The true Subject or author of all knowing and doing is infinite Consciousness, appearing according to its divine nature as the multitude of worldly subjects, who conduct their mundane activities in a variety of ways. The mundane subjects of worldly actions are not, in fact, different from the Absolute Lord, who alone assumes the forms of all finite beings by virtue of His divine, independent, and playful nature. He thereby conducts the wonderful varied play of all knowing and doing in accordance with His independent divine will. The manifestation of the Lord's divine play does have time sequence—past, present, and future—as part of its character, although He is not Himself conditioned at all by such sequence.

The second *kārikā* points out that mutual relations between objects become possible only when one and the same knowing subject perceives them and connects them by his thoughts.

Verse 2

तत्तद्विभिन्नसंवित्तिमुखैरेकप्रमातरि ।
प्रतितिष्ठत्सु भावेषु ज्ञातेयमुपपद्यते ॥ २॥

tat-tad-vibhinna-saṃvitti-mukhair eka-pramātari /
pratitiṣṭhatsu bhāveṣu jñāteyam upapadyate //

Relations between mundane objects can be explained and justified only when they [the objects] are established in one and the same knowing subject. [These relations are achieved] through different psychic channels of his thought-process.

Commentary

Inanimate substances on their own cannot develop mutual relationships. These relationships become possible only when such substances are perceived by one person, one knowing subject. Entering through the different channels of a person's external senses, the images of objects create their impressions, which become definitely established in him through the subsequent process of forming ideas. 'Relationship' is thus not an absolute truth but merely a mundane truth, based on the imagination and calculations of finite beings, who move and work within the realm of *māyā*.

A seed is a seed and a sprout is a sprout. Neither of the two can say anything with regard to the other. But when the images of both of them, along with the idea of the essential presence of one of them before the rise of the other, are impressed on the mind of a knowing subject, he forms the concept of their mutual relationship, which is thus based on mere imagination.

The next couplet again states that no mutual relationship between objects is possible if not established within the mind of a single subject.

Verse 3

देशकालक्रमजुषामर्थानां स्वसमापिनाम् ।
सकृदाभाससाध्योऽसावन्यथा कः समन्वयः ॥ ३ ॥

deśa-kāla-krama-juṣām arthānāṃ sva-samāpinām /
sakṛd-ābhāsa-sādhyo 'sāv anyathā kaḥ samanvayaḥ //

The 'relationship' between self-limited objects, found in different sequences of time and space, can be established only with the help of a single simultaneous manifestation [in one subject's awareness]. Otherwise, how can there be a relationship?

Commentary

Mutual relations between two different perceptions, like a rose and its redness, can be established only when both become manifest in a person's single cognition. But if they shine in his different thoughts at different times, and so are absolutely self-contained and not touching each other in any way, then their simultaneous existence cannot be asserted, nor can their mutual relationship. A similar case might include a horse and a cart being viewed in a person's thought as the unified picture of a horse-cart. Therefore, it must be accepted that both objects shine together simultaneously in a person's individual consciousness, which witnesses them together and brings to light their mutual relationship by means of imagination. In this way, all phenomenal entities enjoy their ideal existence in the mundane plane of human psychology.

The same truth is pointed out with respect to inference.

Verse 4

प्रत्यक्षानुपलम्भानां तत्तद्भिन्नांशपतिनाम् ।
कार्यकारणतासिद्धिहेतुतैकप्रमातृजा ॥ ४ ॥

pratyakṣān upalambhānāṃ tat tad bhinnāṃśa-patinām /
kārya-kāraṇatā siddhi-hetutaika-pramātṛ-jā //

The basic establishment of the principle of causation—depending on perceptions and non-perceptions and aimed at particular different elements such as causes, non-causes, effects, and non-effects—emerges fundamentally out of one common knowing subject.

Commentary

A person may see objects like (1) fire and smoke in a hearth; (2) lack of both in a lake full of water; (3) fire without smoke in a red, heated iron; and (4) smoke rising from a forest situated far away. He thus comes to know from his experience that smoke billows up from fire and it does not rise anywhere without the pre-existence of fire. On the basis of these frequent perceptions, he draws a conclusion that fire is the source or cause of smoke. In the same way, the person finds numerous pairs of entities in this world that are mutually related as causes and effects. All of his conclusions are possible only because the objects of causation shine together within his conscious mind. This conclusion proves, too, that the rules of causation are based on the fact that respective causes and effects were already resting within the spiritual light of the I-Consciousness of this one person. Otherwise, how could any conclusions be drawn?

The next couplet adds that the psychic unity of the individual, knowing subject is essential for the phenomenon of memory as well, because it is based on the past experience of the same person.

Verse 5

स्मृतौ यैव स्वसंवित्तिः प्रमाणं स्वात्मसम्भवे ।
पूर्वानुभवसद्भावे साधनं सैव नापरम् ॥ ५ ॥

smṛtau yaiva sva-saṃvittiḥ pramāṇaṃ svātma-sambhave /
pūrvānubhava-sadbhāve sādhanaṃ saiva nāparam //

Only the Self-awareness that serves as proof of the emergence of a memory, and no other, is the means of proving the existence of the [impressions of] past experiences.

Commentary

It is an undeniable fact that particular experiences, and the impressions and recollections based on them, must lie in one and the same I-Consciousness. A person alone remembers what he or she experienced. The Self-awareness of the person's I-Consciousness establishes both the existence of past impressions and the emergence of memory. No recollection could otherwise become possible. This proves the constant existence of the Self-aware I-Consciousness that serves as the basis of both memory and past impressions in each of us.

Couplet 6 points out that the refutation of incorrect knowledge by its opposite—correct knowledge—becomes possible only on the basis of one common knowing Subject.

Verse 6

बाध्यबाधकभावोऽपि स्वात्मनिष्ठाविरोधिनाम् ।
ज्ञानानामुदियादेकप्रमातृपरिनिष्ठितेः ॥ ६ ॥

bādhya-bādhaka-bhāvo 'pi svātma-niṣṭhāvirodhinām /
jñānānām udiyād eka-pramātṛ-pariniṣṭhiteḥ //

Mutual refutation by different [opposite] cognitions, that are mutually unopposed because they are self-centred, emerges out of their basis in one common knowing Subject.

Commentary

If the existence of one common knowing Subject, existing constantly and conducting all psychological functions, were not accepted, all cognitions would prove to be self-centred, self-limited, and mutually unrelated. There would be no way that opposite propositions, for example 'That is a tree' and 'No, that is not a tree', could be argued or mutually refuted. But the refutation of incorrect knowledge by correct knowledge is an undeniable fact. Therefore, the constant existence of one common knowing Subject, serving as the basis of all such momentary perceptions, conceptions, ideations, recollections, refutations, and so forth, must be accepted. An individual living being called *Ātman* is meant here, though ultimately there is only one common *Ātman,* Śiva.

The next five couplets (7-11) discuss the topic of *anyonyābhāva,* 'mutual non-existence', as propounded in Nyāya-Vaiśeṣika philosophy, and explain the truth about it according to Kashmir Śaivism. It is then argued that the concept of mutual differential existence also becomes justifiable only when the existence of one common knowing Subject, bearing all such different ideas in him, is accepted and not otherwise.

Verse 7

विविक्तभूतलज्ञानं घटाभावमतिर्यथा ।
तथा चेच्छुक्तिकाज्ञानं रूप्यज्ञानाप्रमात्ववित् ॥ ७ ॥

vivikta-bhūtala-jñānaṃ ghaṭābhāva-matir yathā /
tathā cec chuktikā-jñānaṃ rūpya-jñānāpramātva-vit //

If it is argued, 'Just as knowledge of a vacant place is taken as knowledge of the non-existence of a water vessel [there] . . .', in the same way, the knowledge of a shell refutes the correctness of [one's original] perception of silver, [then we say as follows]:

Commentary

Just as a person in search of a water vessel, seeing the concerned place empty, takes his knowledge of that empty place as proof of the non-existence there of the vessel, so does the recognition of a gleaming piece of shell as a shell refute the correctness of a previous perception, where a person mistakenly saw that shell as a piece of silver. This argument is then refuted.

Verse 8

नैवं शुद्धस्थलज्ञानात्सिद्ध्येत्तस्याघटात्मता ।
न तूपलब्धियोग्यस्याप्यत्राभावो घटात्मनः ॥ ८ ॥

naivaṃ śuddha-sthala-jñānāt siddhyet tasyāghaṭāt matā /
na tūpalabdhi-yogyasyāpy atrābhāvo ghaṭāt manaḥ //

It is not so. The knowledge of a vacant place can only assert that the concerned place is different from a vessel. It cannot assert that a vessel, being visible by its nature, does not exist there.

Commentary

Non-existence in the case of a vacant place and a vessel is primarily of two kinds: (1) 'There is no vessel at the place concerned'. Such non-existence is known in philosophy as *saṃsargābhāva*. (2) 'The place concerned is not a vessel'. This is called *anyonyābhāva*. A vacant place can indicate such *anyonyābhāva,* but it cannot prove the previous type called *saṃsargābhāva*. This principle of non-existence is further explained in the next four couplets.

Verse 9

विविक्तं भूतलं शश्वद्भावानां स्वात्मनिष्ठितेः ।
तत्कथं जातु तज्ज्ञानं भिन्नस्याभावसाधनम् ॥ ९ ॥

viviktaṃ bhūtalaṃ śaśvad bhāvānāṃ svātma-niṣṭhiteḥ /
tat kathaṃ jātu taj-jñānaṃ bhinnasyābhāva-sādhanam //

A place is always different from all other objects, because [all] existent entities are restricted to their own selves. How then could its perception be used as a proof of the non-existence of anything other than itself?

Commentary

The perception of a vacant place can manifest just what it is and nothing else. Being thus self-contained and self-limited, the perception cannot presume to deny the existence of any other thing, because it has no concern with anything other than itself.

Verse 10

किंत्वालोकचयोऽन्धस्य स्पर्शो वोष्णादिको मृदुः ।
तत्रास्ति साधयेत्तस्य स्वज्ञानमघटात्मताम् ॥ १० ॥

kiṃtv āloka-cayo 'ndhasya sparśo voṣṇādiko mṛduḥ /
tatrāsti sādhayet tasya sva-jñānam aghaṭātmatām //

> There is either just a flow of light or, in the case of a blind person, a soft and unrestricting touch [in the vacant space]. These cognitions prove it to be something other than a vessel.

Commentary

A person finds just sunlight or the touch of wafting air in a vacant place. He knows it is something other than a vessel by concluding, through the principle of *anyonyābhāva,* that the light or air in this empty place is different from a vessel. The person then says that there is no vessel in that place.

Verse 11

पिशाचः स्यादनालोकोऽप्यालोकाभ्यन्तरे यथा।
अदृश्यो भूतलस्यान्तर्न निषेध्यः स सर्वथा ॥ ११ ॥

piśācaḥ syād anāloko 'py ālokābhyantare yathā/
adṛśyo bhūtalasyāntar na niṣedhyaḥ sa sarvathā //

> For instance, a ghost, though not being light, can be invisibly present within the light at a place, so his existence [there] cannot thus be denied from all viewpoints.

Commentary

Suppose there is a ghost *(piśāca)* not made visible by the light in a particular place. His existence, from the viewpoint of *saṃsargābhāva,* cannot be denied, though it can be denied from that of *anyonyābhāva.* That is, we can surely say that the light at a place or the place itself is not a ghost, but it cannot be said that the ghost does not exist there.

The twelfth couplet applies the conclusion of the discussion about *anyonyābhāva* to the matter of erroneous experience. It claims the essential necessity of one common knowing Subject whenever the validity of such erroneous experience is refuted. Such a refutation cannot be accomplished on the basis of the principle of *anyonyābhāva.*

Verse 12

एवं रूप्यविदाभावरूपा शुक्तिमतिर्भवेत् ।
न त्वाद्यरजतज्ञप्तेः स्यादप्रामाण्यवेदिका ॥ १२ ॥

evaṃ rūpya-vidābhāva-rūpā śukti-matir bhavet /
na tv ādya-rajata-jñapteḥ syād aprāmāṇya-vedikā //

Thus, the perception of a gleaming shell can be taken as the non-existence of the perception of silver, but it cannot make known the invalidity of the previously risen perception of silver [concerning the same object].

Commentary

Suppose a person, finding some shining object, believes at first sight that he is seeing silver. Subsequently, however, he understands that it is a shell. Both of his cognitions are self-centred and self-limited by their own nature, and so neither can say anything about the validity of the other. The perception of a shell is, no doubt, quite different from that of silver; but it cannot refute the validity of the former perception, as it does not actually have any relation to it.

The basis of any connection between the two perceptions, and the invalidation of a wrong perception, is the constantly existent I-Consciousness that pervades the perceptions of both the silver and the shell. Therefore, the logical process of invalidating an erroneous cognition cannot become possible if the divine I-Consciousness, the knowing Subject, does not exist as the basis on which such mutually opposite cognitions stand. One and the same I-Consciousness, the supreme Subject of all doing and knowing, is thus the basis of all logical refutations. These refutations prove the constant existence of the perfect I-Consciousness, which serves as the basis of all types of argumentations, refutations, and other logical processes.

Kārikā 13 points out that even inference cannot prove the incorrectness of an erroneous assumption. It can be proved only on the basis of one common subject, bearing in it both the correct and incorrect cognitions of a shell and silver.

Verse 13

धर्म्यसिद्धेरपि भवेद्बाधा नैवानुमानतः ।
स्वसंवेदनसिद्धा तु युक्ता सैकप्रमातृजा ॥ १३ ॥

dharmya-siddher api bhaved bādhā naivānumānataḥ /
sva-saṃvedana-siddhā tu yuktā saika-pramātṛ-jā //

A logical refutation cannot be worked out even through inference because of the non-existence of the refuting cognition [at the time of such ignorance]. It [the refutation] can, however, be established correctly on the basis of self-knowledge, based on the unity of the knowing Subject.

Commentary

A logical refutation of the validity of some past incorrect cognition cannot be worked out even by the means of inference, because of an involvement in the logical defect known as *āśrayā-siddhi* or *pakṣā-siddhi*, known here also as *dharmya-siddhi*. However, it can be worked out correctly on the basis of the self-knowledge of a permanently existent single subjective Master of knowing.

Āśrayā-siddhi is a defect in logical calculations. A calculator has to establish the existence or non-existence of some entity in some other entity that must itself be enjoying a well-proved existence. If the latter's existence is doubtful, the inference becomes invalid. The entity in which something's existence is to be proved is called *pakṣa* in Indian logic, referred to here as *dharmin,* or *dharmya-siddhi*. Such *dharmin* in the present context could be the past momentary conscious mind, which does not exist at the time of the inference concerned and is intent upon establishing falseness in the perception of silver, or any other object, because of its momentary character. Therefore, the past experience of silver cannot be proved to be invalid by the present experience of a shell, even by means of inference. Since all psychic activities are momentary and temporary in nature, the permanent existence of *Ātman* as the ruling Master of both the past and present mind can alone serve here as the *dharmin* in which the emergence of the past knowledge of silver can be refuted by the present knowledge of a shell. The I-Consciousness, the knowing Subject, alone can retain impressions of both the past erroneous cognition and the present correct one.

The last couplet in the chapter, asserting the principle of one common Subject of all types of knowing, proves the existence of the Lord, by logical conclusion, as the single Master of all types of mental activities occurring in all beings in the universe.

Verse 14

इत्थमत्यर्थभिन्नार्थावभासखचिते विभौ ।
समलो विमलो वापि व्यवहारोऽनुभूयते ॥ १४ ॥

ittham aty-artha-bhinnārthāvabhāsa-khacite vibhau /
samalo vimalo vāpi vyavahāro 'nubhūyate //

Thus the whole world's activities, whether pure or impure, are experienced within the Lord, who shines, decorated by the [reflective] manifestations of various different phenomena.

Commentary

'Pure' mundane transactions in the world consist of religious, philosophical, and theological activities, and the so-called 'impure' ones are considered to be the other diverse occupational and professional activities. All of them are manifest within the light of the pure and infinite Consciousness of the Lord, in whom they shine like reflections brought about by His divine powers. The Lord's shining is beautifully decorated by the reflective manifestation of all phenomenal existence. He is thus the sole basis of the world's show. Nothing can become manifest if it is not based on Him.

Chapter 8

THE ALL-POWERFUL ESSENCE

In this last chapter of Book I, Utpaladeva means to establish the all-powerful divine essence, the Maheśvara nature, of Absolute Consciousness. The first six couplets in the chapter explain the character of the differing manifestations of knowing that occur in the course of mundane affairs.

Verses 1-2

तात्कालिकाक्षसामक्ष्यसापेक्षाः केवलं क्वचित् ।
आभासा अन्यथान्यत्र त्वन्धान्धतमसादिषु ॥ १ ॥
विशेषोऽर्थावभासस्य सत्तायां न पुनः क्वचित् ।
विकल्पेषु भवेद्भाविभवद्भूतार्थगामिषु ॥ २ ॥

tāt kālikākṣa-sāmakṣya-sāpekṣāḥ kevalaṃ kvacit /
ābhāsā anyathānyatra tv andhāndhatamas-ādisu //
viśeṣo 'rthāvabhāsasya sattāyāṃ na punaḥ kvacit /
vikalpeṣu bhaved bhāvi-bhavad-bhūtārtha-gāmiṣu //

It is only when objects depend on timely contact with [a person's] senses [that they become clear]. Elsewhere, as in the case of a blind person or at a place under pitch darkness, these [objects] are otherwise [not clearly visible]. But nowhere is there any difference in the existence of an entity, whether among the ideas of present, past, or [even] future objects.

Commentary

An object's existence is its existence, whether it is visually clear or dim to the viewer or whether the object is manifest in a past, present, or future time. Clarity in manifestation is the result of the fitness of the viewer's senses and the availability of aids to clear perception, such as a lantern or a pair of glasses. But neither clarity nor unclarity results in any difference in the basic existence and character of whatever manifests. The object remains the same in both cases. Thus, the universe that lies latent and invisible within Absolute Consciousness is the same as the universe that appears outwardly in phenomenal existence. It is only the Lord who bears the cosmos in both its aspects.

Verses 3-4

सुखादिषु च सौख्यादिहेतुष्वपि च वस्तुषु ।
अवभासस्य सद्भावेऽप्यतीतत्वात्तथास्थितिः ॥ ३ ॥
गाढमुल्लिख्यमाने तु विकल्पेन सुखादिके ।
तथा स्थितिस्तथैव स्यात्स्फुटमस्योपलक्षणात् ॥ ४ ॥

sukhādiṣu ca saukhyādi hetuṣv api ca vastuṣu /
avabhāsasya sad-bhāve 'py atītatvāt tathāsthitiḥ //
gāḍham ullikhyamāne tu vikalpena sukhādike /
tathā sthitis tathaiva syāt sphuṭam asyopalakṣaṇāt //

[This is similar to remembered] interior experiences like joy, and the objective means yielding them; although these do not [now] shine in the same charming way [as at the time of their direct experience] because of being in the past. But if this experience is brought about through very deep contemplation, its situation becomes exactly like that [past experience] because of its being felt quite clearly.

Commentary

An aspirant can recollect his basic nature of being none other than Almighty God through the yogic practice of contemplative meditation on the real nature and character of the Self. This is what the author wants to subtly suggest. He can thus realise the fact that the whole outward universe does, in fact, lie in his own real Self, while its externality is just a characteristic imposed on it by *māyā*.

Verse 5

भावाभावावभासानां बाह्यतोपाधिरिष्यते ।
नात्मा सत्ता ततस्तेषामान्तराणां सतां सदा ॥ ५ ॥

bhāvābhāvāvabhāsānāṃ bāhyatopādhir iṣyate /
nātmā sattā tatas teṣām āntarāṇāṃ satāṃ sadā //

Exteriority is just an outward attribute, imposed on manifest existent and non-existent phenomena. It is not their essence or Self. Therefore, the interior existence of such entities is the eternal Truth.

Commentary

Exteriority, or objectivity, is imposed on all phenomena by human beings and others working in the field of *māyā*. This illusion is the source of their ignorance. All phenomena do, in reality, exist internally within the monistic Absolute, the pure and infinite Consciousness, which bears them in the form of its divine essence. This divine essence manifests *māyā*, thus imposing exteriority on all phenomena. At the same time, the Lord contracts the Self-Consciousness of beings in such a way that they take only a particular finite entity as their personal Self and see the remaining whole world as objectively external, that is, outside their own I-Consciousness.

Verse 6

आन्तरत्वात्प्रमात्रैक्ये नैषां भेदनिबन्धना ।
अर्थक्रियापि बाह्यत्वे सा भिन्नाभासभेदतः ॥ ६ ॥

āntaratvāt pramātr-aikye naiṣāṃ bheda-nibandhanā /
artha-kriyāpi bāhyatve sā bhinnābhāsa-bhedataḥ //

Being one with the knowing Subject, these [objective phenomena] in their interior aspect do not demonstrate any utility based on mutual differences. Even in their exterior aspect, [this utility] is of various types only because [the objective phenomena] manifest in varied ways.

Commentary

Utility in the world becomes possible only in the field of diversity. One needs objects separate from their subjects in order to employ these objects, to 'use' them in various ways. For example, a carpenter's tool, wood, and so on are used by a person to build a house. Objects must thus appear to be different from the subject, the person. Therefore the special utility of various objective entities ceases to be possible when these entities shine in complete oneness with the Subject, the Lord.

The seventh couplet establishes the fact that all phenomena manifested outwardly as objective existence also have an everlasting existence within infinite Consciousness. They shine therein as a reality that is perfectly non-different from pure Consciousness. This is precisely the principle of spiritual realism, discovered and propagated by the ancient masters of Kashmir Śaivism.

Verse 7

चिन्मयत्वेऽवभासानामन्तरेव स्थितिः सदा ।
मायया भासमानानां बाह्यत्वाद्बहिरप्यसौ ॥ ७ ॥

cin-mayatve 'vabhāsānām antar eva sthitiḥ sadā /
māyayā bhāsa-mānānāṃ bāhyatvād bahir apy asau //

Only the interior existence of phenomenal entities is their eternal existence, because they are one with pure Consciousness. [Their existence] is an exterior phenomenon as well, because they are brought into outward manifestation by *māyā*.

Commentary

All phenomena exist in Absolute Consciousness and shine there as pure I-Consciousness alone, without even the faintest tinge of objective 'this-ness'. That is their noumenal, their true spiritual, existence. *Māyā,* the differentiating and deluding power of the Lord, makes them shine objectively as 'these things' as well. Objects thus shine as entities different from 'I-ness', as well as from one another; that is their phenomenal existence. Both the inner and outer aspects of all phenomena exist and shine as one complete whole in the yogic revelation attained by a Śiva yogin who is devoted to the practice of the Trika yoga of Kashmir Śaivism. The noumenal existence of the phenomenon is everlasting, while the objective, phenomenal existence has a beginning and an end.

The eighth and the ninth couplets focus on the exact character of the internality and externality of manifestations as discovered by the ancient masters of Kashmir Śaivism.

Verse 8

विकल्पे योऽयमुल्लेखः सोऽपि बाह्यः पृथक्प्रथः ।
प्रमात्रैकात्म्यमान्तर्यं ततो भेदो हि बाह्यता ॥ ८॥

vikalpe yo 'yam ullekhaḥ so 'pi bāhyaḥ pṛthak-prathaḥ /
pramātr-aikātmyam āntaryaṃ tato bhedo hi bāhyatā //

The imaginary manifestation of something that occurs in ideation is also accepted as exterior in character, because it appears [objectively] as something different from a person, according to its exteriority. Perfect unity with divine I-Consciousness is (taken in Kashmir Śaivism as) the interior nature of an entity. Its actualised existence, appearing as something different from that nature, is known here as its exteriority.

Commentary

All mental imagery, though shining inside the mind of a person, appears as a thing different from him, and so is taken here to be an exterior element. Whatever appears as 'I' is thus to be taken as interior in character, and everything appearing as 'this' or 'that' is to be counted as an exterior entity. Such is the terminology used in Kashmir Śaivism. All mental objective manifestations, all thoughts and objects, have the nature of exteriority, and everything appearing as identical with true 'I-ness' has interiority as its essential character.

Verse 9

उल्लेखस्य सुखादेश्च प्रकाशो बहिरात्मना ।
इच्छातो भर्तुरध्यक्षरूपोऽक्ष्यादिभुवां यथा ॥ ९॥

ullekhasya sukhādeś ca prakāśo bahir ātmanā /
icchāto bhartur adhyakṣa-rūpo 'kṣyādi-bhuvāṃ yathā // [24]

Just as objects of the exterior senses, like the eyes, appear in [human] perceptual knowledge to be in a position of exteriority by the Lord's authority, so imagination and imagined pleasure, pain, and so on shine in a position of exteriority on the authority of the same divine will, as these also are counted as perceptual knowledge.

Commentary

The objects perceived by the external senses, by the eyes or ears for instance, in fact exist interiorly within pure Consciousness. But the authority of the Lord's divine will manifests them as exterior phenomena as well. They are manifested as being different from Consciousness, as already discussed at length. The same is the case with mental imagination, fancy, supposition, visualisation, and other inner processes, which are generally known as varieties of interior knowledge. Objective knowledge, whether exterior or interior in character, is thus counted in Kashmir Śaivism as an exterior phenomenon, because to be one with the knowing Subject, the I-Consciousness, is taken to be interiority, and to be different from it is counted as exteriority. All mental objective knowledge, although occurring inside one's mind, is considered in this philosophy to be an exterior, or non-essential, self phenomenon, because it appears as something other than I-Consciousness.

The tenth couplet concludes the principle of establishing one common divine basis of perceptions, conceptions, recollections, and other mental processes, as established through the previously expressed valid logical arguments.

Verse 10

तदैक्येन विना न स्यात्संविदां लोकपद्धतिः ।
प्रकाशैक्यात्तदेकत्वं मातैकः स इति स्थितम् ॥ १० ॥

tad aikyena vinā na syāt saṃvidāṃ loka-paddhatiḥ /
prakāśaikyāt tad-ekatvaṃ mātaikaḥ sa iti sthitam //

Therefore, worldly activities are not possible without the existence of unity among different psychological activities and functions. Such a unity can be provided by the unity of *prakāśa* (the light of Consciousness). *Prakāśa* is the one common Subject (the Master of all psychic functions). This principle thus stands established as correct.

Commentary

Complex and varied mundane transactions—like eating, speaking, and operating machinery—are not possible if momentary mental flickers of the conscious mind alone are accepted as the basis of all human psycho-physical functions. The flickers of mental consciousness require a common support that can successfully build and maintain their mutual relations, which are so essential for the character and finite nature of all mundane dealings and the flow of all universal functions. Such a single foundation can only be the infinite, all-pervading, and pure I-Consciousness, which is aware of itself and its own comprehensive basic nature. In Śaivism, I-Consciousness is called *pramātā* (or *pramātṛ*), the active Subject of willing, knowing, doing, and other activities. However, it appears as many because it inhabits different bodies, which are manifested diversely by *māyā,* the differentiating and obscuring power of the Lord.

The last couplet in the chapter establishes emphatically the reality that the Self-awareness of Absolute Consciousness is both pure knowing and pure doing, by virtue of which it is undoubtedly Almighty God.

Verse 11

स एव विमृशत्त्वेन नियतेन महेश्वरः ।
विमर्श एव देवस्य शुद्धे ज्ञानक्रिये यतः ॥ ११ ॥

sa eva vimṛśattvena niyatena maheśvaraḥ /
vimarśa eva devasya śuddhe jñāna-kriye yataḥ //

It is only He [*pramātā,* the absolute Subject] who is Almighty God, by virtue of His constant Self-awareness, because Self-awareness is the pure knowledge, as well as the pure action, of the Lord.

Commentary

Absolute Consciousness, being always aware of itself and its divine nature, is accepted as Maheśvara, Almighty God. It is His awareness that is the very basis of His Godhead. Being aware of His divine nature, He is always inclined to express it externally. Such external expression, happening as a reflective manifestation, results in the Lord's five divine activities of creation, preservation, absorption, Self-concealment, and Self-revelation. The first three are primarily aimed at phenomenal existence as a whole, and the last two are expressed only with created worldly and heavenly beings.

The Self-awareness of Absolute Consciousness, the basis of all the five divine activities, is also known as the pure power of knowledge *(jñāna)* and the power of action *(kriyā)*. By virtue of having such divine powers, Absolute Consciousness is accepted as the omniscient and omnipotent God. He is the fundamental base of all existence that functions successfully as a cosmos on the basis of His divine powers. He is the integrating, organising, and administering authority behind all activities of the universe, although he partially delegates powers to superior created beings known as supergods, like Brahmā, Viṣṇu, and Rudra, as well as to gods in heaven like Indra, Varuṇa, and Yama. Nothing in the universe can function successfully if His existence is not accepted.

Book II

KRIYĀDHIKĀRA

Divine Creative Action

Chapter 1

THE POWER TO ACT

Book II of the *Īśvara-pratyabhijñā-kārikā* establishes the existence of *kriyā-śakti,* the divine active power of the Lord, as discussed in the theistic scriptural schools of thought. This book has been apportioned by Āchārya Abhinavagupta into four chapters. The first presents the fact that the active power, *kriyā,* which is the essential nature of Absolute Consciousness, appears in mundane efforts as action with time sequence as part of its character, although from the perspective of basic reality, such power is absolutely free from all types of sequence. This book is also aimed at neutralising the arguments put forth by Vijñānavāda Buddhism against the principle of the Lord's *kriyā-śakti,* as well as against the very existence of the phenomenon known as *kriyā.*

The first couplet in the chapter refutes Vijñānavāda's assertion that *kriyā* (activity) does not exist. The Buddhist argument is based on some apparently conflicting views of scriptural thinkers about *kriyā*'s nature.

Verse 1

अत एव यदप्युक्तं क्रिया नैकस्य सक्रमा ।
एकेत्यादि प्रतिक्षिप्तं तदेकस्य समर्थनात् ॥ १ ॥

ata eva yad apy uktaṃ kriyā naikasya sa-kramā /
ekety-ādi pratikṣiptaṃ tad ekasya samarthanāt //

By this establishment of the principle of unity, all logical objections raised [by the Vijñānavādins] against the principle of action *(kriyā)* are automatically invalidated. For instance: the impossibility of its being sequential and one single entity [simultaneously] and its not being related to any single reality, and so on.

Commentary

The masters of Buddhist idealism raised several objections against the Śaivite principle of the power of action, *kriyā,* which belongs to the one Absolute Consciousness. This topic was discussed previously in Book I, chapter 2. The central point of all their objections was that one cannot be many. Therefore they objected to the principle of monism developed by the Śaiva yogins of Kashmir. But the Śaiva philosophers have established clearly that one monistic Absolute Consciousness has blissful vibratory activity, *kriyā,* as its essential character. This *kriyā-śakti* manifests itself externally in manifold variety, by virtue of its own divine capacities. All objections raised by the Buddhist thinkers thereby stand rejected and invalidated. The sound arguments that succeeded in establishing the *jñāna-śakti* of the Lord, the power of knowledge, are extremely useful in establishing His *kriyā-śakti* as well.

Couplet two draws a distinction between the nature of the active aspect of the Absolute, on one hand, and the mundane actions that are manifested in phenomenal existence, on the other. By doing so, it justifies the sequential nature of all mundane actions.

Verse 2

सक्रमत्वं च लौकिक्याः क्रियायाः कालशक्तितः ।
घटते न तु शाश्वत्याः प्राभव्याः स्यात्प्रभोरिव ॥ २॥

sa-kramatvaṃ ca laukikyāḥ kriyāyāḥ kāla-śaktitaḥ /
ghaṭate na tu śāśvatyāḥ prābhavyāḥ syāt prabhor iva //

Sequentiality *(sa-kramatvam)* in a mundane action is worked out by that divine power of the Lord that manifests time sequence; but, as it is not the character of the Lord, so it is not that of His eternal activity.

Commentary

Kāla-śakti is that divine power of God that manifests time sequence in all mundane actions. In this world actions occur yesterday, today, tomorrow, or over time. But the Lord Himself, being the Absolute Reality, is not conditioned by such sequences of time, nor is His divine activity conditioned by it, because it is eternal in character.

The next couplet explains that it is only because of the regular sequential nature of some phenomenal entities and their changing conditions that human beings believe in the insubstantial concept of time.

Verse 3

कालः सूर्यादिसंचारस्तत्तत्पुष्पादिजन्म वा ।
शीतोष्णे वाथ तल्लक्ष्यः क्रम एव स तत्त्वतः ॥ ३॥

kālaḥ sūryādi-saṃcāras tat-tat-puṣpādi-janma vā /
śītoṣṇe vātha tal-lakṣyaḥ krama eva sa tattvataḥ //

[The concept of] time signifies either changes such as the position of the sun, or the growth of different flowers, or [changes in atmospheric] heat or cold; or, it is better to say, some sequence [of events] indicated by them.

Commentary

Time is not a real, existent substance. It is just an imagined idea of regular sequence, modelled after certain regular phenomenal happenings, like changes in the positions of the planets within the zodiac, the blossoming of different varieties of flowers, the ripening of fruits, harvesting of crops, changes in seasons, and other phenomena. It is, in fact, a definite and regular system of sequence, imagined by the human mind and applied to mundane events and actions.

Human activities and events in human lives do not usually proceed in accordance with any definite order or regular system of sequence. So people, measuring them by the above-mentioned regular systems of sequence, say that a person lived for a hundred years, a work was completed in six months, a thing will happen after about a week, and so on. Just as a lengthy sheet of cloth comes out of a factory and is measured with a rod bearing the marks of yards, feet, and inches, so mundane activities and events are measured with the rod of time. This rod bears the conceptual marks of different units of time, such as years, months, days, and hours.

This is the principle held by Kashmir Śaivism with regard to time. Time is thus not any real existent substance, but just an entity imagined by beings residing inside the sphere of *māyā.* There is no such time sequence in the higher realms of existence, the realms beyond the reach of *māyā*. Kashmir Śaivism thus disagrees with Nyāya-Vaiśeṣika philosophy, which recognises time as an eternal substance, and it also disagrees with the theory of modern physics, which announces time and space as two basically existent realities.

The next couplet throws light on the character and origin of the manifestation of sequence *(krama)* in the world.

Verse 4

क्रमो भेदाश्रयो भेदोऽप्याभाससदसत्त्वतः ।
आभाससदसत्त्वे तु चित्राभासकृतः प्रभोः ॥ ४ ॥

kramo bhedāśrayo bhedo 'py ābhāsa-sad-asattvataḥ /
ābhāsa-sad-asattve tu citrābhāsa-kṛtaḥ prabhoḥ //

[Mutual] difference is the base on which the sequence [of time or space] stands. That difference is based on the manifestation and non-manifestation [of particular entities]. Such manifestations and non-manifestations are due to the Lord, who brings these wonderful displays into [apparent] existence.

Commentary

There is sequence created in the very process of world creation, between the cosmic energy known as *prakṛti* and the phenomenal existence it creates. This sequence is based on the mutual differences between the two, differences having to do with manifestations and non-manifestations of different qualities in each. For instance, in the fundamental cosmic energy *(mūla-prakṛti)* the qualities of unity, tranquillity, and inactivity manifest, and those of plurality, turbulence, and activity do not. On the other hand, in the universe there is diversity, activity, and turbulence, and the opposite qualities are more rarely found. These examples prove that there are differences between the two. Such varieties in the qualities of entities are basically brought into existence by the Lord, who is Himself manifesting these multifaceted, wonderful entities.

The fifth couplet explains the fact that the Lord manifests two types of sequence based on the concepts of time and space.

Verse 5

मूर्तिवैचित्र्यतो देशक्रममाभासयत्यसौ ।
क्रियावैचित्र्यनिर्भासात्कालक्रममपीश्वरः ॥ ५ ॥

mūrti-vaicitry ato deśa-kramam ābhāsayaty asau /
kriyā-vaicitrya-nirbhāsāt kāla-kramam apīśvaraḥ //

The Lord, being all-powerful, manifests spatial sequence by creating wonderful variety in the forms [of creation], and He also brings about time sequence by manifesting variations in actions.

Commentary

Physical forms that all adjoin one another—such as a house, its compound, the lane outside, a nearby temple, park, and market—are the basis by which a person uses his imagination to form concepts of sequence in space. An astronomer forms similar concepts on the basis of the visible variety of heavenly bodies like the sun, moon, planets, stars, Milky Way galaxy, and their mutual proximity.

Actions are also very often divided into several steps or sub-actions. For instance, a person sitting in a chair puts a piece of paper on the table in front of him, takes a pen in his hand, dips its tip into an inkpot, and writes different lines indicating letters and words on the paper. He then folds it, puts it in an envelope, gums it, affixes a postal stamp to it, and addresses the envelope, feeling at last that he has written a letter. The action of writing a letter includes all these steps, or sub-actions, which come into being one after another in a definite order. This order is calculated, formed in the mind, and imposed on the main action by the writer through his own imagination. The sub-actions do not by themselves manifest or present anything that could be taken as an order. This example illustrates time sequence, which is imposed by the person on the successive variety of sub-actions within the main action.

Both types of sequence—spatial and temporal—emerge out of the playful divine will of the Lord, who manifests them in phenomenal entities and activities. Neither type of sequence has any substantial existence in the outer world, but both enjoy an imaginary existence, worked out by worldly beings, which takes into consideration the variety in form and action. All variety, with the laws governing it, basically is manifested by the Lord through His playful divine essence. This principle of Kashmir Śaivism will be elucidated in greater detail later on, and the reader may also consult one of the author's smaller works, the *Sambandha-siddhi,* the third booklet in the *Siddhitrayī.*

The next two couplets explain that both varieties of sequence—space and time—have their scope only within the limited viewpoint of finite beings and not with respect to the Absolute Lord, who exists beyond the sequential fields of time and space.

Verse 6

सर्वत्राभासभेदोऽपि भवेत्कालक्रमाकरः ।
विच्छिन्नभासः शून्यादेर्मातुर्भातस्य नो सकृत् ॥ ६ ॥

sarvatrābhāsa-bhedo 'pi bhavet kala-kramākaraḥ /
vicchinna-bhāsaḥ śūnyāder mātur bhātasya no sa-kṛt //

The variety in manifestation that is the source of time sequence pertains everywhere only to a finite subject, who takes entities like the void of dreamless sleep as his Self. [This is] because he is manifestly cut off [from other similar beings]. Such is not the case with the infinite Subject, who shines on forever.

Commentary

The infinite Subject, consisting of pure and limitless Consciousness and not bound by anything like time, space, causation, individuality, and mental or physical form, has been shining forever. A finite individual, taking finite substances like *śūnya,* the void, *prāṇa,* the animating life-force, *buddhi,* the understanding faculty or intelligence, and *deha,* the physical body, as his Self, sees the great variety of manifestations in the world and forms ideas of time sequence in relation to them. While the finite subject considers his physical body and mind to be limited by time sequence, this is not the case with the infinite Subject, who is not bound by time sequence.

Verse 7

देशक्रमोऽपि भावेषु भाति मातुर्मितात्मनः ।
स्वात्मेव स्वात्मना पूर्णा भावा भान्त्यमितस्य तु ॥ ७ ॥

deśa-kramo 'pi bhāveṣu bhāti mātur mitātmanaḥ /
svātmeva svātmanā pūrṇā bhāvā bhānty amitasya tu //

Spatial sequence, pertaining to different objects, also occurs in relation to a finite subject; [by contrast] all beings appear to the infinite Subject as His own Self, perfect by themselves and filled with His own existence.

Commentary

It is only the finite I-consciousness, a person with awareness of himself as an individual, who sees spatial sequence, *deśa-krama,* when he encounters the items of everyday life. There is no scope for the manifestation of this sequence in the unitary view of God, the infinite Subject. He sees Himself and everything else as perfect, infinite, unconditioned by spatial sequence, and filled to the brim by His own existence. The same is true for beings in the pure *tattvas* (principles of creation) above *māyā.*

The last couplet discusses the power of the Lord that manifests the multitude of sequential relations between subjects and objects in the phenomenal world.

Verse 8

किंतु निर्माणशक्तिः साप्येवं विदुष ईशितुः ।
तथा विज्ञातृविज्ञेयभेदो यदवभास्यते ॥ ८॥

kiṃtu nirmāṇa-śaktiḥ sāpy evaṃ viduṣa īśituḥ /
tathā vijñātṛ-vijñeya-bhedo yad avabhāsyate //

Nevertheless, there is that power of creative action, belonging to the Self-aware Master of the powers of will and gnosis, by which the variations in subjects and objects of knowing are manifested in wonderfully different ways.

Commentary

The divine Master possesses the powers of will and gnosis. Being aware of these powers and activating His power of action, He vibrates them eternally. This results in the manifestation of differences between one knowing subject and another, between one known object and another, and between subject and objects. This three-pronged variation produces situations in which human beings, in their diverse seeing, form the ideas of sequences of time and space. These two concepts of time and space, though not being any eternal truth, work predominantly in the created phenomenal world, leaving nothing in it untouched.

Chapter 2

UNITY AND DIVERSITY

The aim of the second chapter of Book II is to clarify the viewpoint of existential realism. Kashmir Śaivism adopts a partial agreement with the views of the Nyāya-Vaiśeṣika school on this topic. The first couplet in the chapter emphasises transactional realism in relation to principles like action, relativity, and generality, comparing the Śaiva viewpoint with that of schools like Nyāya-Vaiśeṣika.

Verse 1

क्रियासंबन्धसामान्यद्रव्यदिक्कालबुद्धयः ।
सत्याः स्थैर्योपयोगाभ्यामेकानेकाश्रया मताः ॥ १ ॥

kriyā-saṃbandha-sāmānya-dravya-dik-kāla-buddhayaḥ /
satyāḥ sthairyopayogābhyām ekānekāśrayā matāḥ //

Ideas about action, relation, generality, compound substances, direction [in space], time sequence, and similar concepts are accepted as real entities because of their durability and practical utility.

Commentary

Kashmir Śaivism maintains three complementary views: (1) absolute realism, (2) ideal or transactional realism, and (3) non-realism. Absolute Consciousness is the only entity that enjoys absolute realism. It exists absolutely, permanently, and is totally real, and so it is called *pāramārthika-satya*. On the other hand, ideas like 'the son of a barren woman', 'the horns of a hare', and 'flowers in the sky', are totally unreal, *asatya,* although they appear in a person's imagination. But principles like action, relation, and generality, although also not having any substantial reality and appearing only in the mind, are accepted as transactional reality, *vyāvahārika-satya.* These principles are considered real entities in all mundane transactions because of their durability and practical utility in these transactions.

The second couplet establishes a justifiable compromise between the inward, experientially evident spiritual monism and the outwardly apparent transactional pluralism of the world, a pluralism based on the concepts of time and space.

Verse 2

तत्रैकमान्तरं तत्त्वं तदेवेन्द्रियवेद्यताम् ।
संप्राप्यानेकतां याति देशकालस्वभावतः ॥ २॥

tatraikam āntaraṃ tattvaṃ tad evendriya-vedyatām /
saṃprāpyānekatāṃ yāti deśa-kāla-sva-bhāvataḥ //

There the interior Reality is only one, and that One alone develops multiplicity in its character because of the effect of time and space touching the realm of objects knowable through the senses.

Commentary

Pure Consciousness, the Absolute Subject, is the only interior reality, which alone appears as many by manifesting itself in the form of objects knowable with the help of senses. Such is the effect of the manifestations of time and space working in the realm of objectivity.

The third couplet explains how concepts of unity are combined with those of diversity. The human mind employs diversity in dealing with ideas such as action, relativity, and generality.

Verse 3

तद्द्वयालम्बना एता मनोऽनुव्यवसायि सत् ।
करोति मातृव्यापारमयीः कर्मादिकल्पनाः ॥ ३ ॥

tad-dvayālambanā etā mano 'nuvyavasāyi sat /
karoti mātṛ-vyāpāra-mayīḥ karmadi-kalpanāḥ //

A person's mind, becoming conscious of both thought-free revelations, *nirvikalpa,* and conceptual ideation, depending on unity as well as multiplicity, employs ideas such as action, etc., as the activities of the knowing subject.

Commentary

One's mind, while employing the ideas of action, relation, and other processes, depends on both the unity of the Knower and the diversity of varied phenomena in the world. The mind employs multiple ideas that establish the ideal existence of the entities on which the mundane transactions depend. The unity of pure Consciousness is thus the basic truth, and the diversity appearing in processes like action, relation, and generality is also a sort of truth.

Diversity can conveniently be called the truth existing in ideation, because human ideas about the world are multiple. These diverse concepts are then taken by Kashmir Śaivism as dialectic truth. Śaivism says that unity is the eternal truth and diversity is the dialectic truth. Therefore, action, relation, and the objects they concern are not to be pushed into the field of total non-existence. These are not 'the sons of barren women'.

The next couplet explains the development of ideas of relativity about separate, limited objects.

Verse 4

स्वात्मनिष्ठा विविक्ताभा भावा एकप्रमातरि ।
अन्योन्यान्वयरूपैक्ययुजः संबन्धधीपदम् ॥ ४ ॥

svātma-niṣṭhā viviktābhā bhāvā eka-pramātari /
anyonyānvaya-rūpaikya-yujaḥ saṃbandha-dhī-padam //

Self-contained and separately shining entities become the objects of the idea of relationship when, resting in one knowing subject, they form a unity known as their mutual relationship.

Commentary

Relativity, or relationship, is not a substantial entity. It is merely a special type of idea formed by human beings with respect to ideas about different objects. These objects are themselves totally self-contained and mutually indifferent; they have nothing in common with each other, nothing that could be taken as their mutual relation. 'Relation' is thus merely an idea, without substantial existence.[25]

The fifth couplet aims to justify the presence of both ideas—unity and diversity—in all thoughts about generality and compound substances, including all exterior human affairs.

Verse 5

जातिद्रव्यावभासानां बहिरप्येकरूपताम् ।
व्यक्त्येकदेशभेदं चाप्यालम्बन्ते विकल्पनाः ॥ ५ ॥

jāti-dravyāvabhāsānāṃ bahir apy eka-rūpatām /
vyakty-eka-deśa-bhedaṃ cāpy ālambante vikalpanāḥ //

Unity encompasses both ideas of manifest generalities and compound substances lying outside one's person [in the world], as well as the diversity of compound substances and their component parts, even in their exterior aspects.

Commentary

The concept of unity in diversity is emphasised here as the very important basis of human ideas. It serves as the key in understanding how all mundane transactions, activities, and complex thinking in the world are conducted.

The sixth couplet explains the essence of relationship between agents of action, as well as of concepts such as direction.

Verse 6

क्रियाविमर्शविषयः कारकाणां समन्वयः ।
अवध्यवधिमद्भावान्वयालम्बा दिगादिधीः ॥ ६ ॥

kriyā-vimarśa-viṣayaḥ kārakāṇāṃ samanvayaḥ /
avadhy-avadhimad-bhāvānvayālambā dig-ādi-dhīḥ //

The mutual [cooperative] relationship of the *kārakās* (agents involved in performing an action) is based on the consideration of the parts played by them in action. The concepts regarding direction, for example, depend on the ideas of the extent and limit of actual entities in space.

Commentary

All conceptions involved in mundane dealings are based both on the concept of central interior unity and on that of exterior diversity. 'Unity in diversity' *(bhedābheda)* is therefore the central concept in all types of relations that occur in mundane affairs.

The concluding couplet in the chapter refutes the Vedāntic theory that worldly activities are merely illusory. Kashmir Śaivism says that they are carried out successfully with the help of substances or ideas that have both unity and diversity as their nature.

Verse 7

एवमेवार्थसिद्धिः स्यान्मातुरर्थक्रियार्थिनः ।
भेदाभेदवतार्थेन तेन न भ्रान्तिरीदृशी ॥ ७ ॥

evam evārtha-siddhiḥ syān mātur artha-kriyārthinaḥ /
bhedābhedavatārthena tena na bhrāntir īdṛśī //

In this way the objectives of a person desirous of mundane attainments are fulfilled—with the help of entities [in the world] that have [both] unity and diversity as their character. Such a thing is therefore not an illusion.

Commentary

Concepts like 'the horns of a hare' or 'the son of a barren woman' are considered by Śaivism to express untruth, something non-existent. Ideas about the actual existence of such substances are, no doubt, delusionary. But the world as a whole is not an illusion when practical objectives are considered. To eat, drink, and enjoy many types of mundane experiences, and also to say that the whole world is an illusion, is self-deceit. The phenomenonal world is not the Absolute Truth, but it is not totally false, because it enjoys a long-lived and utilitarian relative reality. It should not be compared with 'the son of a barren woman', which is a physical impossibility. Even the teachings of the Upaniṣads are, after all, part and parcel of mundane phenomenal existence.

The Vedāntin practically depends on the two theories of delusion and pure knowledge. But Śaiva thinkers add a third theory of relative knowledge, and it is this knowledge that serves as a means to attain pure knowledge. This is the same practical philosophical view expressed in the *Īśavasya-upaniṣad* (8-14) and repeated with emphasis throughout the *Bhagavad-gītā*. One could easily argue that negligence of this realistic principle, which is found in early Vedic philosophy, has been one of the main causes of the miseries of the Indian nation over the past one thousand years.

Chapter 3

EPISTEMOLOGY

The third chapter of Book II addresses Kashmir Śaiva epistemology. The Mīmāṃsā philosophy discusses the various *pramāṇas,* or means of correct knowledge. Most of these means have been accepted by modern philosophers as valid for all mundane activities.[26] But these *pramāṇas* are not capable of proving the existence of God, who is the fundamental basis of all of them and thus beyond their reach. This epistemological point is discussed here with great emphasis.

The first two couplets in the chapter present the Śaivite definition of *pramāṇa* as well as its general character and results.

Verse 1

इदमेतादृगित्येवं यद्वशाद्व्यवतिष्ठते ।
वस्तु प्रमाणं तत्सोऽपि स्वाभासोऽभिनवोदयः ॥ १ ॥

idam etā-dṛg ity evaṃ yad vaśād vyavatiṣṭhate /
vastu pramāṇaṃ tat so 'pi svābhāso 'bhinavodayaḥ //

An entity is known as a *pramāṇa* (the means of correct knowledge) when through it a conclusion is reached about an object of knowledge, such as 'This is, and it is like this'. Such an entity is even self-evident and newly arises [in each instance of knowing].

Commentary

The means to ascertain the very existence, as well as the essential character, of something is known as a *pramāṇa*. It is the means of correct understanding about an object. Such a *pramāṇa* is, in fact, a self-revealing entity,[27] which belongs to some concerned knowing subject and always newly arises within him. It is never taken by him as something second-hand or outdated in character. A person goes on ascertaining the nature of certain objects by means of ever-new assertions. Even if he were to enjoy an everlasting existence, the manifestation of *pramāṇas* in his Consciousness would keep occurring. Each momentary mental assertion has its own *pramāṇa,* which always arises newly within the Self of the knowing Subject. It is, in fact, a person's own divine manifestation, because his own Consciousness appears in its form.

Verse 2

सोऽन्तस्तथाविमर्शात्मा देशकालाद्यभेदिनि ।
एकाभिधानविषये मितिर्वस्तुन्यबाधिता ॥ २ ॥

so 'ntas tathā vimarśātmā deśa-kālādy-abhedini /
ekābhidhāna-viṣaye mitir vastuny abādhitā //

That very [*pramāṇa*], being an inward corresponding awareness that does not have any variation based on time or space as its object, is known as [a *pramiti* or a *pramā*, that is,] an accurate conception, provided it is not invalidated.

Commentary

The psychic activity that shines outwardly as *pramāṇa* is also known as *pramā,* an accurate objective conception, in its corresponding inner aspect of awareness, provided its validity is not disproved. If it is disproved in a particular case, then both the *pramāṇa* and the *pramā* are refuted.[28]

The next three couplets express the fact that a single object may be known in different ways, by different persons, and in accordance with different conditions based on different likes, moods, aims, objects, speech, and so on—all on the same occasion.

Verse 3

यथारुचि यथार्थित्वं यथाव्युत्पत्ति भिद्यते ।
आभासोऽप्यर्थ एकस्मिन्ननुसंधानसाधिते ॥ ३ ॥

yathā-ruci yathārthitvaṃ yathā-vyutpatti bhidyate /
ābhāso 'py artha ekasminn anusaṃdhāna-sādhite //

The manifest character of a single object, taken up for the purpose of scrutiny, differs in accordance with one's liking, purpose, verbal knowledge, and so on.

Commentary

It is not necessary that everyone should form the same conception of an object or express it in the same way. Such things do differ according to human differences in aims, objects, likes, and verbal expressions.

Verses 4-5

दीर्घवृत्तोर्ध्वपुरुषधूमचान्दनतादिभिः ।
यथावभासा विभिद्यन्ते देशकालाविभेदिनः ॥ ४ ॥
तथैव सद्घटद्रव्यकाञ्चनोज्ज्वलतादयः ।
आभासभेदा भिन्नार्थकारिणस्ते पदं ध्वनेः ॥ ५ ॥

dīrgha-vṛttordhva-puruṣa-dhūma-cāndanatādibhiḥ /
yathāvabhāsā vibhidyante deśa-kālāvibhedinaḥ //
tathaiva sad-ghaṭa-dravya-kāñcanojjvalatādayaḥ /
ābhāsabhedā bhinnārtha-kāriṇas te padaṃ dhvaneḥ //

Just as a manifest object, without any internal variation caused by time, space, etc., appears differently [to different people] as, for example, something long, round, or tall or as a man or [perhaps as] smoke, sandalwood smoke, etc., in the same way, different [ideas] manifest concerning a single object. For instance, [it may be] taken as merely something existent, a water vessel, some substance, gold, or a glittering object, [each] satisfying different purposes and becoming an object of knowledge accompanied by different word-images.

Commentary

A single object seen by different people in dim light appears to each one differently, either as a tall object or as a thick and round one or as a man. A substance may be taken simply as smoke or, more particularly, as sandalwood smoke. In the same way, a golden water vessel is viewed differently by different people in accordance with their ideas. One person may want some object, so he takes it merely as an object. Someone desiring to fetch water takes it as a water vessel; someone in need of some hard substance takes it as that. Another person, looking at it from an economic point of view, sees it as costly gold, while an excitable or more emotional person takes it as a brightly glittering substance.

Thus there are wonderfully different variations in how objects are perceived, and these perceived manifestations invariably become the primary objects of all types of mundane transactions in the world, where they are known and talked about accordingly. That is the multiple character of *pramā,* correct knowledge. As we can see, such knowledge is based on subjective as well as objective criteria.

The sixth and seventh couplets throw light on the fact that different types of cognitions concerning a single object take into consideration different details of the object's nature, and so are aimed at different objectives. However, thinking about the object holistically, in a single overarching cognition, produces quite different results. This phenomenon is compared, on one hand, with tiny lamp lights shining together and, on the other hand, with small rivulets that flow into and become one with the ocean.

Verse 6

आभासभेदाद्वस्तूनां नियतार्थक्रिया पुनः ।
सामानाधिकरण्येन प्रतिभासादभेदिनाम् ॥ ६ ॥

ābhāsa-bhedād vastūnāṃ niyatārtha-kriyā punaḥ /
sāmānādhikaraṇyena pratibhāsād abhedinām //

The utility of substances is different according to their different manifest [qualities]. But it is quite another thing to take these manifestations together as one overarching entity, without any differentiation.

Commentary

The mere appearance of an object removes the idea in a person's mind that nothing is there. That is, apparent substance removes the idea of insubstantiality. Take the example of a gold vessel. The vessel itself provides the idea of utility in fetching water. Its gold substance creates a high estimation of its value and a sense of its wonderful beauty. All such manifest qualities, the different aspects of an object, when taken together as a whole, produce in the viewer a joyful satisfaction. For instance, for a worshipper of Śiva the vessel is seen as worthy of being placed on the stand over a *śiva-liṅga,* a symbolic image of Lord Śiva. This demonstrates the joint utility of all the above-mentioned manifest qualities.

Verse 7

पृथग्दीपप्रकाशानां स्रोतसां सागरे यथा ।
अविरुद्धावभासानामेककार्या तथैक्यधीः ॥ ७ ॥

pṛthag-dīpa-prakāśānāṃ srotasāṃ sāgare yathā /
avirūddhāvabhāsānām eka-kāryā tathaikya-dhīḥ //

Mutually unopposed manifest objects are taken as one single entity because they appear to be mixed together, just like the lights of different lamps or currents of water in an ocean.

Commentary

When individual lights of several lamps are placed together in a room to illumine it, they are not perceived as different from one another. They join together to shine as one single bright light. The case of waves and currents in an ocean is similar. Just as these phenomena are perceived as a single entity simply because they appear together, so in worldly dealings all the various appearances of one and the same substance may occasionally be taken to be one single entity.

The eighth couplet states the fact that one single proof can validate the position of an object, along with all its essential basic qualities. A separate means of knowing may not be required for the purpose concerned.

Verse 8

तत्राविशिष्टे वह्न्यादौ कार्यकारणतोष्णता ।
तत्तच्छब्दार्थताद्यात्मा प्रमाणादेकतो मतः ॥ ८ ॥

tatrāviśiṣṭe vahny-ādau kārya-kāraṇatoṣṇatā /
tat tac chabdārthatādyātmā pramāṇād ekato mataḥ //

There, in the case of simple fire, all its particulars like cause, effect, character [warmth], the word that denotes it, and so on, are the results of one single *pramāṇa.*

Commentary

Fire is a self-sufficient entity, without having any real relation with any other thing, because all existent substances are basically self-limited, *sva-lakṣaṇas,* without having any relation with any other *sva-lakṣaṇa.* That is the principle of Buddhism which has been accepted in Śaivism as well.

But even then it is a fact that simple self-sufficient fire comes to be known, along with its essential particulars mentioned above, through one single *pramāṇa.* Such is the character and power of *pramāṇa.*

Verse 9

सा तु देशादिकाध्यक्षान्तरभिन्ने स्वलक्षणे ।
तात्कालिकी प्रवृत्तिः स्यादर्थिनोऽप्यनुमानतः ॥ ९ ॥

sā tu deśādikādhyakṣāntar-abhinne sva-lakṣaṇe /
tāt kālikī pravṛttiḥ syād arthino 'py anumānataḥ //

The generally prevalent, timely propensity of beings aimed toward [affecting or knowing] certain objects, which are limited by a particular time, space, etc., becomes possible only when they are inwardly non-different from the interior I-Consciousness. Such a thing happens in the case of inference as well. [Such is the working of *pramāṇas.*]

Commentary

All objective entities, though self-limited in their character and having no mutual relation, still become the objects of knowing with the help of the senses and mind. This becomes possible only when they are not inwardly different from the Consciousness of the concerned knowing Self, working with the help of the *pramāṇas,* which, along with the objects, are merely the manifestations of one and the same infinite, divinely potent, and pure Consciousness. Such is the working of *pramāṇas,* even in the case of inferential knowing. Several perceptions joining together thus do create certain propensities in finite beings.

The next two couplets state that an object does not become different just because of different conditions or types of means and aids to knowing it. It remains one and the same entity.

Verses 10-11

दूरान्तिकतयार्थानां परोक्षाध्यक्षतात्मना ।
बाह्यान्तरतया दोषैर्व्यञ्जकस्यान्यथापि वा ॥ १० ॥
भिन्नावभासच्छायानामपि मुख्यावभासतः ।
एकप्रत्यवमर्शाख्यादेकत्वमनिवारितम् ॥ ११ ॥

dūrāntikatayārthānāṃ parokṣādhyakṣatātmanā /
bāhyāntaratayā doṣair vyañjakasyāny athāpi vā //
bhinnāvabhāsa-cchāyānām api mukhyāvabhāsataḥ /
eka-pratyavamarśākhyād ekatvam anivāritam //

The oneness and sameness of [individual] objects stands unquestioned due primarily to their mutual unity, even though they may have appeared with shades of mutual difference. [This may happen] because they are stationed very close or far away [from the observer], or are interior [mental] or exterior in character, or due to defects in one's senses, or because of deficiencies in the aids of perception.

Commentary

A person sometimes perceives an object to be different from another similar object because the two are in different locations, appear differently, or because the person's physical sight or understanding is flawed. But the objects can be definitely taken as one in nature on the authority of clear subsequent knowledge. Unity or diversity will thus appear because of different internal and external causes. But false perceived diversity with respect to one and the same object, or several similar objects, may be refuted in mundane activities when the true sameness and unity are brought to light by subsequent definite knowledge.

The twelfth couplet states that an object does not become a different object even if, on account of certain obstacles, it does not serve its main purpose. It still remains the same object because its actual utility depends on several other causes and conditions in accordance with the Lord's will, which is working as the law of spatial restriction.

Verse 12

अर्थक्रियापि सहजा नार्थानामीश्वरेच्छया ।
नियता सा हि तेनास्या नाक्रियातोऽन्यता भवेत् ॥ १२ ॥

artha-kriyāpi sahajā nārthānām īśvarecchayā /
niyatā sā hi tenāsyā nākriyāto 'nyatā bhavet //

Even utility is not the basic character of objects, as that [utility] is ordained by the will of the Lord. Therefore an object cannot be taken as anything other than itself even if it does not produce.

Commentary

To give an example: An imagined mango fruit is not anything other than itself, even when it does not yield its own taste. Even then, it is still a mango. Or, a genuine mango tree is not anything other than itself, even when it does not yield mangoes. Even then, it is still a mango tree.

The next couplet expresses the Śaivite view on mistaken perception.

Verse 13

रजतैक्यविमर्शेऽपि शुक्तौ न रजतस्थितिः ।
उपाधिदेशासंवादाद्द्विचन्द्रेऽपि नभोऽन्यथा ॥ १३ ॥

rajataikya-vimarśe 'pi śuktau na rajata-sthitiḥ /
upādhi-deśāsaṃvādād dvi-candre 'pi nabho 'nyathā //

Silver does not exist in a shell, even though that may be the sole perception, because the place [where one falsely saw a glittering shell as silver] does not continue to appear like that. A sky bearing two moons also [eventually] will appear differently.

Commentary

The existence of silver at a place, known through mistaken perception, is refuted by a subsequent perception that there was just a glittering shell there. Similarly, a region of sky wrongly seen to bear two moons does not for long continue to appear like that. Therefore, in these cases the existence of silver and a second moon is surely refuted.

The next couplet states that perceptions of difference and sameness between objects ultimately depend only on the concepts of the perceiving person, the single knowing Subject.

Verse 14

गुणैः शब्दादिभिर्भेदो जात्यादिभिरभिन्नता ।
भावानामित्थमेकत्र प्रमातर्युपपद्यते ॥ १४ ॥

guṇaiḥ śabdādibhir bhedo jātyādibhir abhinnatā /
bhāvānām ittham ekatra pramātary upapadyate //

Difference and unity between knowing subjects is established, respectively, through conceptions of their attributes, such as sound [touch, colour] and concepts like generality. The only proprietary base is thus the one [common] knowing Subject.

Commentary

Objects appear to have unity when they are viewed with the help of a concept like generality. They appear to be different when thought about in the terms of their different attributes like sound, touch, appearance, and smell. Mundane dealings that utilise these perceptions thus become possible only when these ideas about the objects shine in one knowing Subject. It is the person, or his inner Self, who establishes their unity and differences. The knowing Subject is thus the central base of any concepts of unity and diversity about phenomenal objects.

The next two couplets throw light on the fact that no presently emerging proofs or means of knowing can ever claim to have the power to establish the existence of the Lord, the eternally existent and self-evident Absolute. He Himself shines as the main basis of all the means of knowledge that have been discussed and established in any school of philosophy.

Verses 15-16

विश्ववैचित्र्यचित्रस्य समभित्तितलोपमे ।
विरुद्धाभावसंस्पर्शे परमार्थसतीश्वरे ॥ १५ ॥
प्रमातरि पुराणे तु सर्वदाभातविग्रहे ।
किं प्रमाणं नवाभासः सर्वप्रमितिभागिनि ॥ १६ ॥

viśva-vaicitrya-citrasya sama-bhitti-talopame /
viruddhābhāva-saṃsparśe paramārtha-sat-īśvare //
pramātari purāṇe tu sarvadā-bhāta-vigrahe /
kiṃ pramāṇaṃ navābhāsaḥ sarva-pramiti-bhāgini //

Of what use is a newly manifest means of mundane knowledge in proving the existence of the truly existent God, who is the ever-shining, eternal Knower with the correct knowledge of everything, who can never be touched by any idea of non-existence, and who resembles a plain canvas on which the paintings of the wonderful variations of phenomenal existence are painted?

Commentary

All means of correct knowledge rise and fall within the spiritual lustre of the eternal, infinite, self-aware, and pure I-Consciousness, which shines always through its own psychic luminosity. Therefore no means of knowledge can ever be applied to this pure I-Consciousness. Even the finite I-Consciousness—the individual Self that shines as worldly beings—is self-luminous and self-aware. I-Consciousness is thus its own proof. Illuminating everything in the universe, it is an omniscient, eternal Reality. Even the idea of non-existence cannot touch it. I-Consciousness alone has a real and independent infinite existence, and it is known as Almighty God (Paramaśiva) because it manifests all phenomenal existence through the divine activities of creation, maintenance, absorption, and so on. As the single base on which the whole show of universal manifestation stands, Paramaśiva can be compared to a plain, smooth canvas, on which are painted a multitude of fascinating paintings. Epistemology thus cannot be applied to such an eternal and self-evident Reality. This principle has already been discussed in the beginning of the present work.

The last couplet in the chapter states that the aim of the *Īśvara-pratyabhijñā-kārikā* is not to establish the existence of the ever-existent God, but simply to restore the active understanding of the Godhead. This understanding has stagnated because of human ignorance about Absolute Reality and the fact that the Lord appears as one's finite Self. This renewed understanding is called *pratyabhijñā,* the recognition of the true divine nature of the Self.

Verse 17

अप्रवर्तितपूर्वोऽत्र केवलं मूढतावशात्।
शक्तिप्रकाशेनेशादिव्यवहारः प्रवर्त्यते ॥ १७ ॥

apravartita-pūrvo 'tra kevalaṃ muḍhatā-vaśāt /
śakti-prakāśeneśādi-vyavahāraḥ pravartyate //

[The aim of this scripture is] to initiate a concern with God, etc., [in relation to I-Consciousness], by illuminating the divine power *(śakti),* [a task] that had not been initiated due to delusion.

Commentary

I-Consciousness is in fact Almighty God. But human beings, having forgotten that this is their nature due to a deep-rooted delusion, do not take themselves as God. The treatise in hand is meant to destroy human delusion and to help people recognise that in truth their basic nature consists of the Absolute Godhead. The Lord within each person has playfully pushed awareness of the true 'I' into oblivion. Recognition would again empower aspirants to renew and employ again this understanding about their real Self. The work has for this reason been given the name *Īśvara-pratyabhijñā,* 'the recognition of (one's own Self as) the Lord'.

Chapter 4

CAUSATION

The fourth chapter of Book II promotes deliberation on the principle of causation, as discovered by the ancient masters of Kashmir Śaivism through their successful practice in the highest methods of Trika yoga. The first couplet in the chapter declares that the Absolute Lord is the basic source and the main cause of the creation of all phenomena. He manifests them outwardly in accordance with His independent and playful divine will power. This activity on His part is due to the creative aspect of His Godhead.

Verse 1

एष चानन्तशक्तित्वादेवमाभासयत्यमून् ।
भावानिच्छावशादेषा क्रिया निर्मातृतास्य सा ॥ १ ॥

eṣa cānanta-śaktitvād evam ābhāsayaty amūn /
bhāvān icchā vaśad eṣā kriyā nirmātṛtāsya sā //

The Lord, by virtue of His infinite divine power, manifests these apparent phenomena simply through the power of His divine will [without resorting to the use of any other cause or means]. That is what is known as His active nature and His creative aspect.

Commentary

The authors of other schools of Indian philosophy explain creation by referring to external causes such as *avidyā* (ignorance) or *māyā* (illusion) or *prakṛti* (cosmic energy) or the existence of atoms. But

Kashmir Śaivism says that the Lord creates all external phenomena out of His own being merely by exercising His divine, creative will power. In reality, everything exists in Him in the form of the divine powers of His pure and potent infinite Consciousness, which alone shines within as 'I'. By exercising His divine will, the Lord manifests these phenomena outwardly so that they appear objectively as 'this' or 'these', shining as entities seemingly different from His I-Consciousness. All this creation happens through a process of the outward reflection of His inwardly shining divine powers. This fundamental cosmogonic principle of Kashmir Śaivism is hinted at in this first couplet and is explained at greater length in the third chapter of Abhinavagupta's *Tantrāloka*.

The next three couplets (2-4) argue that an insentient substance is completely incapable of creating anything. They emphasise the Śaivite principle that the essence of the law of causation depends basically on the relation between the conscious Subject and unconscious objective existence.

Verse 2

जडस्य तु न सा शक्तिः सत्ता यदसतः सतः ।
कर्तृकर्मत्वतत्त्वैव कार्यकारणता ततः ॥ २ ॥

jaḍasya tu na sā śaktiḥ sattā yad-asataḥ sataḥ /
kartṛ-karmatva-tattvaiva kārya-kāraṇatā tataḥ //

It cannot be within the power of any inanimate object to bring into existence anything that is non-existent. Therefore, the essence of the relation between a cause and its effect is, in fact, the relation between a [manifesting] subject and a [manifestable] object.

Commentary

Neither *māyā* nor *avidyā* nor *prakṛti,* all of them inanimate in nature, can ever bring any non-existent phenomenon into existence. This is because the power of creation lies in 'animation', that is, in Self-consciousness. Inanimate entities or principles like *māyā* are not even conscious of their own selves, so how can they be conscious of any thing or idea in phenomenal creation? Therefore, only the independent, creative will of the Lord can manifest the external phenomenal world. It shines in Him in the form of His pure I-Consciousness (which is not an 'ego'). This happens through the outward objective reflection of His own subjective capacities, and it is brought about by the independent power of His supreme, divine will.

Verses 3-4

यदसत्तदसद्युक्ता नासतः सत्स्वरूपता ।
सतोऽपि न पुनः सत्तालाभेनार्थोऽथ चोच्यते॥ ३॥
कार्यकारणता लोके सान्तर्विपरिवर्तिनः ।
उभयेन्द्रियवेद्यत्वं तस्य कस्यापि शक्तितः॥ ४॥

yad-asat tad-asad yuktā nāsataḥ sat-sva-rūpatā /
sato 'pi na punaḥ sattā-lābhenārtho 'tha cocyate //
kārya kāraṇatā loke sāntar-viparivartinaḥ /
ubhayendriya-vedyatvaṃ tasya kasyāpi śaktitaḥ //

A non-existent entity is always non-existent; the existence of a non-existent entity is not possible. Nor has an existent entity anything to gain by attaining existence once more. If, even then, the cause-and-effect relation is talked about in the world, [the effect] can [at the most] be just an exterior manifestation of some internally existent entity, [the cause, which assumes] the position of an object of knowing through [a person's] interior and exterior senses. Such a thing can happen through the divine power of that unknowable Authority (God).

Commentary

If a phenomenon is basically non-existent, it can never become existent even through its so-called creation. Even some newly invented mechanical object does basically exist in an invisible form inside its source matter. (That is the *sat-kārya-vāda* in Indian philosophy.) Its invention is such a manifestation, which makes it actually known as the object and as something useful in producing certain desirable mundane results. Besides, it also exists in the person of the inventor, shines in his imagination, and is brought out by his skill. But if some object is accepted to be already existent, then what benefit or even enjoyment would there be in bringing it again into existence? Even the existence of a particular cause-and-effect relation in the world is only an external manifestation of entities that are ever existent. They are already present within the powers of infinite Consciousness and shine there as 'I'. A phenomenon of relation manifests them outwardly as 'this' through an outwardly expressed reflection, brought about by the supreme Artist of this wonderful universal creation. A great poet and an expert painter can be cited here as examples of such an exterior manifestation of interior powers. The Lord, being the supreme Artist, manifests outwardly from His own being this multifarious phenomenal existence as a reflective manifestation of His inner powers.

The next three couplets (5-7) stress the principle of Śaivite realism, explaining the fact that Absolute Consciousness alone, containing in it the whole universe, is the only creative cause that can manifest the cosmos outwardly as the object of universal creation.

Verse 5

एवमेका क्रिया सैषा सक्रमान्तर्बहिःस्थितिः ।
एकस्यैवोभयाकारसहिष्णोरुपपादिता ॥ ५ ॥

evam ekā kriyā saiṣā sa-kramāntar-bahiḥ-sthitiḥ /
ekasyaivobhayā-kāra-sahiṣṇor upapāditā //

Action, being a single phenomenon, exists both inwardly and outwardly and has time sequence as its quality. It thus belongs to whatever single entity can include both these indications. The truth [about action] is therefore well established.

Commentary

Action has its start as a person's inner volition. He wills something to happen through him. Then it becomes manifest in the forms of his internal (mental) and external (physical) movements. There is a definite order of manifestation here: will, then thought, followed by action. Action thus shines both inwardly and outwardly. This same volition assumes the character of both interior and exterior movements, and it belongs to the capability of one and the same active Subject. This is Kashmir Śaivism's understanding regarding action.

Verses 6-7

बहिस्तस्यैव तत्कार्यं यदन्तर्यदपेक्षया।
प्रमात्रपेक्षया चोक्ता द्वयी बाह्यान्तरस्थितिः ॥ ६ ॥
मातैव कारणं तेन स चाभासद्वयस्थितौ।
कार्यस्य स्थित एवैकस्तदेकस्य क्रियोदिता ॥ ७ ॥

bahis tasyaiva tat kāryaṃ yad antar yad-apekṣayā/
pramātr-apekṣayā coktā dvayī bāhyāntara-sthitiḥ //
mātaiva kāraṇaṃ tena sa cābhāsa-dvaya-sthitau/
kāryasya sthita evaikas tad-ekasya kriyoditā //

Only such a [master] can be the author of some particular exterior creation in whom [that creation] is already present internally. Besides, both exteriority and interiority are spoken about [only] concerning the conscious knowing subject. Therefore, the [basic] cause [of creation] is only this conscious subject. He thus stands as the only master of created objects and so the action [of creation] belongs to him alone.

Commentary

Objects to be created first exist in the person who creates them, generated in his mind in the form of particular ideas. These ideas afterward take the form of the actual material creation of articles that exist outside their creator. It is thus clear that objects to be created originally exist within the person of the creator, and it is his or her will, assisted by ideation and outward action, that brings them into existence in the mental and material planes. Similarly, all of phenomenal existence exists originally within infinite Consciousness, only appearing in the phenomenal sphere through the power of His divine will.

The next two *kārikās* apply this principle to the relation between a seed and its sprout, and a pot and its potter.

Verse 8

अत एवाङ्कुरेऽपीष्टो निमित्तं परमेश्वरः ।
तदन्यस्यापि बीजादेर्हेतुता नोपपद्यते ॥ ८ ॥

ata evāṅkure 'pīṣṭo nimittaṃ parameśvaraḥ /
tad-anyasyāpi bījāder hetutā nopapadyate //

For this reason, God has been accepted as the cause of a sprout [coming out of a seed]. The appropriateness of [understanding] sole causation in terms of other substances, such as the seed, cannot be established.

Commentary

A conscious entity alone can be the main active cause of a particular effect. God has therefore been determined by philosophers to be, for example, the active cause of a seed sprouting. Other causes like the seed itself, soil, moisture, or warmth serve only as aids to growth, and even their utility in this regard is dependent on the free will of God. He establishes the laws of causation in accordance with His will and delegates the powers of effective causation and restriction. In fact, only a sentient cause can make use of the secondary types of causes at all. It is thus established that only a conscious being can become a truly effective and fruitful cause of a desired effect.

Verse 9

तथा हि कुम्भकारोऽसावैश्वर्यैव व्यवस्थया ।
तत्तन्मृदादिसंस्कारक्रमेण जनयेद्घटम् ॥ ९ ॥

tathā hi kumbhakāro 'sāv aiśvaryaiva vyavasthayā /
tat-tan-mṛdādi-saṃskāra-krameṇa janayed ghaṭam //

This principle is established by the fact that a potter can make a pitcher [only] through some definite sequence in the process of perfecting it, such as by using clay, in accordance with the laws of nature established by God.

Commentary

A potter, while manufacturing earthen pots, is not quite free to use his own will independently. He has to follow some unavoidable sequential processes in his activity, processes such as moistening the earth and shaping it step by step. These are features of natural law, and they have been ordained by God Himself, who is the only primary cause of creation. Even the great gods like the creator, Lord Brahmā, have to work in accordance with divine law and the divine will of the Absolute God.

The tenth couplet presents the example of powerful yogins to prove the validity of these main principles of causation. The illustrations include the materialisation of objects out of the divine will and the application of these examples to the phenomenon of inferential calculations.

Verse 10

योगिनामपि मृद्बीजे विनैवेच्छावशेन तत् ।
घटादि जायते तत्तत्स्थिरस्वार्थक्रियाकरम् ॥ १० ॥

yoginām api mṛd-bīje vinaivecchā-vaśena tat /
ghaṭādi jāyate tat-tat-sthira-svārtha-kriyā-karam //

Earthen pots, etc.—of normal utility and able to stand firmly [rather than vanishing like magic]—can be created by some yogins through [the materialisation of] their will, without making use of anything like seeds or soil.

Commentary

Advanced yogins can create substances that stand firm in time; they do not vanish like magic shows and yield their desired practical use. The yogin need not resort to the use of any material causes like seeds or soil to accomplish this purpose. These creations by yogins prove to be as real as ordinary objects available in the phenomenal world. The yogins can do this simply by materialising their free will. These creations are cited here as examples of creation by mere will, the way in which God creates. When a yogin can create material substances and desired objects through his will power alone, why shouldn't God be accepted as creating all of phenomenal existence through His divine will alone? The divine will of the Lord is thus the main source of all the mundane rules of causation working in the world, as well as every type of subject, object, and activity.

Verse 11

योगिनिर्माणताभावे प्रमाणान्तरनिश्चिते ।
कार्यं हेतुः स्वभावो वात एवोत्पत्तिमूलजः ॥ ११ ॥

yogi-nirmāṇatā-bhāve pramāṇāntara-niścite /
kāryaṃ hetuḥ sva-bhāvo vāta evotpatti-mūla-jaḥ //

It is for this reason that either the effects or the basic characters [of objects]—both of which have their origin in a basic source—are accepted as logical reasons [in an argument]. [But this is] only when it is definitely established, on the basis of other definite proofs, that the concerned object is not a yogin's creation.

Commentary

The existence of a burning fire at some particular place can be inferred on the basis of the perception of a clearly visible rising current of smoke. Similarly, a substance can be inferred to be a tree on the basis of its being known as a pipal. Smoke is born out of fire and to be a tree is the essential nature of a pipal. The mutual relationship in both these cases is basically an inborn phenomenon and therefore may be used in logical syllogisms. But this use of particular pairs of examples can be correct only when a person is sure that neither of the two substances has been created by a yogin through his yogic will power. This is because a yogin can produce smoke without the help of fire and can also materialise a pipal tree in the air that is not a genuine tree.

The next two couplets (12-13) extend the application of the law of causation to general inferential calculations.

Verses 12-13

भूयस्तत्तत्प्रमात्रेकैकवह्न्याभासादितो भवेत् ।
परोक्षादप्यधिपतेर्धूमाभासादि नूतनम् ॥ १२ ॥
कार्यमव्यभिचार्यस्य लिङ्गमन्यप्रमातृगात् ।
तदाभासस्तदाभासादेव त्वधिपतेः परः ॥ १३ ॥

bhūyas tat-tat-pramātr-eka-vahny-ābhāsād ito bhavet /
parokṣād apy adhipater dhūmābhāsādi nūtanam //
kāryam avyabhicāryasya liṅgam anya-pramātṛ-gāt /
tad-ābhāsas tad-ābhāsād eva tv adhipateḥ paraḥ //

Fresh smoke that is seen by people who are present can rise again [at the time of inference] from fire—its master—which may not be visible at the time. Being invariably [fire's] result, [smoke] can serve as a proof in inferring [fire's] existence. Smoke that is seen by another person can [sometimes] rise out of smoke itself, since that [stored smoke] is its master source.

Commentary

A trail of fresh smoke, rising up and seen by everyone present, can have risen directly from fire, although one may not be able to see the fire at the time. Its effect, the smoke, can thus be used as an inferential proof arguing the current existence of fire burning beneath it.

Another example is smoke that has been stored in a big earthen pot by a milkman. When this trail of smoke is seen rising up, it rises up out of smoke and not out of burning fire. It thus cannot prove the existence of fire beneath it. This argument, worked out by authors of Nyāya philosophy, is based on imagination and not on any actual happening. Milkmen in India often employ very big earthen vessels to carry their milk to market. They may well have stored thick smoke in these vessels to destroy any bacteria that might have developed inside. If the lid of the earthen pot is removed, a trail of smoke can be seen rising upward but the smoke cannot prove the existence of burning fire inside the vessel.

The next two couplets (14-15) assert that the validity of the law of causation, existing among inanimate substances like fire and smoke, is also dependent on the observations made by conscious beings and not otherwise. Insentient substances like seeds and sprouts cannot assert anything in this regard.

Verse 14

अस्मिन्सतीदमस्तीति कार्यकारणतापि या ।
साप्यपेक्षाविहीनानां जडानां नोपपद्यते ॥ १४ ॥

asmin satīdam astīti kārya-kāraṇatāpi yā /
sāpy apekṣāvihīnānām jaḍānāṃ nopapadyate //

The law of causation, prevalent generally as—'Such a thing [as smoke] can exist only when another thing [fire] already exists'—cannot be well established by inanimate substances since they cannot consider one another.

Commentary

Neither smoke and fire, nor seeds and sprouts, have any conscious consideration of one another; they are insentient. For this reason, each cause and each effect—such as fire and smoke—is always self-centred and obviously unconcerned with anything other than itself. How could such things themselves establish their mutual relation? Relationship is realised only by a person, the conscious master of the action of knowing, who could establish their mutual relationship, being aware of something as a cause and some other thing as its effect.

Verse 15

न हि स्वात्मैकनिष्ठानामनुसन्धानवर्जिनाम् ।
सदसत्तापदेऽप्येष सप्तम्यर्थः प्रकल्प्यते ॥ १५ ॥

na hi svātmaika-niṣṭhānām anusandhāna-varjinām /
sad-asattāpade 'py eṣa saptamy-arthaḥ prakalpyate //

The idea of the locative *(saptami)* case [as denoted, for instance, by the clause *asmin sati idam asti,* 'This thing is possible only when this other thing is there'] is possible neither in the case of the existence of things [like a seed and a sprout], nor in that of their non-existence, because these objects are absolutely self-limited and unaware of each other.

Commentary

A seed is a seed and a sprout is a sprout. Neither of them has any regard for the other, because each is absolutely separate from and unaware of the other. A person may accept each object either as an existent or a non-existent entity. But in both cases these objects are mutually unconcerned and therefore cannot help to establish any mutual relations between them. This must be accomplished by some conscious third entity, a person who takes both objects jointly into consideration.

The sixteenth couplet applies this principle to the relationship between different agents of action, like subjects and objects.

Verse 16

अत एव विभक्त्यर्थः प्रमात्रेकसमाश्रयः ।
क्रियाकारकभावाख्यो युक्तो भावसमन्वयः ॥ १६ ॥

ata eva vibhakty-arthaḥ pramātr-eka-samāśrayaḥ /
kriyā-kāraka-bhāvākhyo yukto bhāva-samanvayaḥ //

For this reason the mutual relationship between ideas of action and their agents, denoted by the *vibhaktis* (the seven cases in Sanskrit grammar), is established only through their dependence on the knowing subject.

Commentary

It is, in fact, the *pramātṛ,* the knowing subject, who takes into consideration and establishes firmly the mutual relations between the seven grammatical cases—like the nominative, accusative, instrumental, dative, and so forth—as well as their relations with the main action, denoted by the main verb in a sentence. This consideration establishes the relations between persons, substances, actions, and ideas in sentences relating to all mundane dealings. These relations can never be explained if left to themselves, without assistance from the single subject of knowing. He or she takes all such elements jointly into consideration.

The next three couplets (17-19), disproving the validity of the principle of causation as developed and propagated by the masters of the Sāṃkhya school, emphasise the fact that Absolute Consciousness alone is the basic cause and source of all phenomena.

Verse 17

परस्परस्वभावत्वे कार्यकारणयोरपि ।
एकत्वमेव भेदे हि नैवान्योन्यस्वरूपता ॥ १७ ॥

paras-para-sva-bhāvatve kārya-kāraṇayor api /
ekatvam eva bhede hi naivānyonya-sva-rūpatā //

If [according to Sāṃkhya philosophy] both cause and effect have each other's nature, then both should be taken as one and the same entity. If [on the other hand] they are different, their having each other's nature is disproved.

Commentary

Sāṃkhyas say that the nature of a cause is to appear as an effect, and the effect has the same nature as the cause. Further, they maintain that *prakṛti* is the basic cause and original source of the evolved universe; both the cause and the universe are of one and the same basic nature, and thus consist of three *guṇas* or qualities. If their nature is not mutually different, then both cause and universe should be accepted as one, without any distinction. But if there is some difference between them, then they should not be taken as mutually identical in character.

Verse 18

एकात्मनो विभेदश्च क्रिया कालक्रमानुगा ।
हेतोः स्यात्कर्तृतैवैवं तथापरिणमत्तया ॥ १८ ॥

ekātmano vibhedaś ca kriyā kāla-kramānugā /
hetoḥ syāt kartṛtaivaivaṃ tathāpariṇamat tayā //

The varied manifestations of a single, changeless entity —appearing as action in time sequence—can be taken as that entity's [independent] activity by virtue of [the latter] not undergoing any transformation.

Commentary

Cosmic manifest energy or matter, *prakṛti,* being insentient in nature,[29] cannot by itself appear in the form of this purposeful and variegated, wonderful world. It requires goading, guidance, and direction from some sentient and powerful presence for this purpose. It is without a doubt definitely possible for the sentient presence, consisting of pure, infinite, and all-powerful Consciousness, to appear multifariously in the forms of all phenomena, without undergoing any transformation of its basic character of purity, infinity, and divine potency. Its apparent transmutation into thirty-six *tattvas* (cosmic principles) and the entire universe of phenomena is just the outward manifestation of internally existent universal entities. They appear as an outward reflection of the divine powers of Absolute Consciousness. This reflection is brought about by Consciousness itself, due to the innate playfulness of the Lord's nature. This outward and objective manifestation of the Lord's inward and subjective divine powers is known as His *kriyā-śakti,* His power of action.

Verse 19

न च युक्तं जडस्यैवं भेदाभेदविरोधतः ।
आभासभेदादेकत्र चिदात्मनि तु युज्यते ॥ १९ ॥

na ca yuktaṃ jaḍasyaivaṃ bhedābheda-virodhataḥ /
ābhāsa-bhedād ekatra cid-ātmani tu yujyate //

Such a thing is not justifiable and explainable in the case of an insentient entity [like *prakṛti*], on account of contradiction between unity and diversity, but it is quite acceptable in the case of the singular monistic Self *(Ātman),* [which] consists of pure Consciousness with the capability of appearing diversely.

Commentary

The inanimate cosmic material energy *(prakṛti)* cannot appear simultaneously as one and many because there is a contradiction between being a unified substance and being diverse or multiple. But both are possible simultaneously for pure Consciousness, the all-powerful sentient Reality, which can appear as both one and many as it wishes, according to its free will and its natural blissful tendency toward transmutational manifestation. This active nature of Absolute Consciousness is known in Śaivism as *kriyā-śakti.*

The twentieth couplet emphasises the fact that even the monistic, pure Consciousness propounded in Advaita Vedānta could not be of any use in creating this phenomenal existence if it were devoid of divine potency.

Verse 20

वास्तवेऽपि चिदेकत्वे न स्यादाभासभिन्नयोः ।
चिकीर्षालक्षणैकत्वपरामर्शं विना क्रिया ॥ २० ॥

vāstave 'pi cid-ekatve na syād ābhāsa-bhinnayoḥ /
cikīrṣā-lakṣaṇaikatva-parāmarśaṃ vinā kriyā //

The activity [of creation] is not possible at all on the basis of the two apparently different realities [*Ātman* and the world] —in spite of the unitary character of Consciousness—as long as a unitary awareness of the will to create is not accepted as its essential nature.

Commentary

According to the Vedantic concept of creation, the only fully existent reality is infinite Consciousness. Discussion through dialectical logic yields a so-called creator who shines as infinite I-Consciousness, while creation is separate and appears in the form of 'this-ness'. Subject and object are thus two different concepts without any mutual relationship. Now how can one of these be taken as the creator and the other as his 'creation'? The Vedāntins made use of the dialectical arguments of Buddhist philosophy and chose to accept only those Upaniṣadic passages that attribute creation to an imaginary and inexplicable relation between pure Consciousness and a falsely appearing, insentient element known as *māyā,* universal ignorance. *Māyā,* they said, works in all individual beings as their own particular ignorance, called *avidyā*. This Vedantic principle comes close to dualism between Brahman and *māyā,* granting, as it does, all divine powers to *māyā,* and thus reducing Brahman, Absolute Consciousness, to an ontological status similar to *śūnya,* the void of the Buddhist thinkers.

Śaivism, on the other hand, establishes a divine creative will, blissful and playful in its nature, as the essential character of

Absolute Consciousness. This playful will of the Lord is aimed at the five divine activities of world creation, preservation, absorption, Self-oblivion, and Self-revelation. This will is His *kriyā* aspect, known also as His basic *kriyā-śakti*. The Śaiva sages had this truth revealed to them in the *turīya* (Self-revelative) state of awareness, as well as in *turyātīta,* the transcendental state, which shines at a still higher level of pure Self-Consciousness. They said that the phenomenal activities of creation, preservation, and so on become manifest as outward reflections of the Absolute Lord's inward divine powers. Thus, they do not involve Him in any sort of change or transformation, putting to rest the apprehensions of the Vedāntins. This principle of absolute theism, or 'theistic absolutism' as one might call it, is the basic ontological view of the masters of Kashmir Śaivism. Most schools of Vaiṣṇavism similarly accept the theistic nature of God, but tend to avoid absolutism in favour of more mythological concepts of God. Kashmir Śaivism, however, expresses a beautiful and satisfying unity between theism and absolutism of a monistic character.

The last verse, concluding the chapter, declares that the divine will of the Lord alone is His *kriyā-śakti,* His power of action. It is the fundamental means by which He appears as the wonderfully varied phenomenal world.

Verse 21

इत्थं तथा घटपटाद्याभासजगदात्मना ।
तिष्ठासोरेवमिच्छैव हेतुता कर्तृता क्रिया ॥ २१ ॥

ittham tathā ghaṭa-paṭādy-ābhāsa-jagad-ātmanā /
tiṣṭhāsor evam icchaiva hetutā kartṛtā kriyā //

It is thus [the Lord's] will to appear in the form of the mundane manifestation of worldly objects like a pot, a cloth, etc.—which is the real cause [of the phenomenal world]—and this is His active aspect, known as his *kriyā*[-*śakti*].

Commentary

Everything is present in God in the form of the pure power of sentience and shines therein as one infinite and all-powerful, pure Consciousness. Infinite Consciousness, being fully aware of its divine powers, and also being ever charged with infinite blissful and playful will due to its basic nature, is always manifesting its character outwardly in the playful divine activities of creation, preservation, dissolution, concealment, and revelation. The whole universe, shining in God as the infinite and pure I-Consciousness, is thus manifested by Him objectively as 'this', and so it is that creation occurs. It becomes possible only when the Lord's 'willing' activity vibrates out from Him. His divine power to vibrate out is His *kriyā-śakti,* and the activity itself is known as His *kriyā,* his divine action. The whole universe shines in Him as His 'I', but its outward reflection appears as 'this', the objective world. The Lord's *kriyā-śakti* is the highest essence of His Godhead. Devoid of such unfathomable power and an active nature, God would come very close to the *śūnya* (void) of the Vijñānavāda Buddhists.

This Śaiva principle of absolute theism has many illustrious antecedents in India's past. For instance, the *Vāgāmbhṛṇīya* hymn of the *Ṛg Veda* (X.125) presents it in quite clear terms. Here, absolute theism is not presented as merely the Lord's *upādhi* or external attribute, giving rise to a semblance of conditions in His character, but as His own essential nature. This divine essence of the Absolute has also been recounted in clear terms in the *Bhagavad-gītā* (chapter 11). When the Śaiva yogins of Kashmir discovered this same truth about Absolute Reality in the *turīya* and *turyātīta* states of awareness, they developed and expressed these truths by using a philosophical method; the result is presently known as Kashmir Śaivism.

Book III

ĀGAMĀDHIKĀRA

Scriptural Knowledge

Chapter 1

THE TATTVAS IN ŚAIVISM

Chapter 1 begins with vague hints as to the character of the first two *tattvas* usually known as Śiva and Śakti, the two perennial principles of the universe.

Verse 1

एवमन्तर्बहिर्वृत्तिः क्रिया कालक्रमानुगा ।
मातुरेव तदन्योन्यावियुक्ते ज्ञानकर्मणी ॥ १ ॥

evam antar-bahir-vṛttiḥ kriyā kāla-kramānugā /
mātur eva tad-anyonyāviyukte jñāna-karmaṇī //

Thus the [divine] action, vibrating inwardly as well as outwardly in accordance with time sequence, belongs to none other than the [infinite] Subject of knowing. Therefore infinite knowledge and action are mutually inseparable.

Commentary

The philosopher Svatantrāṇandanātha, in his *Mātṛkā-cakra-viveka,* remarks: 'Knowledge, by coagulating its form, becomes action. It is action which, having assumed liquidity, becomes knowledge. Therefore both of them [knowledge and action] indeed have a twin character in the view of the *Siddhas,* the perfected beings. [The distinguishing] of their antecedence and subsequence is only a sort of antagonistic [or dualistic] view'. (MCV I.15-16)

To explain from the highest philosophical point of view: The monistic Absolute Reality, known in Śaivism as Paramaśiva, has the nature of infinite transcendent Consciousness and infinite awareness of itself and its nature, as its essential character. This Absolute Reality shines always and, because it is aware of possessing divine powers of action, becomes active in manifesting them outwardly. The Absolute is thus the only transcendent reality, without any second; its infinite nature, called *prakāśa,* is quiescent, while its active nature, known as *vimarśa,* is always manifesting its divine powers outwardly in the form of phenomenal creation. *Prakāśa* also includes the *jñāna* (knowledge) aspects of enlightenment and creative action, called *kriyā.*

When Paramaśiva is meditated upon in His *prakāśa* aspect, one is calling upon the Absolute as *śiva-tattva* (the Śiva principle), is deliberating upon the truth of Śiva. When the predominant focus is on His *vimarśa* aspect, this is called *śakti-tattva* (the Śakti principle). *Śiva-tattva* is the eternal existence of knowing. It has the *śakti-tattva,* infinite active energy, as its essential and inseparable nature. Therefore, Absolute Reality is the infinite I-Consciousness known as *prakāśa,* and its Self-awareness, *vimarśa,* is part of its essential character.

Śiva-tattva is thus the noumenal aspect of the Absolute and *śakti-tattva* is its phenomenal aspect. Although the former is dominated by the manifestation of *prakāśa* and the latter by that of *vimarśa,* both are in fact one inseparable whole. They are explained like this just for the purpose of a correct and perfect understanding. *Śiva-tattva* can also be called the introversive aspect of the Absolute Knower and *śakti tattva* the extroversive aspect. These two *tattvas* thus form two aspects of one and the same Absolute, as expressed mystically in this couplet.

The pure and infinite I-Consciousness, charged with the infinite vibration of Self-bliss, is *śiva-tattva;* and its natural tendency toward outward manifestation of its divine powers, resulting in the five divine activities—known as phenomenal creation, preservation, absorption, concealment, and revelation—is to be meditated upon as *śakti-tattva*. These introversive and extroversive aspects of Paramaśiva, Absolute God, do not undergo creation and absorption under any time sequence, although counted as the first two among the thirty-six principles of creation.

The next thirty-four *tattvas* are all elements involved in and undergoing creation and absorption in the world process. *Sadāśiva-tattva* and *īśvara-tattva,* the third and the fourth in the series, are the first and the second among such principles of creation. These two are dealt with in the second couplet of the present chapter, as follows.

Verse 2

किंत्वान्तरदशोद्रेकात्सादाख्यं तत्त्वमादितः ।
बहिर्भावपरत्वे तु परतः पारमेश्वरम् ॥ २ ॥

kiṃtv āntara-daśodrekāt sādākhyaṃ tattvam āditaḥ /
bahir-bhāva-paratve tu parataḥ pārameśvaram //

Yet, in the beginning [of creation], the *sādākhya-tattva* (also known as the *sadāśiva-tattva*) emerges first as the interior aspect. Later, through an emphasis on its exterior aspect, *Pārameśvara* (meaning the *īśvara-tattva* here) emerges.

Commentary

The results of the divine objective manifestation of Almighty God do not become clearly manifest in the *tattvas* above *īśvara* due to the overwhelming absorption in the subjective reality of God. The fourth *tattva* is named *īśvara-tattva,* and the master ruling over it is known as *īśvara-bhaṭṭāraka*. Beings residing in this *tattva* are known as *mantreśvaras,* while those living in *sadāśiva-tattva* are called *mantra-maheśvaras*. Both belong to the pure and non-human creation, consisting only of pure and Self-aware Consciousness. The only activity conducted by these two classes of beings is tasting the ecstasy rising out of the awareness of their unity with the Lord, experienced either as *'aham idam'* or as *'idam aham'*, as such is the awareness manifested by *sadāśiva* and *īśvara*. The masters of these planes are named after their respective *tattvas: śiva-bhaṭṭāraka* is the master of *śiva-tattva,* followed by *śakti-bhaṭṭāraka* and *īśvara-bhaṭṭāraka,* and so forth, down through *sadāśiva-tattva.*

The whole of existence is analysed into three broad planes of *śakti, vidyā,* and *māyā,* wherein one finds the perspectives of unity, unity in diversity, and clear diversity, respectively. The first four *tattvas—śiva, śakti, sadāśiva,* and *īśvara*—and the fifth one, *śuddha-vidyā* or *sad-vidyā,* are called pure *tattvas* because subject and object are still seen as a single entity. The remaining thirty-one *tattvas,* beginning with *māyā,* which is the sixth *tattva* in the series, are known as impure *tattvas* because with the introduction of the principle of delusion *(māyā),* apparent duality is created. (See cosmology chart, page 209).

Lord Sadāśiva *(sadāśivanātha)* and the beings residing in the third *tattva* have the awareness 'I am this', with 'I-ness' being the awareness of the pure and subjective Self-consciousness and 'this-ness' meaning the undifferentiated objective existence. Just a faint reflection of objectivity appears there. Lord Īśvara and the beings residing in His domain (the state of the fourth *tattva*) are aware of themselves and the world as 'This is myself'. The subjective focus on the 'I-ness' of Sadāśiva is pushed here to the position of predicate and the focus on 'this-ness', objectivity, is raised to the position of subject. That shows a difference in the emphasis on the Self or on the object of knowing in these two *tattvas.* *Sadāśiva-tattva* maintains a subjective emphasis, showing an 'upward' domination (toward the Lord), while *īśvara-tattva* focuses 'downward' (toward the objective world) because of its objective emphasis.

The first half of the next couplet, which mentions the technical terms used in the Śaiva Āgamic scriptures for *sadāśiva-* and *īśvara-tattvas,* explains these as the introversive and the extroversive awareness of the Absolute.

Verse 3

ईश्वरो बहिरुन्मेषो निमेषोऽन्तः सदाशिवः ।

. . . ॥ ३ ॥

īśvaro bahir unmeṣo nimeṣo 'ntaḥ sadā-śivaḥ /

. . . //

Īśvara is the extroversive aspect of the Absolute and *Sadāśiva* is the introversive one, the former being known [in the Āgamas] as *unmeṣa* and the latter as *nimeṣa* . . .

Commentary

Unmeṣa means literally 'opening of the eye', or here, the initial unfolding of the universe of forms. *Nimeṣa* signifies 'closing of the eyes', involution, or world dissolution. These are two other technical terms also used in scriptural works dealing with the practice of Śaiva yoga.

The second half of couplet 3 defines *sad-vidyā,* known popularly as *śuddha-vidyā.* It is the third among the *tattvas* of creation, the last of the pure *tattvas,* and also the fifth in the entire series of thirty-six principles.

. . . ।

सामानाधिकरण्यं च सद्विद्याहमिदंधियोः ॥ ३ ॥

. . . /

sāmānādhikaraṇyaṃ ca sad-vidyāham-idaṃ-dhiyoḥ //

. . . A unitary and joint awareness of both 'I-ness' (subjectivity) and 'this-ness' (objectivity), with respect to one and the same entity, is *sad-vidyā,* correct knowing.

Commentary

Beings residing in the *sadāśiva* and *īśvara* pure *tattvas* see the objective element of an object as partly identical with their subjective person, as well as partly different from it. Had they felt the object to be perfectly identical with themselves, then there could not have been any manifestation of 'this-ness', or objectivity, in their view. On the other hand, if the viewer and the object had appeared to be quite different from each other, then their mutual identity would not have been accepted or expressed.

These two categories of pure beings, those in the *sadāśiva-tattva* and *īśvara-tattva* states, thus have the viewpoints of unity in diversity and diversity in unity respectively. However, in the next *tattva,* called *sad-vidyā* or *śuddha-vidyā* in the Āgamas, partial unity and partial diversity are both tasted by pure beings. *Sad-vidyā* or *śuddha-vidyā* means pure and correct knowledge. Those pure beings who possess this knowledge do not yet have any mind or senses; therefore they see and know through the power of pure intuitional knowing *(vidyā).* It serves them as their instrumental means of awareness of unity in diversity and diversity-in-unity.

How and why such a viewpoint of unity in diversity is accepted as *sad-vidyā,* pure and correct knowledge, is explained in the fourth couplet. This differs from impure *vidyā,* which belongs to *paśu* (bound) beings and is one of the later limitations of *māyā (kañcukas).*

Verse 4

इदंभावोपपन्नानां वेद्यभूमिमुपेयुषाम् ।
भावानां बोधसारत्वाद्यथावस्त्ववलोकनात् ॥ ४ ॥

idaṃ-bhāvopapannānāṃ vedya-bhūmim upeyuṣām /
bhāvānāṃ bodha-sāratvād yathā-vastv avalokanāt //

[This viewpoint is pure and correct knowledge] because one may see even entities that are well established in the objective plane, and well known through an idea of 'this-ness', through the correct perspective; that is, Consciousness is seen as their essence.

Commentary

Knowledge that gives prominence to differences between subjects and objects is, according to Śaivism, incorrect. But *śuddha-vidyā,* pure knowledge, understands divine Consciousness as the essence of all objects; it sees objective existence in its correct perspective and so is called pure and correct knowledge, *sad-vidyā.*

The fifth couplet in this chapter throws light on the status of phenomena that shine in the plane, or state, of *sad-vidyā,* the pure *vidyā tattva.*

Verse 5

अत्रापरत्वं भावानामनात्मत्वेन भासनात् ।
परताहन्तयाच्छादात्परापरदशा हि सा ॥ ५ ॥

atrāparatvaṃ bhāvānām anātmatvena bhāsanāt /
paratāhantayācchādāt parāpara-daśā hi sā //

Phenomena in such a state seem imperfect and inferior because they appear as non-Self. These are [at the same time] perfect and superior by virtue of their being invested with I-Consciousness. Such a state [of *vidyā*] is thus superior and perfect, on one hand, and inferior and imperfect, on the other hand [since it is the state of unity in diversity, indicating both purity and impurity].

Commentary

This *tattva* consists of the viewpoint of beings in the *tattvas* named after *īśvara* and *sadāśiva*. The *śakti* stage is one hundred percent pure, while the next three *tattvas* are partly pure and partly impure. Even so, these are counted among the pure creation, along with those in the *vidyā* stage.

It is important to recognise that the term *vidyā* is used in at least three different ways in this system of understanding: (1) the stage of *vidyā* is the broadest, referring to the second plane of existence, which includes *tattvas* three to five, and encompasses relatively more or less pure types of knowledge; (2) the *sad-vidyā* or *śuddha-vidyā-tattva,* 'the principle of true or pure knowledge', is the fifth out of the thirty-six *tattvas,* and (3) *vidyā-kañcuka,* the limitation of knowledge, which is one of the later *tattvas* (numbers seven through eleven) influenced by the viewpoint of *māyā* delusion.

Phenomena at the *vidyā* stage or plane—including the three *tattvas: sadāśiva, īśvara, and śuddha-vidyā*—appear either as 'I am this' or as 'This is myself' *(aham-idam* or *idam-aham).* Their unity with I-Consciousness shines in both states. Therefore the phenomena shining there can be taken as superior and perfect. But since diversity between them and I-Consciousness also shines in both aspects of the *vidyā* stage, these are accepted there as inferior and imperfect as well (in comparison with *śiva-* and *śakti-tattvas*). Such is the nature of *vidyā,* the plane or state lying between *śakti,* the plane of absolute unity, and *māyā,* the plane of manifest diversity. The plane of *vidyā* along with the three categories of beings known as *mantra-maheśvaras, mantreśvaras,* and *mantras* thus represents the middle stage of unity in diversity and is accepted as an intermediate, partly pure and partly impure, state of existence.

The next couplet throws light on one of the types of *vidyā* that is included in this semi-pure plane of existence.

Verse 6

भेदधीरेव भावेषु कर्तुर्बोधात्मनोऽपि या ।
मायाशक्त्येव सा विद्येत्यन्ये विद्येश्वरा यथा ॥ ६ ॥

bhedadhīr eva bhāveṣu kartur bodhātmano 'pi yā /
māyā-śakty eva sā vidyety anye vidyeśvarā yathā //

Others say that the viewpoint of sheer diversity toward phenomena, resembling that imposed by the *māyā-śakti*, is *vidyā*. This pertains even to active beings who take pure Consciousness alone as themselves, for example, the *vidyeśvara* beings.

Commentary

Some Āgamic teachers of Śaivism have used the term *vidyā* to represent the viewpoint of such pure beings as *vidyeśvaras*, known also as *mantra* beings.[30] Such beings feel the pure and divinely potent I-Consciousness alone as their Self, but still they see objective phenomena as different from their subjective Self. Besides, they take themselves as different from other fellow beings as well as from the Lord. The *vidyeśvaras* maintain a viewpoint of diversity because they possess some impurity of *māyā* in their outlook. In fact there are several levels of *vidyā*, one of them being that of the *vidyeśvaras* and the other two belonging to the *mantreśvaras* and *mantra-maheśvaras* residing in *īśvara-tattva* and *sadāśiva-tattva* respectively. Different Śiva yogins have thus used the term *vidyā* in different senses.

The first half of the next couplet throws light on yet another type of *vidyā*, or rather, on another sense in which the term has been frequently used. It has been referred to as *vidyā-śakti*.

Verse 7

तस्यैश्वर्यस्वभावस्य पशुभावे प्रकाशिका ।
विद्याशक्तिः . . .

. . . ॥ ७ ॥

tasyaiśvarya-sva-bhāvasya paśu-bhāve prakāśikā /
vidyā-śaktiḥ . . .

. . . //

Vidyā-śakti is that [divine revelatory] power that reveals to an aspirant his divine nature, while he is yet living as a bound being . . .

Commentary

Vidyā, knowledge, is not only a benevolent power of Śiva, it is a power possessed by a worldly human being as well, because it reveals his divine nature to him as soon as it is aroused in him. It results in a clear feeling of being one with the Almighty Lord Śiva, even while an aspirant is still living as a bound being in his physical body. In fact this is the *vidyā,* the awakened knowledge, that is being sought for diligently by yogins practicing Śaivism. The term *vidyā* is thus used in a variety of ways in different Āgamas, and has therefore been depicted as such in the present book of the *Īśvara-pratyabhijñā.*

The remaining portion of the couplet defines *māyā-śakti.*

. . . ।

. . . तिरोधानकरी मायाभिधा पुनः ॥ ७ ॥

. . . /

. . . tirodhāna-karī māyābhidhā punaḥ //

. . . Māyā-śakti is, on the other hand, that power of God that conceals the truth under [a cloak of] ignorance.

Commentary

Māyā-śakti is that divine power of Śiva that makes impossible things possible for Him. Although he always shines as Almighty God, He hides His divine nature and appears both as a bound human being and also as unconscious phenomenal objects. Śiva does this through His power known as *māyā*. A bound human being, under the effect of *māyā,* feels himself to be either his physical body or his mind, and he finds himself able to know and to do just a little bit in this life, with the help of his senses and organs. For long, long aeons of birth and rebirth, he forgets his real nature, which is the infinite and divinely potent Godhead. Veiling that knowledge and power is one role of *māyā-śakti*.

The other role of *māyā* lies in the exterior manifestation of *māyā-tattva*. *Māyā-tattva* serves as the source of all other insentient elements that cover the *Ātman* and reduce a human being to a position where he finds himself limited, capable of doing and knowing just a little. In other words, it provides the conditions imposed on him by *māyā*. The Lord, having descended to lower levels in the heavenly world, and appearing there as deities like the great trinity of Hindu gods—Brahmā, Viṣṇu, and Maheśvara—uses *māyā* and its mental and physical evolutes as the means to conduct all divine phenomenal actions. *Māyā* also takes up the forms of time, space, and so on, and under their conditions appears as the two basic *tattvas* of the Sāṃkhya system, *puruṣa* and *prakṛti*.

Māyā thus serves as the basic source of creation of all the mental and physical *tattvas* of Indian philosophy, for these are said to emanate from *prakṛti* (the material energy). *Sad-vidyā* is the fifth, and *māyā* the sixth *tattva* in the series of thirty-six. The word *māyā* is employed in several senses in Śaiva philosophy. Its main meanings, which are not exclusive of one another, are: (1) *māyā-śakti,* the divine power of the Lord; (2) *māyā-tattva,* the source of the world's psychophysical principles; (3) *māyāvaraṇa*, or *māyā-moha,* the binding power of the Lord; and (4) *māyā-kañcuka,* the veil or mask hiding the real nature of a being.

The next couplet enumerates the main fields where the illusion of *māyā* has its sway.

Verse 8

भेदे त्वेकरसे भातेऽहंतयानात्मनीक्षिते ।
शून्ये बुद्धौ शरीरे वा मायाशक्तिर्विजृम्भते ॥ ८॥

bhede tvekarase bhāte 'haṃtayānātmanīkṣite /
śūnye buddhau śarīre vā māyā-śaktir vijṛmbhate //

When an uninterrupted diversity shines everywhere and some non-Self entity, like the physical gross body, the animated intelligence, or the Buddhist void, is seen as one's Self, then *māyā-śakti* has its full sway.

Commentary

When *māyā-śakti* fully prevails upon the whole world, it deludes all worldly (and even heavenly) beings. Because of this, they see only through an all-pervasive viewpoint of diversity, and taking unconscious entities as their Self, they feel themselves to be either: (1) the gross physical body in the waking state; (2) the understanding capacity in the dreaming state; (3) the functions of simple life-force *(prāṇa)* in the state of deep sleep; or (4) the vacuum-like, finite I-Consciousness, free from all objective manifestation and known as *śūnya,* in the absolutely dreamless sleep state. Such are the effects of the deluding powers of *māyā,* the sixth *tattva* in the series.

The causal state of Vedānta, as represented by numbers three and four above, is analysed here into two states: *praṇa,* including the awareness of hunger, thirst, heaviness, lightness, rest, and so on, taken as the particulars of the life-force or the simple awareness of one's living state; and *śūnya* (the void), the awareness of one's simple existence, freed from all such feelings. These two states of awareness correspond to the *savedya* and *apavedya* types of *suṣupti,* the deep sleeping 'causal' state of awareness.

The ninth couplet in the chapter is devoted to the description of the twelfth *tattva, puruṣa-tattva.*

Verse 9

यश्च प्रमाता शून्यादिः प्रमेये व्यतिरेकिणि ।
माता स मेयः सन्कालादिकपञ्चकवेष्टितः ॥ ९ ॥

yaś ca pramātā śūnyādiḥ prameye vyatirekiṇi /
mātā sa meyaḥ san kālādika-pañcaka-veṣṭitaḥ //

That subjective condition [or situation, discussed above as] *śūnya*, having entities other than itself as its objects, and being wrapped by five limiting elements known as time and so on, is itself an objective element, appearing as a subjective one.

Commentary

The finite subject, or individual soul, is known as *puruṣa,* and it consists of limited I-Consciousness. Its finitude is caused by *māyā (tattva* six) as well as by the five following *tattvas* of limitation (seven through eleven) known as *kañcukas,* or sheaths. These sheaths limit the divine powers of a person, and they are in fact an extension or outward expansion of *māyā*. Because of these imposed limiting sheaths, a person sees himself either as his physical body, as his mind, as functions of a simple animated state *(prāṇa),* or as an empty and inactive finite I-Consciousness called *śūnya,* where the finite 'I' seems to be without any form or movement. A subject limited in this way is, in fact, more like an object, having just a few subjective powers delegated to him, such as the capacity to know certain things and to do a few actions. The soul's feeling of Selfhood is thus limited to the ego, or individual I-Consciousness, alone.

A being in a perfectly thought-free, sound sleep, or swoon, has only a feeling of his self-limited and finite individual 'I-ness'. Then, in the state of a less sound sleep, he has only an egoistic feeling of living animation. In the state of dreaming, one's egoistic feeling is centred around the mind and its contents. In the waking state, this feeling extends itself to one's physical form as well.

Paradoxically, in all four cases the finite subject is in fact identifying itself wrongly as an objective element, while still working as a subjective one by virtue of the I-Consciousness saturating it constantly. Therefore, the process of true understanding of Self becomes skewed by this subjective-objective confusion. Finite Consciousness that has covered itself with the five limiting sheaths is *puruṣa-tattva,* also known as *aṇu* (the atomic), *paśu* (the bound one), and *jīva* (the living soul).

The five *kañcukas,* or sheaths of limitation, are: (1) *kalā,* a limited capacity to conduct objective actions, restricting divine omnipotence; (2) impure *vidyā,* a limited capacity to know, restricting divine omniscience; (3) *rāga,* interest in doing and knowing only particular actions and in desiring only particular objects, restricting the experience of divine fulfilment and narrowing the field of knowing and doing; (4) *kāla,* the limitation caused by self-imposed time sequence, restricting the experience of eternality; and (5) *niyati, māyā's* law of restriction, restricting further, at each step, the functions of *kalā, vidyā,* and *rāga.*[31] *Māyā,* being itself the basic *kañcuka,* and giving rise to the five above-mentioned restrictions, is counted among them, raising their number to six. These impure *tattvas,* as well as the previously discussed pure *tattvas,* have been discovered by Śiva yogins and have been philosophically discussed only in Kashmir Śaivism. The origin of the *puruṣa-tattva* has also been located and discussed only in this school of Indian philosophy. The late Jayasankar Prasad, a celebrated Hindi poet of the twentieth century, sang sweet songs about the *kañcukas* in his highly popular poetical work, *Kāmāyanī.* But neither his admirers nor the commentators have so far succeeded in explaining his exact views on the topic.

The tenth couplet of this chapter mentions briefly the creation of *prakṛti-tattva* (or *pradhāna-tattva*) and its thirteen evolutes; which had been discussed previously in Sāṃkhya philosophy.

Verse 10

त्रयोविंशतिधा मेयं यत्कार्यकरणात्मकम् ।
तस्याविभागरूप्येकं प्रधानं मूलकारणम् ॥ १० ॥

trayo-viṃśati-dhā meyaṃ yat kārya-karaṇātmakam /
tasyā-vibhāga-rūpy ekaṃ pradhānaṃ mūla-kāraṇam //

Knowable existence [the objective world], which consists of twenty-three objective and instrumental elements, has *pradhāna* (or *mūla-prakṛti,* cosmic energy) as its root cause; which is always identical with this existence and contains all this as only itself.

Commentary

The *aham* element, or subjective existence, shining in pure *vidyā* as pure I-Consciousness, appears in phenomenal creation as the *puruṣa-tattva*. The *idam* element, or the simple and undiversified objective world, shining there as more 'this-ness', also evolves out of *māyā* in the form of the *prakṛti-tattva.* The whole objective and instrumental existence lies in *prakṛti* as that alone, just as all milk products are present in milk only as milk, and not at all in their later transformations.

The eleventh couplet briefly describes the twenty-three evolutes of *prakṛti-tattva.*

Verse 11

त्रयोदशविधा चात्र बाह्यान्तःकरणावली ।
कार्यवर्गश्च दशधा स्थूलसूक्ष्मवभेदतः ॥ ११ ॥

trayo-daśa-vidhā cātra bāhy-āntaḥ-karaṇāvalī /
kārya-vargaś ca daśa-dhā sthūla-sūkṣmav abhedataḥ //

The series of internal and external instrumental elements is of thirteen kinds, and the class of objective elements is of ten kinds, divided into subtle and dense.

Commentary

This refers to the organs of knowledge (five senses of cognition, five senses of action, plus sensory mind, ego, and intellect—a total of thirteen) and the objective elements (five dense elements and five subtle elements—a total of ten) discussed previously in the Introduction.

Chapter 2

THE CLASSIFICATION OF SENTIENT BEINGS

This chapter is devoted to an analysis of the seven categories of beings residing in the above-mentioned world planes of *śakti, vidyā,* and *māyā.* The *śakti* plane consists of the highest Śiva-Śakti state. The plane of *vidyā* includes *sadāśiva-, īśvara-,* and *śuddha-vidyā-tattvas.* The *māyā* plane starts from *māyā-tattva* and extends down to the plane of earth.

The first couplet in the chapter throws light on the nature and position of the trinity of the famous supergods of Hinduism —Brahmā, Viṣṇu, and Rudra (or Śiva)—as these are the most important divine beings in the view of worldly people. The couplet describes the position of these three supergods as follows:

Verse 1

तत्रैतन्मातृतामात्रस्थितौ रुद्रोऽधिदैवतम् ।
भिन्नप्रमेयप्रसरे ब्रह्मविष्णू व्यवस्थितौ ॥ १ ॥

tatraitan-mātṛtā-mātra-sthitau rudro 'dhidaivatam /
bhinna-prameya-prasare brahma-viṣṇū vyavasthitau //

Rudra is the deity who presides there when the subject alone remains existent [and objective and instrumental elements get absorbed in this subject]; but Brahmā and Viṣṇu preside when the objective element becomes prominent as an entity differing from the subject.

Commentary

Brahmā creates the objective universe, while Viṣṇu carries it forward. That is to say, Viṣṇu preserves the universe for a long span of time and maintains it in accordance with the divine laws of restriction. Then Rudra absorbs it back again into its original subjective existence. He thus presides over the quiescent state of being of the Absolute, before creation begins again.

The next couplet throws light on the positions of bound and liberated beings respectively.

Verse 2

एष प्रमाता मायान्धः संसारी कर्मबन्धनः ।
विद्याभिज्ञापितैश्वर्यश्चिद्घनो मुक्त उच्यते ॥

eṣa pramātā māyāndhaḥ saṃsārī karmabandhanaḥ /
vidyābhijñāpitaiśvaryaś cid-ghano mukta ucyate //

The worldly person, blinded by delusion and lying in the bondage of past deeds, moves on in the cycles of transmigration; but having been enlightened by knowledge about his divine potency, and being the great mass of Consciousness, he is said to be liberated.

Commentary

Māyā (delusion) and *vidyā* (knowledge) are thus the binding and liberating forces of the Absolute Lord. They come into action by turns, with respect to ordinary beings and liberated persons. A bound person takes either the physical body or the mind or the functions of life or the nihilistic void as his Self, while a liberated person sees himself as pure and divinely potent, the great scintillating mass of Consciousness *(cid-ghana)* alone.

The next couplet defines two types of beings counted as *paśus* and *patis*.

Verse 3

स्वाङ्गरूपेषु भावेषु प्रमाता कथ्यते पतिः ।
मायातो भेदिषु क्लेशकर्मादिकलुषः पशुः ॥ ३ ॥

svāṅga-rūpeṣu bhāveṣu pramātā kathyate patiḥ /
māyāto bhediṣu kleśa-karmādi-kaluṣaḥ paśuḥ //

A person who sees objects as his own form is called a *pati* (a master), while one lying under the effects of delusion and seeing objects as different from him is called a *paśu* (a bound being).

Commentary

Both *paśus* and *patis* are of several categories. Beings moving under the effects of *māyā* are counted in the *paśu* category. Beings of the *pati* category take the pure and potent Consciousness as their Self. In addition, most of them look upon objective existence as non-different from their subjective Self. *Paśus,* on the other hand, take inanimate entities, like the physical body, the mind, the functions of life and breathing, or the nihilistic void, as their Self. They see objective existence as something different from their subjective Self. There are, however, categories of living beings who possess wholly or partly the qualities of these two main groups of living beings; these are classified accordingly into seven main groups.

The next couplet takes up *mala,* defilement or impurity, as the topic to be discussed, because the complex mixture of types of defilement and purity divides beings into seven categories, worked out in the Śaiva Āgamas and discussed philosophically in Kashmir Śaivism alone. Couplet four describes the two types of *āṇava-mala,* the defilement of finitude.

Verse 4

स्वातन्त्र्यहानिर्बोधस्य स्वातन्त्र्यस्याप्यबोधता ।
द्विधाणवं मलमिदं स्वस्वरूपापहानितः ॥ ४ ॥

svātantrya-hānir bodhasya svātantryasyāpy abodhatā /
dvi-dhāṇavaṃ malam idaṃ sva-sva-rūpāpahānitaḥ //

The two types of *āṇava-mala,* the impurity of finitude, are pure Consciousness losing its independent active power and an active entity identifying itself with some unconscious element. Both proceed out of the loss of [awareness of] one's real nature.

Commentary

Pure and infinite I-Consciousness is, however, always conscious, or rather, aware of itself and its nature, and it is always capable of manifesting its divine nature through the activities of cosmic creation, preservation, and so on. These are the two essential aspects of the pure and infinite Reality. The loss of either of these two aspects—Self-awareness or basic power—causes the limitation of finitude, the impurity known as *āṇava-mala.* This type of impurity thus has two varieties: not knowing or feeling that pure Consciousness is one's essential nature and not being divinely active and potent in one's nature. These two types of *āṇava* impurity are found among beings in all the worlds, including the heavens.

The next couplet describes the other two impurities known as the *māyīya-mala* and *kārma-mala.*

Verse 5

भिन्नवेद्यप्रथाऽत्रैव मायाख्यं जन्मभोगदम् ।
कर्तर्यबोधे कार्मं तु मायाशक्त्यैव तत्त्रयम् ॥ ५ ॥

bhinna-vedya-prathātraiva māyākhyaṃ janma-bhoga-dam /
kartary abodhe kārmaṃ tu māyā-śaktyaiva tat-trayam //

The diverse manifestation of the objective world, when it appears under the effect of that very [*āṇava*] impurity, is called *māyā (māyīya-mala). Kārma* [*mala*] exists in a being who is [something] other than Consciousness, who is [cycling in rebirth], and who tastes [pleasure and pain] as the results [of his past deeds]. All these three have illusion *(māyā)* as their source.

Commentary

The viewpoint that sees diversity in the world is based originally on the *āṇava* impurity, and it is here called *māyīya-mala.* This is the second type of impurity. The third type of impurity is known as *kārma-mala,* and it is caused by one's attachment to actions and impressions or feelings of responsibility for past deeds. It is based on both good and bad past actions committed by a person in his previous lives, and it is the cause of the cycle of birth and rebirth and also of the experience of pleasure and pain in life, which are direct results of these past actions. *Māyā* is generally the base of all three of these impurities, and therefore it is not the *māyīya-mala* alone that is based on delusion *(māyā). 'Māyīya'* is thus simply a technical term used here to denote the viewpoint of diversity maintained by most impure living beings.

The sixth couplet defines a category of living beings who are neither excellently pure nor totally impure. These are known in Śaivism as *vijñānākalas.*

Verse 6

शुद्धबोधात्मकत्वेऽपि येषां नोत्तमकर्तृता ।
निर्मिताः स्वात्मनो भिन्ना भर्त्रा ते कर्तृतात्ययात् ॥ ६ ॥

śuddha-bodhātmakatve 'pi yeṣāṃ nottama-kartṛtā /
nirmitāḥ svātmano bhinnā bhartrā te kartṛtātyayāt //

Those beings who, in spite of consisting of pure Consciousness, do not possess the superior power of divine action, are a creation of the Lord. They appear to be different from Him, just because they lack His power of action.

Commentary

According to this view, people who practise Self-contemplation, as taught in Advaita Vedānta, do actually contemplate their Self as being pure Consciousness. Yet this Self is devoid of all propensity and capacity to conduct any divine or mundane action. In their view, 'activity' appears falsely in the nature of Consciousness, due to the beginningless contact of *Ātman* with *māyā,* universal ignorance. Such people attain a spiritual position in which they feel themselves to be pure but absolutely inactive Consciousness. They have the realisation of their *prakāśa* aspect, but do not discover the *vimarśa* aspect of their own nature. Due to possessing this one type of *āṇava* impurity—the lack of the power of action—they have been created by the Lord as beings appearing to be different from Him.

More light is thrown on the nature of the *vijñānākalas* in the next couplet.

Verse 7

बोधादिलक्षणैक्येऽपि तेषामन्योन्यभिन्नता ।
तथेश्वरेच्छाभेदेन ते च विज्ञानकेवलाः ॥ ७ ॥

bodhādi-lakṣaṇaikye 'pi teṣām anyonya-bhinnatā /
tatheśvarecchā-bhedena te ca vijñāna-kevalāḥ //

In spite of their being mutually similar in the basic character of being Consciousness, and so on, they have been created as beings who are different from one another just through the [independent] will of God. Such beings are known as the *vijñāna kevalins.*

Commentary

Vijñāna-kevalin is another name given to the *vijñānākalas—kevalin* meaning 'one who is alone'. They are called this because their conscious awareness *(vijñāna)* is Consciousness lacking the power of divine action. Elsewhere, they have been called by Utpaladeva *sāṃkhya-puruṣa-prāyāḥ*—that is, 'resembling in some respects the *puruṣas,* or independent souls, of the Sāṃkhya system'. (IPVV III.18) All of them have Consciousness, purity, eternity, and so on, as their character. They enjoy freedom from *māyā* and *prakṛti* and do not have subtle or gross bodies. They do not experience any pleasure or pain and have a common nature among them.

The next couplet mentions another type of being called here the *pralayākala.*

Verse 8

शून्याद्यबोधरूपास्तु कर्तारः प्रलयाकलाः ।
तेषां कार्ममलोऽप्यस्ति मायीयस्तु विकल्पितः ॥ ८॥

śūnyādy-abodha-rūpās tu kartāraḥ pralayākalāḥ /
teṣāṃ kārma-malo 'py asti māyīyas tu vikalpitaḥ //

The inactive beings who take the unconscious void, and so on, as their Self, are the *pralayākalas*. They have the *kārma* impurity as well, though the existence of the *māyīya* impurity in them is not certain. [Some of them may have it and some may not.]

Commentary

Beings who take either a mere feeling of being alive or the nihilistic void as their Self are known as *pralayākalas*. They have the impression of having performed various deeds and are thus under the effect of *kārma* impurity. Some of them rest in the state of the void *(śūnya)* and do not become conscious about any objectivity lying beyond them. But others rest in the function of living and moving animation, so they do have some slight objective experience. For this reason they have a slight tendency toward the viewpoint of diversity, as well. The full existence of the *māyīya* impurity in them is thus uncertain. Some of them do have it while some others are free from it. Such beings are said to lie in a constant sleep for aeons, waiting until the close of the present age, the *pralaya*, or cosmic dissolution, after which they will wake up when the universe is created anew out of cosmic energy. Being free from the element of finite creative power *(kalā)* up to the age of the next *pralaya*, they are consequently known as *pralayākalas*. In fact, all living beings lose their *kalā*, the finite active power, at the time of world dissolution and become *akalas*, inactive beings. They also become *pralayākalas* for an aeon. They are known as *pralaya-kevalins* as well.

The ninth couplet in the chapter defines *vidyeśvaras*, who are a class of pure beings.

Verse 9

बोधानामपि कर्तृत्वजुषां कार्ममलक्षतौ ।
भिन्नवेद्यजुषां मायामलं विद्येश्वराश्च ते ॥ ९ ॥

bodhānām api kartṛtva-juṣāṃ kārma-mala-kṣatau /
bhinna-vedya-juṣāṃ māyā-malaṃ vidyeśvarāś ca te //

Beings who have pure Consciousness as their Self and activity as their nature, but who still see objective existence as different from them, have [only] the defilement of *māyā*. They are known as the *vidyeśvaras*.

Commentary

There is a class of pure beings who do not have the *āṇava* and the *kārma* impurities. They see themselves as pure and infinite Consciousness, and have the feeling of their infinite omnipotence as well; but they see the universe of objective existence as something different from their subjective Self. This viewpoint of diversity is called the *māyīya* impurity. Such beings are called either *vidyeśvaras* or *mantra*-beings. In spite of their partial impurity of viewpoint, they are counted among the pure beings who live in a lower level of the plane of pure *vidyā*. This level is called *mahāmāyā*.

The next couplet counts the limited beings who have all three impurities.

Verse 10

देवादीनां च सर्वेषां भविनां त्रिविधं मलम् ।
तत्रापि कार्ममेवैकं मुख्यं संसारकारणम् ॥ १० ॥

devādīnāṃ ca sarveṣāṃ bhavināṃ tri-vidhaṃ malam /
tatrāpi kārmam evaikaṃ mukhyaṃ saṃsāra-kāraṇam //

All [bound] beings, including the gods in heaven, are undergoing rebirth and are defiled by the three impurities; but among these, the defilement caused by past deeds is the most important cause of their transmigratory existence.

Commentary

All finite beings—including even the gods in heaven like Indra and semigods like the *gandharvas, kinnaras, yakṣas,* and *apsarases,* as well as the ancestors, human beings, animals, birds, fish, worms, insects, plants, and so on—all are moving under the effects of the three types of impurity. However, among these three, it is *kārma-mala* alone, responsibility for past deeds, which specifically generates the cyclic course of repeated birth and death in all creatures.

The actual situation of bound beings is shown in the next couplet.

Verse 11

कलोद्वलितमेतच्च चित्तत्त्वं कर्तृतामयम् ।
अचिद्रूपस्य शून्यादेर्मितं गुणतया स्थितम् ॥ ११ ॥

kalodvalitam etac ca cit-tattvaṃ kartṛtām ayam /
acid-rūpasya śūnyāder mitaṃ guṇatayā sthitam //

Subjective Consciousness, being wrapped by finite creative power *(kalā,* counted among the *kañcukas),* and appearing finite in character, stands here [only] as a quality of unconscious elements like the void *(śūnya).*

Commentary

Though the basic foundation of manifest elements in existence, like the void, is in reality the spiritual lustre of Consciousness, yet at the stage of transmigratory existence, Consciousness becomes wrapped by *kalā,* and so appears only to be a quality of the void or other element. This element seems to shine as the main subject of knowing and doing, rather than Consciousness revealing its own light.

The next verses highlight the Śaiva experience of *samāveśa,* the sudden and direct revelation of the real Self.

Verse 12

मुख्यत्वं कर्तृतायास्तु बोधस्य च चिदात्मनः ।
शून्यादौ तद्गुणे ज्ञानं तत्समावेशलक्षणम् ॥ १२ ॥

mukhyatvaṃ kartṛtāyās tu bodhasya ca cid-ātmanaḥ /
śūnyādau tad-guṇe jñānam tat samāveśa-lakṣaṇam //

On the other hand, a flash of true knowledge that gives prominence to the activity and psychic brilliance of the real Subject, pure Consciousness, with the void, etc., appearing as subordinate to it, is called a *samāveśa*.

Commentary

Samāveśa is a sudden flash of Self-realisation in which the Self is intuitively felt to be pure and infinite Consciousness. One knows he is the universal power who can, in a state of total independence, conduct all universal divine activities in accordance with his free will. It is the direct realisation of one's real nature as the infinite divine essence. This special philosophical principle finds its place in Kashmir Śaivism alone. *Samāveśa* can yield liberation quickly, even while one is living in a physical form—liberation while alive being called *jīvan-mukti*. This happens when the state experienced in *samāveśa* becomes possible at one's will. The development of a yogin's supernatural powers is the other main result of the *samāveśa* experience. No yogin can remain alive long if he stays constantly in *samāveśa*. Only a regular practice in it is possible for a living being. It, however, leaves a deep impression of the Truth on the person of the yogin.

A yogin who lives in this experience rests in the *turyā* (or *turīya*) state—the fourth, revelatory state of awareness. Sometimes he is said to rise into a still higher condition, which shines as *turyātīta,* the supertranscendental state of awareness. These two states of awareness are enjoyed by yogins known as *patis,* or masters, who were discussed at the beginning of this chapter.

Living beings entangled in the delusion of *māyā* are known here as *paśus,* which literally means bound beasts or cattle. They do not generally have any clear experiences of *turyā* or *turyātīta.* They roam in three states, known as *suṣupti, svapna,* and *jāgrat* (deep sleep, dreaming sleep, and waking). These states of bondage are discussed in the next six couplets. The first three are devoted to examining in detail the state of deep, dreamless sleep.

Verses 13-15

शून्ये बुद्ध्याद्यभावात्मन्यहन्ताकर्तृतापदे ।
अस्फुटारूपसंस्कारमात्रिणि ज्ञेयशून्यता ॥ १३ ॥
साक्षाणामान्तरी वृत्तिः प्राणादिप्रेरिका मता ।
जीवनाख्याथवा प्राणेऽहन्ता पुर्यष्टकात्मिका ॥ १४ ॥
तावन्मात्रस्थितौ प्रोक्तं सौषुप्तं प्रलयोपमम् ।
सवेद्यमपवेद्यं च मायामलयुतायुतम् ॥ १५ ॥

śūnye buddhy-ādy-abhāvātmany ahantā-kartṛtā-pade /
asphuṭārūpa-saṃskāra-mātriṇi jñeya-śūnyatā //
sākṣāṇām āntarī vṛttiḥ prāṇādi-prerikā matā /
jīvanākhyāthavā prāṇe 'hantā pury-aṣṭakātmikā //
tāvan mātr-asthitau proktaṃ sauṣuptaṃ pralayopamam /
savedyam apavedyaṃ ca māyā-mala-yutāyutam //

Sometimes [a being's] self-identity, along with its active aspect, rests in the void *(śūnya),* a state in which there is no understanding sense, etc. Here the being bears only vague and unclear impressions, without having any objects to know. This situation consists simply of his senses functioning inwardly to activate animation alone. Otherwise, his self-identity, while resting in the animated state, feels itself to be the group of eight subtle entities [including five finer objective elements like sound, and the three elements of mind]. Such a situation is known as *suṣupti,* the state of deep dreamless sleep, which resembles the [world] situation during the cosmic dissolution.

[*Suṣupti*] is of two types, one with some slight objective experience and the other totally free even from that, due either to the presence or to the absence of the impurity of *māyā*.

Commentary

A person's finite I-Consciousness that has withdrawn itself even from the functions of the mind is called in Śaivism *śūnya,* vacuum. This I-Consciousness is known here as *prāṇa* when it extends itself into a faint objective feeling, while yet resting beyond a person's mind in the state of simple animation. This *prāṇa* and *śūnya* are taken by the person as his Self while he is in the deep sleep state. Similarly, when one looks into one's own times of deep sleep, one can observe only gentle breathing and an awareness of a void without content. *Prāṇa-suṣupti* (deep sleep with faint objective feeling) is said to be *savedya* (with knowing), while the *śūnya* state is called *apavedya-suṣupti* (deep sleep without knowing). A faint impurity of *māyā* has its effect on the former, but the latter is free even from that.

Different methods of spiritual practice, worked out in the Nyāya-Vaiśeṣika, Sāṃkhya yoga, and other schools, are said to lead to the state of *prāṇa-suṣupti,* while those of Vijñānavāda and Śūnyavāda Buddhism are said to lead an aspirant to *apavedya-suṣupti*. Most likely, at the time when Utpaladeva composed his work, it was not an uncommon practice among philosophical circles to attribute to the followers of competing schools of philosophy limited states of attainment, quite short of the mark of final liberation. It is further said that such beings, resting in the deep sleep state, are awakened from it by Śrīkaṇṭhanātha Śiva, at the time of the next world creation, when the finer mental *tattvas* emerge out of the cosmic energy, *mūla-prakṛti*.

The next couplet throws light on the nature of *svapna avasthā,* the dream state.

Verse 16

मनोमात्रपथेऽप्यक्षविषयत्वेन विभ्रमात् ।
स्पष्टावभासा भावानां सृष्टिः स्वप्नपदं मतम् ॥ १६ ॥

mano-mātr-apathe 'py akṣa-viṣayatvena vibhramāt /
spaṣṭāvabhāsā bhāvānāṃ sṛṣṭiḥ svapna-padaṃ matam //

In the dream state, the clear manifestation of objective existence, which is brought about only through the mind but, through misapprehension, seems to be brought about by the senses, is taken as actual existence.

Commentary

All knowledge gained while one is asleep and dreaming is clearly the result of the activities of one's mental faculties. But in spite of this fact, because of his misapprehension about the matter, a dreaming person feels at the time that he is attaining his knowledge through his exterior senses. Such is the nature of the dreaming existence, which is subtle in its character. The next couplet throws light on the nature of the waking state.

Verse 17

सर्वाक्षगोचरत्वेन या तु बाह्यतया स्थिरा ।
सृष्टिः साधारणी सर्वप्रमातॄणां स जागरः ॥ १७ ॥

sarvākṣa-gocaratvena yā tu bāhyatayā sthirā /
sṛṣṭiḥ sādhāraṇī sarva-pramātṝṇāṃ sa jāgaraḥ //

The creation that proves to be externally stable, on the basis of being commonly known to all knowing subjects through all their senses, is the waking state.

Commentary

Gross exterior existence is what is known in the waking state. It is commonly knowable as a fully existent reality to all knowing subjects through both their internal and external senses.

The next couplet expresses a poor opinion of the three types of existence: waking, dream, and deep sleep.

Verse 18

हेया त्रयीयं प्राणादेः प्राधान्यात्कर्तृतागुणे ।
तद्धानोपचयप्रायसुखदुःखादियोगतः ॥ १८ ॥

heyā trayīyaṃ prāṇādeḥ prādhānyāt kartṛtā-guṇe /
tad-dhānopacaya-prāya-sukha-duḥkhādi-yogataḥ //

This trinity [of states] deserves to be avoided, because of the supreme importance it gives to *prāṇa* (the animating life-force), etc., and the secondary place it allots to the real Master of action; and also because of the occurrence of pleasure, pain, and so on, which represent precisely its rise and fall.

Commentary

The body, the mind, and the system of breathing, as well as the void-like *śūnya* awareness, attain particular importance for human beings in the waking, dreaming, and deep sleep states, respectively. The result of this is that pure Consciousness, having the independent power to know and to do, is pushed into the background of human awareness. With Consciousness suppressed and forgotten, experiences of pleasure and pain, among others, tend to dominate in our lives. Therefore, these three states of animated awareness should be avoided; and the fourth state, the supercausal, transcendental *turīya* state, is worthy of being awakened and illuminated. The *turīya* state illuminates pure divine Consciousness as the supreme Master of all knowing and doing, in accordance with its free will. Whereas oblivion of the blissful fourth state of Consciousness results in experiences of pain, its inner illumination yields within the seeker pleasure in the other three states. The fourth state illumines the real nature of divine I-Consciousness, and so is to be realised for attainment of constant bliss in all states of awareness.

The next couplet throws light on the fields of the first three varieties of life-force, known as *prāṇa, apāna,* and *samāna.*

Verse 19

प्राणापानमयः प्राणः प्रत्येकं सुप्तजाग्रतोः ।
तच्छेदात्मा समानाख्यः सौषुप्ते विषुवत्स्विव ॥ १९ ॥

prāṇāpāna-mayaḥ prāṇaḥ praty-ekaṃ supta-jāgratoḥ /
tac-chedātmā samānākhyaḥ sauṣupte viṣuvatsv iva //

The life-force, in both the waking and dreaming states, consists of both inhalation *(prāṇa)* and exhalation *(apāna)*. Both of these are [at times] suspended in the deep sleep state, when the *samāna* type of life-force functions, representing the suspension of the two *(prāṇa* and *apāna)*. This is similar to what happens during an equinox *(viṣuvat)*.

Commentary

The word *viṣuvat* is generally used to signify the equinoxes, when day and night are of equal length. It is mentioned here to indicate the perfect equality and consequent unity between *prāṇa* and *apāna*. *Prāṇa* is the activity of elimination and *apāna* that of assimilation. Both these activities stop in the state of dreamless sleep, which is compared here with the balanced or suspended state of the equinoxes. The correct view of Kashmir Śaivism about the topic is as follows: All activities of elimination, conducted through the breathing process, the mind, the senses, and the various organs, are mystically termed *prāṇa;* and all activities of assimilation are termed *apāna.* Both activities of the life-force go on, hand-in-hand, in the waking and dreaming states of life.

The third function of life is called *samāna*. It consists of a sort of equanimity between these two activities of elimination and assimilation, shining as a kind of vibrant rest. It is experienced by yogins in the yogic state of dreamless sleep and has been compared poetically to equinoxes.

The fourth function of the life-force has been called, by *Śaiva Siddhas, udāna*. It is an experience of sweet sensation, proceeding upward through one's central, vertical spinal nerve and moving toward the crown of the head, called the *sahasrāra-cakra*. This upward movement of the life-force, upon reaching the *brahma-randhra,* its central point, vibrates there as the universal I-Consciousness, which also operates the functions of the entire universe. Such is the view of the Śiva yogins of Kashmir regarding the five functions of *prāṇa,* the life-force. The generally known view of the topic comes closer to physiology than it does to practical philosophy.

The last couplet in the chapter is devoted to throwing light on the character of *udāna* and *vyāna,* the fourth and fifth types of life-force. These two can be taken, respectively, as the revelatory and the absolute types of life-force.[32]

Verse 20

मध्योर्ध्वगाम्युदानाख्यस्तुर्यगो हुतभुङ्मयः ।
विज्ञानाकलमन्त्रेशो व्यानो विश्वात्मकः परः ॥ २० ॥

madhyordhva-gāmy udānākhyas turyago huta-bhuṅ-mayaḥ /
vijñānākala-mantreśo vyāno viśvātmakaḥ paraḥ //

The type of life-force that is fiery in character and functions in the *turyā* state, moving upward through the centre of one's spine, is *udāna*. It works in the *vijñānākalas, mantras,* [*mantreśvaras,* and *mantra-maheśvaras*]. The *vyāna* is the superior, all-pervading one.

Commentary

Advanced yogins, practicing the Śaiva yoga of the Trika system, often have the sweet feeling of a wonderful, fiery sensation moving upward through their spinal cord toward the crown of their head. When such a sweet sensation moves up the six nerve centres, known as *cakras,* one feels it burning to ashes mental ideas of all sorts, known as *vikalpas.* At the same time, it illuminates the inner infinite I-Consciousness that exists behind the mind's concepts and can shine more and more in the mind as it gradually becomes purer and purer. This Self-revelatory function of the vital energy is known in Śaivism as *turyū* or *turīya.* In its nearly (not perfectly) pure aspect, it functions in beings known as *vijñānākalas;* its increasingly purer aspects are seen working in *mantras (vidyeśvaras), mantreśvaras,* and *mantra-maheśvaras.* A still purer and more superior type of vital breath is known as *vyāna.* In this state one tastes the revelation of one's all-pervading, omniscient, omnipotent, all-blissful, and infinite I-Consciousness. This happens in *akala* beings only.

The *turyā* state thus has four varieties: *turyā jāgrat,* the state of the *vidyeśvaras* or *mantra*-beings; *turyā svapna,* the state of the *mantreśvaras; turya suṣupti,* the state of the *mantra-maheśvaras;* and *turyā turyā,* the supreme state of *akala* beings.

Book IV

TATTVA-SAṂGRAHĀDHIKĀRA

The Treasury of Divine Principles

Chapter 1

CONCLUSION

The overall conclusion of the *Īśvara-pratyabhijñā-kārikā* is drawn together in this single and final chapter of Book IV. Besides that, there are also a few topics included here that previously found no proper occasion for discussion. Couplet 1 refers to the exact nature and character of the real Self.

Verse 1

स्वात्मैव सर्वजन्तूनामेक एव महेश्वरः ।
विश्वरूपोऽहमिदमित्यखण्डामर्शबृंहितः ॥ १ ॥

svātmaiva sarva-jantūnām eka eva maheśvaraḥ /
viśva-rūpo 'ham idam ity akhaṇḍāmarśa-bṛṃhitaḥ //

> The great God is, in fact, none other than the real Self of each and every being. He alone endures, having evolved into all phenomenal existence through [His] undiversified Self-awareness, 'I am this'.

Commentary

God shines always as infinite and pure I-Consciousness. The whole phenomenal world lies in Him, merged into His pure I-Consciousness. His pure Consciousness, blissful in nature, inclines toward exhibiting the playful outward show of the world, including all types of beings stationed at different levels of awareness and material creation. God alone thus appears as each individual person who lives in this world, which is an outward manifestation of His divine powers. Therefore, the Self of each and every being is not any third person, but the first person, God. He, being One, appears playfully to be many. The world is the show of His universal aspect, and He always takes all of objective existence as His pure and infinite I-Consciousness. As the Lord creates, His constant awareness—'I am this', 'I am all this'—becomes outwardly manifest, by stages, as the gradual exterior evolution of the entire universe. But God is not most beneficially searched out within these outward phenomenal displays. He is to be realised, in His essence, as one's own real Self. He is now appearing playfully on the world's stage as you or him or her, the individual being.

The next couplet throws light on the creation of finite beings, who mistakenly take the intellect or body or any other element as their Self.

Verse 2

तत्र स्वसृष्टेदंभागे बुद्ध्यादिग्राहकात्मना ।
अहंकारपरामर्शपदं नीतमनेन तत् ॥ २॥

tatra sva-sṛṣṭedaṃ-bhāge buddhyādi-grāhakātmanā /
ahaṃ-kāra-parāmarśa-padaṃ nītam anena tat //

The active knowing entity there in the intellect, etc., in relation with the self-created objective existence, has been manifested as the target of the egoistic 'I'.

Commentary

All of phenomenal existence shines in the Lord as His 'I', that is, His Self. While He manifests outwardly as an objective existence, He also appears as the subjective elements, for instance, as the intellect or sense of understanding *(buddhi),* the life-force, the physical form, and so on. The subjective elements appear as active entities of knowing and doing that act upon objective substances. The world thus contains the two varieties of elements, the objective and the subjective; the latter appearing as the egoistic finite 'I', the subject, and the former as 'this', the object.

The next couplet discusses the nature of finite beings known as *puruṣas.*

Verse 3

स्वस्वरूपापरिज्ञानमयोऽनेकः पुमान्मतः ।
तत्र सृष्टौ क्रियानन्दौ भोगो दुःखसुखात्मकः ॥ ३ ॥

sva-sva-rūpāparijñāna-mayo 'nekaḥ pumān mataḥ /
tatra sṛṣṭau kriyānandau bhogo duḥkha-sukhātmakaḥ //

He [God] is taken to be numerous types of finite persons when He apprehends [only] Self-oblivion. In such a position He has to experience created tensions and releases known as *bhoga,* consisting of pleasure and pain [the result of the person's past deeds].

Commentary

God, playfully pushing His real, divine nature into forgetfulness, appears in the form of numerous living beings having various natures and characters, and known in philosophy as *puruṣas* or *jīvas.* Such beings are bound by destiny to reap the results of their past deeds, both good and bad. For such purpose they have to undergo births, deaths, and rebirths, in cyclic courses in heavens, hells, and the world of mortal beings. The experience of the results of their past deeds is called *bhoga,* as its taste is of both pleasure and pain. This *bhoga,* resulting from one's involvement in *rajo-guṇa* and *sattva-guṇa* (see verse 4), is said here to be painful and pleasurable. *Tamas* is not mentioned verbally because it is not felt so consciously, although its existence is also implied.

The next couplet throws light on the origin of the well-known three *guṇas.*

Verse 4

स्वाङ्गरूपेषु भावेषु पत्युर्ज्ञानं क्रिया च या ।
मायातृतीये ते एव पशोः सत्त्वं रजस्तमः ॥ ४ ॥

svāṅga-rūpeṣu bhāveṣu patyur jñānaṃ kriyā ca yā /
māyā-tṛtīye te eva paśoḥ sattvaṃ rajas tamaḥ //

The (1) knowledge and (2) action of a *pati* (a master, a liberated being), aimed toward objects taken [by him] as his own, as well as (3) his power to manifest the viewpoint of diversity, become respectively [the three *guṇas* named] *sattva, rajas,* and *tamas* of a bound being.

Commentary

When Śiva the Master takes up the position of a bound being, His three divine powers, named *jñāna* (knowledge), *kriyā* (action), and *māyā* (illusion), assume the positions of the three *guṇas* *(sattva, rajas,* and *tamas)* that function in these beings, called here *paśus* (lower animals, cattle, literally 'bound ones'). The illuminating power of the Lord takes up the form of *sattva-guṇa,* and His active power appears as *rajo-guṇa.* The power of the Lord that is capable of manifesting diversity in phenomenal existence is called *māyā-śakti.* This *māyā* takes up the form of *tamo-guṇa,* producing in a bound person a confusion of diversity.

The search for the specific origin of these three *guṇas,* mentioned frequently in Sāṃkhya philosophy, has been talked about very widely in nearly all the philosophical systems and religious traditions of India. Sāṃkhya generally claims the *guṇas* emerge out of *prakṛti* (nature, or the material energy), not from the Lord at all. But the ancient masters of Kashmir Śaivism have done a great service in specifying the exact sources for each *guṇa.* They hold, from their experience, that each *guṇa* has its source in a specific power of God.

The fifth couplet in the chapter explains the significance of the name *'guṇa'* given to the particular qualities of the nature of a bound being.

Verse 5

भेदस्थितेः शक्तिमतः शक्तित्वं नापदिश्यते ।
एषां गुणानां करणकार्यत्वपरिणामिनाम् ॥ ५ ॥

bheda-sthiteḥ śakti-mataḥ śaktitvaṃ nāpadiśyate /
eṣāṃ guṇānāṃ karaṇa-kāryatva-pariṇāminām //

These [three] *guṇas*, becoming transformed into [thirteen] instrumental and [ten] objective elements, are not spoken of as the powers of the powerful One *(puruṣa)* because [as *tattvas*] they stand separate from *puruṣa*.

Commentary

A power is always unified with the powerful entity that possesses it, and so cannot be separated from it. Such is the relation between the three *śaktis (jñāna, kriyā,* and *māyā),* on the one hand, and their Master, Śiva, on the other hand. But this is not the case between the three *guṇas* and *puruṣa.* When the *guṇas* become transformed into the twenty-three *tattvas* during world creation, they begin to stand separately from *puruṣa.* Therefore, these elements can be taken only as His *guṇas* (qualities) and not as His *śaktis.*

The next couplet explains the nature of these three *guṇas.*

Verse 6

सत्तानन्दः क्रिया पत्युस्तदभावोऽपि सा पशोः ।
द्वयात्मा तद्रजो दुःखं श्लेषि सत्त्वतमोमयम् ॥ ६ ॥

sattānandaḥ kriyā patyus tad abhāvo 'pi sā paśoḥ /
dvayātmā tad rajo duḥkhaṃ śleṣi sattva-tamo-mayam //

The constant experience of the bliss of his existence is the [natural] activity of a realised master *(pati)*. A bound being has this bliss occasionally and simultaneously also lacks it. This dual experience of Self is his *rajas* [*guṇa*], which, being a mixture of *sattva* and *tamas*, [yields] pain and turbulence.

Commentary

A realised master, living as he does in the fourth state, has the constant experience of his own blissful existence. A bound being also has the experience of happiness on some joyful occasions, such as when meeting a near and dear person after a long separation. Then he is experiencing his quality of purity and truth, his *sattva-guṇa*. At times, however, he does not have this unalloyed experience at all—in deep sleep, for example, or falling into an unconscious swoon. That is his state of *tamo-guṇa* (darkness, unconsciousness). But sometimes he both has joy and at the same time does not have it. For instance, when a father's desired meeting with a dear son takes place after a long separation, but the father finds the son fatally ill, the father does have a wonderful experience on seeing his son, but in thinking of the terrible result of the disease, he feels no joy at all. Such a mixed experience of the existence and non-existence of Self-bliss is sheer turbulence and pain. This experience, being thus a mixture of *sattva* and *tamas,* is his *rajo-guṇa* (activity, passion). Here we have the essential character of the three *guṇas,* as explored and explained by the masters of Kashmir Śaivism.

The next couplet throws light on the manner in which the world exists in the Lord.

Verse 7

येऽप्यसामयिकेदन्तापरामर्शभुवः प्रभोः ।
तेऽविमिश्रा विभिन्नाश्च तथा चित्रावभासिनः ॥ ७ ॥

ye 'py asāmayikedantā-parāmarśa-bhuvaḥ prabhoḥ /
te vimiśrā vibhinnāś ca tathā citrāvabhasinaḥ //

This world's phenomena about which the Lord is [ever] aware, through a perception lying beyond the scope of any verbal conventions, invariably become manifest either collectively or separately in wonderful variety.

Commentary

The Lord becomes disposed toward creating outwardly, giving form to the objective world beginning with such a faintly objective quality that it does not yet depend on any conventional usage of words. Such visualisation of 'this-ness' is nearly like that which is assumed by a newborn baby toward its environment. This divine visualisation is aimed either at the whole world to be created or individually at some particular item or items. Only a faint manifestation of phenomenal existence occurs at the higher stages of *sadāśiva-* and *īśvara-tattvas*. It is extremely faint in *sadāśiva-tattva* and just a little more clear in *īśvara-tattva*. It becomes clear beginning with *māyā-tattva*.

The next couplet discusses the ideal creations constructed by bound beings in their mental activities.

Verse 8

ते तु भिन्नावभासार्थाः प्रकल्प्याः प्रत्यगात्मनः ।
तत्तद्विभिन्नसंज्ञाभिः स्मृत्युत्प्रेक्षादिगोचरे ॥ ८ ॥

te tu bhinnāvabhāsārthāḥ prakalpyāḥ pratyag-ātmanaḥ /
tat-tad-vibhinna-saṃjñābhiḥ smṛty-utprekṣādi-gocare //

In the case of a finite being, all the phenomena that become objects of his cognitions are generally made the objects of thought by [his] using different names during recollection, imagining, and so on.

Commentary

Ideas about different objects and people occur almost continually in the mind of a worldly person. For his raw material he uses the objects of his daily knowledge and action. He generally works out and gives different names to each object, in accordance with his recollections, imagination, and fancy. Whereas God's creation is apparently permanent and is common to all beings, that 'creation' brought about by an individual person through his imagination is limited to him alone, and it is impermanent in character. God's creation is due to the materialisation of His divine will, while that of a finite being is the result of his own ideas.

The next couplet aims to throw more light on the nature and character of the creation brought about by an individual being through his own imagination.

Verse 9

तस्यासाधारणी सृष्टिरीशसृष्ट्युपजीविनी ।
सैषाप्यज्ञतया सत्यैवेशशक्त्या तदात्मनः ॥ ९ ॥

tasyāsādhāraṇī sṛṣṭir īśa-sṛṣṭy-upajīvinī /
saiṣāpy ajñatayā satyaiveśa-śaktyā tad-ātmanaḥ //

His individual creation, not being common to all beings, remains dependent on God's creation. But even such a phenomenon, though appearing erroneously, is 'true' because of its being created by God appearing in the form of this individual being.

Commentary

An individual being can create in his imagination only such things as are already existent in God's universal creation. He cannot create anything new that is not already in some form present in God's creation. He may, at most, imagine certain substances in different combinations; for instance, an elephant with four tusks, a man with wings, flying through the air in an airplane, or building a computer. But all such things do already exist, though not necessarily in that particular combination, in the Lord's creation.

The next couplet explains how God makes ideational creation take place through finite individual beings, under His own directions. It happens internally through His divine powers working in each individual being.

Verse 10

स्वविश्रान्त्युपरोधायाचलया प्राणरूपया ।
विकल्पक्रियया तत्तद्वर्णवैचित्र्यरूपया ॥ १० ॥

sva-viśrānty-uparodhāyācalayā prāṇa-rūpayā /
vikalpa-kriyayā tat-tad-varṇa-vaicitrya-rūpayā //

It happens through the unstable activity of thought, which stands in the way of [a finite being's] Self-reliance and which becomes manifest in different forms with the help of the complex combinations of sounds and letters, bringing about the activities of life [at different levels of being].

Commentary

The activity of thinking, or ideation, which beings engage in at different levels of phenomenal existence, stands in the way of their correct understanding of themselves and consequent higher Self-reliance. The tendency to cogitate happens in all finite beings, even up to the level of supreme beings like Brahmā and Viṣṇu. Thinking activity is, in fact, basically manifested by God Himself; it appears in the forms of complex and different combinations of sounds and letters, which make up the words of thoughts. These words are the vehicles for the different ideas that beings think about in all the varied states of existence.

The next couplet throws light on the nature of a Śiva yogin's clear vision, which yields the correct realisation of the real nature of the Self and its divine potency, as taught in Kashmir Śaivism. This illustrates the *śāmbhava* method of Self-realisation.

Verse 11

साधारणोऽन्यथा चैश सर्गः स्पष्टावभासनात् ।
विकल्पहानेनैकाग्र्यात्क्रमेणेश्वरतापदम् ॥ ११ ॥

sādhāraṇo 'nyathā caiśa sargaḥ spaṣṭāvabhāsanāt /
vikalpa-hānenaikāgryāt krameṇeśvaratā-padam //

Clearly manifest universal and individual creations, brought into being by God, lead [a spiritual seeker] by stages to the position of the Lord, through the practice of constant elimination of all thought.

Commentary

This is the *śāmbhava* method of Trika yoga, which directly reveals the real nature of the Self as God. In fact, everything in the whole world is God alone. It is just our objective activity of thinking that portrays the world to us as an object of our individual knowing, standing apart from our subjective Self. Besides, it is our activity of ideation that makes us believe we are identical with an individual body, either a physical or a mental one. Constant regular practice in avoiding all thought leads to a psychological position in which our mind stops thinking and our intellect does not indulge in forming any ideas. Then, our I-Consciousness alone shines through its own lustre. It shakes off its presumed identity with the physical body and the mind, for both appear as they do only on account of incorrect thought. This practice also shakes off the limits of time and space, imposed by ideation. Regular yogic spiritual practice reveals to a practitioner the truth of his being nothing other than pure and infinite Consciousness, which has the absolute Godhead as its essential nature.

The next couplet throws light on the *śākta* method *(śākta-upāya)* of Trika yoga.

Verse 12

सोऽहं ममायं विभव इत्येवं परिजानतः ।
विश्वात्मनो विकल्पानां प्रसरेऽपि महेशता ॥ १२ ॥

so 'haṃ mamāyaṃ vibhava ity evaṃ parijānataḥ /
viśvātmano vikalpānāṃ prasare 'pi maheśatā //

A person who feels like this—'I am He. All this is my own exuberant luxury, my own splendour'—goes on feeling himself as none other than Almighty God, even while a multitude of thoughts are still going on [in his mind].

Commentary

That is the character of an aspirant practising *śākta-upāya,* the method of Śakti. Such a Śiva yogin has the knowledge of all objective entities, but feels them to be nothing other than his own Self. The Self shines as none other than Almighty God, whom he sees as his own divine Self and who plays exuberantly the universal drama of the Godhead with respect to all phenomena. *Śākta-upāya* is the practice of reflecting upon one's divine essence while objectively knowing the world.

A similar practice is taken up while performing *āṇava-upāya* as well, but in the latter phenomenal existence as a whole is not made the focus of one's ideas. *Āṇava* practice is conducted with some particular objective element as the target of thought. Such targets are many in number; one may focus on his intellect or understanding, on the function of his vital airs, on the sound of his breathing, on different manifestations of time and space, and so on.

In *śāmbhava-upāya* one practises the direct intuitive realisation of the real Self; in *śākta* one practises mental contemplation on the Self along with its divine character; while in *āṇava* one performs contemplative meditation on particular objective phenomena in the world or within oneself.

The thirteenth couplet shows the difference between the viewpoints of a liberated being and a bound one.

Verse 13

मेयं साधारणं मुक्तः स्वात्माभेदेन मन्यते ।
महेश्वरो यथा बद्धः पुनरत्यन्तभेदवत् ॥ १३ ॥

meyaṃ sādhāraṇaṃ muktaḥ svātmābhedena manyate /
maheśvaro yathā baddhaḥ punar aty-anta-bhedavat //

A liberated being, seeing the objective world that he and all other beings know, takes it as being identical with himself, as does the Lord, while a bound being sees it as absolutely different from himself.

Commentary

A person who has realised his identity with Absolute God is a liberated being, though still living as an individual person. Such a being sees the entire objective universe as his own Self, as does Lord Īśvara. Besides, he feels that the knowledge gained by all beings is his own knowledge, and he knows himself through the understandings of all beings. Thus, he sees the world and its functions as identical with himself, as does Lord Īśvara. He thinks, as do all liberated beings, 'All this is the Self'. A bound being, on the other hand, sees everything as absolutely different from himself.

The next couplet is devoted to expressing the way that the universe exists in the Absolute Lord.

Verse 14

सर्वथा त्वन्तरालीनानन्ततत्त्वौघनिर्भरः ।
शिवश्चिदानन्दघनः परमाक्षरविग्रहः ॥ १४ ॥

sarvathā tv antarālīnānanta-tattvaugha-nirbharaḥ /
śivaś cid-ānanda-ghanaḥ paramākṣara-vigrahaḥ //

Absolute Śiva, perfectly concentrated with blissful Consciousness, has all the countless multitudes of phenomenal elements perfectly absorbed in Him up to the brim He exists essentially as the spontaneously [infinite] and all-perfect transcendental Self-awareness.

Commentary

Absolutely existent Reality, called Paramaśiva, is very often referred to simply as Śiva. He consists of infinite, eternal, and all-blissful pure Consciousness. The entire phenomenal existence basically dwells in Him in the form of Self-aware, pure Consciousness, having bliss as its essential character. Such concentrated and blissful Self-awareness, shining as the infinite 'I' (which is not the same as the ego), is the essential characteristic essence that has been charmingly witnessed by Śiva yogins of the monistic school of Tryambaka. It shines as the all-inclusive 'I' and 'I' alone, without even the faintest appearance of objectivity or 'this-ness' in it.

The final practical aim to be attained by studying the work in hand is expressed in the next couplet.

Verse 15

एवमात्मानमेतस्य सम्यग्ज्ञानक्रिये तथा ।
पश्यन्यथेप्सितानर्थाञ्जानाति च करोति च ॥ १५ ॥

evam ātmānam etasya samyag-jñāna-kriye tathā /
paśyan yathepsitān arthāñ jānāti ca karoti ca //

Thus realising his real Self and its natural divine powers to know and to do, [an aspirant], seeing this, becomes capable of knowing and doing as he likes.

Commentary

An aspirant, becoming enlightened about his real character and divine powers, becomes a *jīvan-mukta,* a being liberated from bondage even while living in a mortal form. Realising his hitherto hidden powers, he becomes capable of knowing and doing and creating whatever he likes. He thus starts to enjoy the sweet taste of his divine essence in this very life and becomes all-pervasively one with Almighty God after shedding his present mortal form.

The next verse is meant to conclude the *Īśvara-pratyabhijñā-kārikā.*

Verse 16

इति प्रकटितो मया सुघट एष मार्गो नवो
महागुरुभिरुच्यते स्म शिवदृष्टिशास्त्रे यथा ।
तदत्र निदधत्पदं भुवनकर्तृतामात्मनो
विभाव्य शिवतामयीमनिशमाविशन्सिध्यति ॥ १६ ॥

iti prakaṭito mayā sughaṭa eṣa mārgo navo
mahāgurubhir ucyate sma śiva-dṛṣṭi-śāstre yathā /
tad atra nidadhat padaṃ bhuvana-kartṛtām ātmano
vibhāvya śivatā-mayīm aniśam āviśan sidhyati //

Thus have I thrown clear light on the new and easy path [of liberation], as clearly expounded by the great master [Somānanda] in his work, the *Śiva-dṛṣṭi*. So [an aspirant], establishing himself in its practice, having experienced [through it] his own Śivahood—including mastery over the creation, and so on, of all abodes of beings [in the universe]—and conducting a regular practice in *samāveśa* (a sudden burst that merges the individual Self into infinite Consciousness), can, no doubt, become a *Siddha* (a perfect being having the correct knowledge of everything and divine power to do everything).

Commentary

This new path consists of the threefold practice of (1) correct theoretical knowledge of Śaiva monism, (2) practice in Śaiva yoga, and (3) maintaining all along the path an attitude of devotional love for the Lord. This path introduces a new attitude toward the mind, the body, and the world when compared with the practices prescribed by the ascetic paths that advocate repression of human instincts and emotions, forcible control of the breath and mind, starvation of the senses, and so on. It is also new in that it neither prescribes the eightfold path *(aṣṭāṅga-yoga)* found in the *Yoga Sūtras* of Patañjali, nor any puritanical discipline like that handed down in the Brahmanic *smṛtis*, such as Manu. The development of such powers confirms the fact that the concerned yogin has attained the merit of becoming one with the Absolute Lord after shedding his mortal frame. Such *siddhis* are thus not prohibited in Śaivism.

The practice of the Trika Śaiva path, described in the last chapter of the *Śiva-dṛṣṭi* by the great teacher Somānanda, yields the recognition of one's identity with the Absolute Lord. Its regular practice results in having sudden experiences of Śivahood, or merging fully into Śiva. These are known as *samāveśas,* and they also result in the natural attainment of supernatural powers called *siddhis.* That is to say, a Śiva yogin who practises merging with God in *samāveśa* will develop powers to liberate beings at his will and can grant them desired boons as well. Besides that, he becomes capable of involving them in bondage if they commit indiscipline. In short, he can conduct some of the Lord's divine activities of creation, bestowal of grace, and so on, at his will.

The next stanza, number 17, describes poetically the wonderfully sweet experience of the correct recognition of one's true Śivahood. Comparing this experience with the previously existent, painful Self-oblivion has been the main aim of this treatise.[33]

Verse 17

तैस्तैरप्युपयाचितैरुपनतस्तन्व्याः स्थितोऽप्यन्तिके
कान्तो लोकसमान एवमपरिज्ञातो न रन्तुं यथा ।
लोकस्यैष तथानवेक्षितगुणः स्वात्मापि विश्वेश्वरो
नैवालं निजवैभवाय तदियं तत्प्रत्यभिज्ञोदिता ॥ १७ ॥

tais tair apy upayācitair upanatas tanvyāḥ sthito 'py antike
kānto loka-samāna evam aparijñāto na rantuṃ yathā /
lokasyaiṣa tathānavekṣita-guṇaḥ svātmāpi viśveśvaro
naivālaṃ nija-vaibhavāya tad iyaṃ tat-pratyabhijñoditā //

Just as a very lovable man, earnestly desired by a beautiful maiden as her lover, being urged on by her profusely eager yearnings, comes to her and stands by her side, but is not recognised and consequently appears [to her] just like any ordinary person, [and so] does not provide her with the immensely desired taste of mutual union, [just] so, the Self of a person, even though being Almighty God Himself, is not able to taste his own divine grandeur, just because he does not recognise [himself].

Commentary

Recognition of oneself as God is liberation, and non-recognition is bondage. A Puranic story tells of the maiden Umā, the daughter of the mountain king Himavat. Although she was deeply in love with Śiva, the truthful damsel Umā could not shake off the pangs of her feeling of separation from Śiva, even when he stood before her in the form of a *brahmacārin* ascetic, because she did not recognise Him as her beloved Lord Śiva.

The concluding stanza briefly gives information about the author's personal history.

Verse 18

जनस्यायत्नसिद्ध्यर्थमुदयाकरसूनुना ।
ईश्वरप्रत्यभिज्ञेयमुत्पलेनोपपादिता ॥ १८ ॥

janasyāyatna-siddhy-artham udayākara-sūnunā /
īśvara-pratyabhijñeyam utpalenopapāditā //

Utpala, the son of Udayākara, composed this work, the *Īśvara-pratyabhijñā,* for the purpose that people attain perfection without any [arduous] effort.

Commentary

Udayākara is also mentioned in the *Vivṛti-vimarśinī* as the father of Utpaladeva. His ancestors had come to Kashmir and settled there permanently sometime in the middle of the eighth century. Since he is said to have come from the Lāṭa lineage, he may well have come to Kashmir from Gujarat. The mother of Utpaladeva was named Vāgīśvarī. His son was called Vibhramākara and he had a class friend named Padmānanda. This information is available from another work by the author, the beginning of his brief paraphrase of the *Śiva-dṛṣṭi* of Somānanda, and from commentaries by Abhinavagupta.

Let us conclude the work with a quotation that is a sweet, poetic expression of the principle of *pratyabhijñā,* or Self-recognition, as given by Utpaladeva in his *Śiva-stotrāvalī, 'A Garland of Songs to Śiva'.*[34]

ईश्वरमभयमुदारं पूर्णमकारणमपह्नुतात्मानम्
सहसाभिज्ञाय कदा स्वामिजनं लज्जयिष्यामि ॥ ४ ६ ॥

īśvaram abhayam udāraṃ pūrṇam akāraṇam apahnutātmānam /
sahasābhijñāya kadā svāmijanaṃ lajjayiṣyāmi //

My beloved Master, being all powerful, perfect, fearless, and broadminded in character, has yet—alas!—been keeping Himself hidden from me! Oh, when will the time come that I may put Him to shame, by finding Him out so suddenly?

Commentary

The *Īśvara-pratyabhijñā-kārikā* represents the head of this master philosopher, while the *Śiva-stotrāvalī* is an outpouring from his heart. The former offers excellent logical thinking and brilliant argumentation, while the latter represents his passionate feelings about the Truth as described here.

APPENDIX

Cosmology of Kashmir Śaivism

Planes of Existence	Masters of the Planes	Beings Living in the Planes	Tattvas in each Plane
PURE			
1. *Śakti* stage	*Śiva-bhaṭṭāraka* *Śakti-bhaṭṭārikā*	*Śambhavas* *Śāktas*	1. *Śiva* 2. *Śakti*
PURE AND IMPURE			
2a. Pure *Vidyā* stage	*Sadāśiva-nātha* *Īśvara-bhaṭṭāraka*	*Mantra-maheśvaras* *Mantreśvaras*	3. *Sadāśiva* 4. *Īśvara*
2b. *Vidyā* stage i) Pure Knowledge ii) Inferior Knowledge or *Mahāmāyā*	*Ananta-nātha* or *Aghoreśa*	*Mantra* beings or *Vidyeśvaras*	5. *Sad-vidyā* or *śuddha-vidyā* influenced by *Mahāmāyā*
IMPURE			
3. Māyā stage			
a) Finer aspect	*Ananta-nātha*	*Vijñānākalas*	6. *Māyā* 7-11. *Kañcukas*
b) Subtle aspect	*Śrīkaṇṭha-nātha*	*Pralayākalas*	12. *Puruṣa* 13. *Prakṛti*
c) Gross aspect	Supergod trinity *Brahmā, Viṣṇu, Rudra*	*Sakala* beings	14-35. instrumental & objective *tattvas* up to water
d) *Pṛthivī* sub-stage	gods in heaven	gross body beings	36. *Pṛthivī* (earth)

NOTES

1. Vijñānavāda does not accept the existence of *Ātman* (the Self or soul) ruling over one's mental consciousness, flowing ahead like a constant stream. The finer logic of this school was totally ignored by all theistic thinkers, and by Śaṅkarācārya.

2. The term 'mono-dualism' is now being popularly used in India for philosophical views that propound theories partly monistic and partly dualistic in their principles. Such schools are now known as mono-dualistic, e.g., Śivādvaita of Śrīkaṇṭha, Viśiṣṭādvaita of Rāmānuja, and so on. Vīraśaivism, though basically a monistic school of philosophy, expressed poetically in the Vacana literature in the Kannaḍa language, is now counted by some present-day masters of Indian philosophy as a school coming close to that of Rāmānuja's Viśiṣṭādvaita.

3. The *devanagari* letters *n* and *v* are written in such a similar fashion that some copyists in the past thought that *Vāmaka* was instead *Nāmaka,* and the mistake has continued up to the present. *Vāmaka-tantra* is still being written as *Nāmaka-tantra.*

4. SDr VI.33-87. Somānanda is the first non-Buddhist philosopher who did justice to the finer logical arguments of Vijñānavāda. Even the Vedānta of Śaṅkarācārya ignored it. Also, it was given due justice later by both Utpaladeva and Abhinavagupta.

5. One of the author's former students tried to go through the whole list of manuscripts, but did not find the one described there. The owner, knowing its high value, may not have sold it to Smt. Vatsyayana. It is also possible that the manuscript may be lying bound with some others preceding it and may not have found its place in the list of manuscripts.

6. The Vijñānavādin, raising an objection against such inference, would say as follows: Since recollection easily becomes possible merely on the basis of mental impressions, what is the use in the supposition of the existence of an additional reality called *Ātman*.

7. A ghost said to be invisibly present within sunlight is surely also considered an entity non-identical with that light. That is the difference in seeing through the two different viewpoints corresponding to the principles of (1) *saṃsargābhāva* (non-existence through contact) and (2) *anyonyābhāva* (mutual non-existence) of the Nyāya-Vaiśeṣika system.

8. An experience at the first moment is just a simple reflection of an object as it is in itself. It is not at all touched by any mental idea or any word image. That is the *nirvikalpa* experience. The mind of an experiencer imposes on it the ideas of its name and form in the next moment, and such experience is called *savikalpa,* that is, a knowing accompanied by the ideas of a definite name and form.

9. *Mahāmāyā* is the name given to *śuddha-vidyā* at its lower stage. Beings residing at this stage of pure knowledge do not retain any ignorance with regard to their own nature of purity and divine potency but, at the same time, they do maintain a viewpoint of diversity with regard to other beings, Lord Śiva, and the objective world

10. The finite I-Consciousness, lying beyond the reach of all mental apparatus and movements of life-force, is called in Śaivism the state of *śūnya,* which resembles the consciousness of a being in deep, dreamless sleep.

11. This upward-moving sensation of *udāna* has been described in a poetic style by some Śākta-yogins as the upward-moving *kuṇḍalinī-śakti,* and several types of paintings of it are also available, but it is only Utpaladeva who started to discuss the topic philosophically. Later it was Abhinavagupta who explained its practical aspect in accordance with the *uccāra-yoga* of the Trika system of *sādhana* in his *Tantrāloka* and *Tantrasāra.* (TS 38, TAV 44-49)

12. *Prāṇa* and *apāna* move during the waking and dreaming states. *Samāna* leads to a sort of dreamlessly sleeping state of tranquillity, while *udāna* carries one gradually through the steps of *turyā,* the state of self-revelation of one's Śakti-Śivahood. Finally, *vyāna* reveals one's transcendental position as Paramaśiva, the supreme state lying beyond *turyā.*

13. Such movements of the life-force represent the inward movements of Śakti, the divine, active essence of God, and lead the individual consciousness of an aspirant finally to the position of the Absolute Consciousness, known as Śiva or Paramaśiva, represented by the finest life-force, *vyāna.* (IPK III.2.19)

14. Development of divine powers makes an aspirant fully sure about his being none other than the Almighty God in reality. Therefore, such *siddhis* are not totally prohibited in Kashmir Śaivism. It is only their unjustifiable use which is to be avoided.

15. Please compare with *samasta-sampat-samavāpti-hetuṃ* in couplet I.1.1.

16. A commentator refers to the Vijñānavādin as *pradhāna-malla,* the most powerful wrestler.

17. Even the *ālaya-vijñāna*, 'storehouse consciousness,' moving ahead as an effulgent flow of momentary I-ness, is nothing more than an aspect of mental consciousness, or *vijñāna,* and cannot be accepted as any other reality called *Ātman*.

18. It appears that the correct reading of the first line of the couplet may have been:

jñānaṃ ca cit-sva-rūpaṃ cet tanna nityaṃ kim ātmavat /

This reading agrees with the text of the *Vimarśinī* by Abhinavagupta on the text. It reads:

'jñānam api' tarhi sva-prakāśam—iti,
tatrāpi eṣaiva vārtā—iti /
tad api kasmāt na nityam? . . . etc. //
(See page 69 KSTS IPV)

19. One case is that of a yogin having an experience of someone's knowledge through telepathy, and the other case is that of a person cognising objectively his own experience. The two are not similar in character and therefore the telepathic observation cannot serve here as an example which may prove a person's ability to know objectively his own past experience.

20. A person, while remembering a past experience, takes it subjectively as 'I saw such and such a person in Delhi', laying the main emphasis on himself. He does not have any objective feeling with respect to his previous knowledge, though he does have it toward that person, the object of the knowledge concerned.

21. No genuinely important principles of philosophy are meant by such terms and discussions, which have been examined here merely to combat the finer but dry logic of Vijñānavāda, as worked out

in *Prāmaṇa-vārtika* of Dharmakīrti and the commentary on it by Dharmottara.

22. All phenomena basically exist in the infinite and eternal pure Consciousness in the form of its divine power, just as the wonderful creation of a poetic world lies fundamentally in the poetic talent of a poet. Such divine Consciousness, being playfully vibratory in its essential nature, manifests the reflection of its powers outwardly, and those appear as creation, and so on, of the whole universe, including the thirty-six *tattvas* and the worlds made of them. This process of creation starts long before the emergence of *prakṛti* and *māyā,* as discovered in Sāṃkhya and Vedānta. This theory of the reflective manifestation of the universe is called *ābhāsa-vāda,* which is the basic cosmogonical theory of Kashmir Śaivism.

23. This method of yoga is the practice of contemplative visualisation of the unity of one's present-day finite Self with its primordial state, the omnipotent, eternal, infinite, and pure Consciousness. It can be conducted either directly or gradually, beginning with visualisation of the Śrīkaṇṭha Śiva of the epics all the way up to Paramaśiva, the monistic Absolute God.

24. IPK and IPV read *akṣādibhuvām,* IPVV and Bhaskari read *akṣyādibhuvām.*

25. Take, for instance, the example of a sweet mango. It is a solid substance to be held in one's hand, while its sweetness is a subtle taste to be relished with the help of one's tongue. Both are mutually different entities, thought about jointly. There is no substantial element lying between the two that could be taken as their mutual relation. This is just an idea imposed on them by one's mind. Relation, or relativity, thus has only a dialectical existence, although it cannot be pushed into the field of total non-existence.

26. *Pramāṇas,* or means of correct knowledge, as discussed in Mimaṃsā and other schools of Indian philosophy, are seven in number: (1) *pratyakṣa* or perception, (2) *anumāna* or inference, (3) *upamāna* or analogy, (4) *arthāpatti,* implication or circumstantial evidence, (5) *śabda* or verbal authority, (6) *anupalabdhi*—non-perception, or negative proof, and (7) *aitihya (prasiddhi),* tradition or fallible testimony. Kashmir Śaivism does not deal in detail with the topic, but accepts the *pramānas* validity in mundane dealings. It agrees with the views of Kumārila Bhaṭṭa.

27. Such means of correct knowledge does not require anything else to reveal it or its validity. The perception of a red rose reveals the existence of such an object, but so far as the perception itself is concerned, it is self-revelatory and thus does not require anything other than itself to reveal its existence. Had it required anything other than itself as a *pramāṇa* to reveal its existence, this other *pramāṇa* would also 'sail in the same boat', so to speak, thus leading to the logical defect known as *anavasthā* or *ad infinitum,* a series of *pramāṇas* without any end.

28. As soon as a glittering object, having at first sight been perceived as silver, is in fact known definitely by careful perception to be just a shell, the previous perception (presenting it as silver) ceases to be a *pramāṇa,* from the moment it appeared as silver.

A yogin, having recognised himself to be none other than God, feels at once that the validity of his previous concept of himself as a finite being is rendered invalid as a *pramāṇa.*

29. The *prakṛti* of Sāṃkhya philosophy, being unconscious in its nature, comes very close to the cosmic energy of modern physics, there being sufficient similarity in their nature. Śakti, on the other hand, is the conscious divine spiritual power of the monistic Absolute, Paramaśiva.

30. The word *mantra,* used in specialised Āgamic terminology related to *tattvas,* does not mean a verbal formula containing mystic words or sounds. These Āgamic terms have been used to denote gradually purer types of beings residing in *tattvas* above *māyā.*

31. Kṣemarāja's view on the meaning of *niyati* is not correct.

32. *Udāna,* which resembles a spiritual fire burning to ashes all the ideational notions and revealing, by stages, the non-ideational pure character of the Self, no doubt is a revelatory sort of life-function. *Vyāna,* the pure and Self-aware life-function shining in its universal and transcendental aspects, is in fact non-different from the nature of Paramaśiva, the Absolute God.

33. Such recognition was later described in a charming poetic style by Śaiva Nāgārjuna in his twelfth-century work, *Citta-santoṣa-triṃśikā* (Jammu: Ranvir Vidyapeeth-Shastri-nagar).

34. The verse concerned is a sweet example of a beautifully poetic figure of speech known as *samāsokti.*

GLOSSARY

ābhāsa. Divine manifestation.

ābhāsa-vāda. The Kashmiri Śaiva doctrine of idealist world creation, wherein the universe shines forth through a reflecting outward manifestation of divine Consciousness.

abhilāpa. A word image imposed upon thought-free *(nirvikalpa)* knowledge.

Abhinavagupta. (tenth to eleventh century C.E.) Brilliant philosopher and commentator of Kashmir Śaivism, belonging to the lineage of Vasugupta and Somānanda. He is the author of the *Tantrāloka* and the *Īśvara-pratyabhijñā-vimarśini,* a commentary on the *Īśvara-pratyabhijñā-kārikā,* among other works.

adhikāra. A book or section of the *Īśvara-pratyabhijñā-kārikā.*

adhyavasāya. Conviction; knowledge limited by the names and visible forms of objects, as proposed by Advaita Vedānta philosophy.

Advaita Vedānta. The Vedic philosophy of the Upaniṣads, as interpreted by Gauḍapāda and Śaṅkarācārya.

Āgamādhikāra. Book III of the *Īśvara-pratyabhijñā-kārika,* dealing with scriptural knowledge.

Āgamas. Scriptures considered to be divinely revealed; sources of the various Śaiva schools.

aham. 'I'; I-awareness, whether limited (ego) or perfected (Supreme Consciousness). In its limited form, the I-awareness becomes separated from *idam,* the objective 'this-ness' of other beings and objects in the world.

āhnika. A daily lesson or chapter.

aiśvarya. Supreme authority of God; divine essence of lordship.

akalas. The highest type of formless, pure beings, also known as *śivas,* who are aware of their own omniscience, omnipotence, and other powers. They see only their infinite 'I-ness' in the whole of existence. Such beings live in the first two *tattvas—śiva* and *śakti-tattvas.*

āṇava-mala. The impurity of finitude or limited selfhood; one of the three impurities or limitations that bring about the bondage of the universal Self and reduce it to a limited, individual being. See also *māyīya-mala* and *kārma-mala.*

āṇava-upāya. In Kashmir Śaivism, a means to Self-realisation whereby the seeker uses his body, senses, breath, sound, etc.; also known as *bheda upāya* or *kriyā upāya.* See also *śākta-upāya* and *śāmbhava upāya.*

anubhava. Higher spiritual experience.

anyonyābhāva. The principle of mutual non-existence (*x* is not *y*). See also *saṃsargābhāva.*

apāna. The vital air of assimilation; one of the five types of *prāṇa,* or life-force.

apoha. A philosophical term meaning avoidance of other options.

apohana-śakti. The Lord's power of differentiation, making a thing appear as something different from other objects; one of the three powers (along with *jñāna* and *smṛti*) that sustain the world as a regulated cosmos.

aṣṭāṅga-yoga. Patañjali's eight-limbed system of yoga propounded in the *Yoga Sūtras.* Includes *yama, niyama, āsana, praṇāyāma, pratyāhāra, dhāraṇā, dhyāna,* and *samādhi.*

Ātman. The individual soul or Self, equivalent to Paramātman or Paramaśiva.

Atrigupta. Ancestor of Vasugupta, the discoverer of the *Śiva-sutras*.

Aurva. A mythological god of fire, consuming the bulk of ocean waters.

avidyā. Ignorance.

bhakti. Loving devotion to God or guru.

Bhaṭṭa Kallaṭa. Ninth-century disciple of Vasugupta and author of the *Spanda-kārikā*.

bhedābheda. Philosophical position of unity in diversity.

bhoga. Worldly experience; the enjoyment and suffering of experiencing the world through the senses.

brahmacārin. A celibate student or ascetic; literally, 'journeying on the path of God'.

brahma-randhra. The subtle energy centre at the crown of the head. When the rising life-force reaches it, one experiences the state of complete freedom.

buddhi. Intellect, understanding sense; also called *mahāt*.

caitta. Mental or intellectual ideas.

cakra. Spiritual nerve centre in the subtle body; traditionally there are seven.

citi. Pure, divine Consciousness.

citta. The mind.

guṇas. The three qualities of nature: *sattva* (purity and enlightenment); *rajas* (activity and turbulence, purity and impurity); and *tamas* (impurity, heaviness, inactivity, darkness).

icchā-śakti. The Lord's power of will.

idam. 'This', or the objective sense; the objective world as opposed to subjective awareness. See also *aham*.

Īśvara. God, the Lord; also the fourth *tattva* among the thirty-six principles of the universe in Kashmir Śaivism.

Īśvara-bhaṭṭāraka. The presiding master of the *īśvara-tattva,* on the plane of pure *vidyā*.

īśvara-tattva. The fourth *tattva* among the thirty-six principles of the universe in Kashmir Śaivism.

jāgrat. The waking state of awareness.

jīva. Individual self; the limited 'living' self.

jīvan-mukti. The state of being spiritually liberated while still alive.

jñāna. Knowledge.

jñāna-śakti. The Lord's perfect and all-embracing cognitive power.

Jñānādhikāra. Book I of *Īśvara-pratyabhijñā-kārikā,* dealing with the nature of the divine power of knowledge inherent in Supreme Consciousness.

kalā-kañcuka. One of the five restrictions or limitations on divine awareness due to the influence of *māyā,* the constriction of creative power, of acting and knowing.

kāla-śakti. Divine power manifesting as time sequence in mundane actions.

kañcukas. Sheaths or constrictions that limit the divine powers of the soul, under the influence of *māyā,* or illusion.

kārakas. Agents involved in performing an action.

kārikās. Couplets; the poetic verse form in which *Īśvara-pratyabhijñā-kārikā* is composed.

kārma-mala. The bondage of action and its consequences; one of the three impurities or limitations that bring about the bondage of the universal Self and reduce it to a limited, individual being. See also *māyīya-mala* and *āṇava-mala*.

Kaulism. A systematic practice of quick realisation of I-Consciousness, achieved through the disciplined taste of the five *makāras:* meat *(māṃsa)*, fish *(matsya)*, wine *(madirā)*, a highly delicious food *(mudrā)*, and sexual intercourse *(maithuna)*. This practice is conducted jointly by a man and a woman, realising one another as Śakti and Śiva and, for the moment, losing their personal individuality.

kriyā. Action, activity.

kriyā-śakti. The inherent divine power by which God acts in creating and maintaining the universe.

Kriyādhikāra. Book II of the *Īśvara-pratyabhijñā-kārikā*, dealing with divine creative action, *kriyā-śakti*.

Kumārila Bhaṭṭa. A primary exponent of Mīmāṃsā philosophy.

Lakṣmaṇagupta. A teacher of Abhinavagupta.

mahāmāyā. Literally, 'the great illusion'; the influence of māyā at the cosmic stage of vidyā. It involves increasing manifestation of subtle ignorance in understanding.

mahāsattā. Absolute existence.

Maheśvara. Śiva in His character of absolute Lordship.

Manorathagupta. The younger brother of Abhinavagupta.

mantra-maheśvaras. Beings living in the plane of pure *vidyā,* at the level of the third *tattva, sadāśiva-tattva*. They experience the 'I am this' level of conscious awareness.

mantreśvaras. Beings living in the plane of pure *vidyā,* at the level of the fourth *tattva, īśvara-tattva*. They experience the 'This I am' level of conscious awareness; their awareness of objectivity has increased beyond that of the *mantra-maheśvaras*.

māyā. Illusion, delusion; the sixth universal *tattva*. In Kashmir Śaivism, *māyā* evolves out of the power of Supreme Consciousness.

māyā-śakti. Divine power of illusion. See also *māyā*.

māyīya-mala. The impurity of duality or deluded understanding; one of Kashmir Śaivism's three impurities or limitations that bring about the bondage of the universal Self and reduce it to a limited, individual being. Also see *kārma-mala* and *āṇava-mala*.

Mīmāṃsā. One of the six traditional schools of Indian philosophy; divided into Pūrva-mīmāṃsā (concerned with correct interpretation of Vedic ritual and texts) and Uttara-mīmāṃsā (concerned with philosophy and commonly known as Vedānta).

moha. Delusion.

mūla-prakṛti. Fundamental energy which becomes the forms of world creation, according to Sāṃkhya philosophy.

Narasiṃhagupta. An ancestor of Abhinavagupta.

nimeṣa. Involution; world dissolution. See also *unmeṣa*.

nirvikalpa. Beyond thought; a thought-free state of experience; one of the forms of *samādhi*. A variety of *suṣupti* according to Kashmir Śaivism. See also *savikalpa*.

niyati-kañcuka. One of the five restrictions or limitations on divine power due to the influence of *māyā;* the constriction of space, knowledge, and action.

Nyāya-Vaiśeṣika. Two of the related six traditional schools of Indian philosophy; the science of logical proof and the discovery of the essential properties of reality. Nyāya is said to have been founded by Gautama (c. 550 B.C.E.); Vaiśeṣika by Kaṇāda (third-century B.C.E.).

pāramārthika-satya. The absolutely highest and most perfect Truth.

Paramaśiva. Supreme Consciousness, the highest Śiva; name for God in Kashmir Śaivism.

Paramātman. Supreme soul.

parāvāk. Supreme speech; initial vibratory or sound-form of God, which manifests prior to and as the source of universal creation. It consists of the self-awareness of the vibratory nature of God.

paśu. The soul in a state of bondage due to ignorance of its true nature and divested of its original divine powers; one who separates his or her own self from God, the objective world, and other beings.

Patañjali. (fourth-century B.C.E.) Philosopher and author of the *Yoga Sūtras*.

pati. A being who takes pure Consciousness as his or her own Self, and who does not differentiate the objective world from his own divine subjective Self.

prakāśa. The light of Consciousness; one of the two aspects of the ultimate reality, Paramaśiva; the principle of self-revelation that illumines everything. See also *vimarśa*.

prakṛti. Material energy; material creation; an independent and eternal, but inanimate, material substratum according to Sāṃkhya philosophy. But in Kashmir Śaivism, *prakṛti* is the thirteenth *tattva* emerging out of Paramaśiva.

prakṛti-tattva. Principle of the undiversified material substratum of the universe, emerging out of Paramaśiva, according to Kashmir Śaivism; also called *pradhāna-tattva*.

pralaya. Universal destruction and reabsorption into Paramaśiva, occurring at the end of a *kalpa* of time, or four thousand three hundred and twenty million years. All beings remain in a dormant condition during the *pralaya*.

pralayākalas. Beings residing at the level of the twelfth and thirteenth *tattvas,* in the subtle *māyā* plane of existence. They possess no physical or mental body, only the subtle body, and their state of awareness is reduced to simple, finite 'I-ness,' as in the *pralaya*.

pramāṇa. A means of correct knowledge or proof.

pramātṛ/pramātā. The knowing subject (as distinguished from the known object, *prameya*); the supreme *pramātṛ* is Paramaśiva, the divine conscious Lord, for whom the entire universe is His own subjective Self.

prameya. The known object (as distinguished from the knower-subject, *pramātṛ*).

pramiti. An accurate conception. See also *pramātṛ* and *prameya*.

prāṇa. The vital life-force of both the individual body and the entire universe; one of five vital forces in the body, often connected with the assimilative functions and inhalation of the breath.

pratyabhijñā. Recognition; especially the higher experiential recognition of one's divine Self and unity with Paramaśiva.

puruṣa. The eternal soul, or Self, according to the Sāṃkhya Yoga system; in Kashmir Śaivism, a *māyā*-influenced state of the soul, and thus limited.

puruṣa-tattva. The twelfth *tattva* of the universal creation in Kashmir Śaivism; the first *tattva* in the Sāṃkhya system.

pūrva-pakṣa. The opponent's view.

rajas. See *guṇas.*

Rudra. In the *Īśvara-pratyabhijñā-kārikā,* one of the three supergods living on the plane of *māyā,* along with Brahmā and Viṣṇu. In other contexts, Rudra can be another name for Śiva or Paramaśiva. Also, in Kashmir Śaivism there are ruling masters of different categories in the hierarchy of divine administrators who are known as Rudras.

Śabda-brahman. God in the form of sound; the vibratory form of self-aware Consciousness.

sābhilāpa. Another word for *savikalpa.*

sadāśiva-tattva. The third *tattva* of universal creation, in the plane of pure *vidyā.*

sādhana. Spiritual practice.

sad-vidyā or *śuddha-vidyā-tattva.* The fifth *tattva* of universal creation.

sahasrāra. The seventh spiritual centre in the crown of the head, often depicted in art as a thousand-petalled lotus.

Śaiva. Of or relating to Śiva; one who worships Śiva or Paramaśiva as supreme Lord; also *Śaivite.*

sa-kramatvam. Sequentiality.

śākta-upāya. In Kashmir Śaivism, a means to Self-realisation whereby the seeker uses his mind in support of the unitive state; also known as *jñāna-upāya* or *bhedābhedopāya*. See also *āṇava-upāya* and *śāmbhava upāya*.

Śakti. General term for the divine power(s) of God; a goddess; wife of Śiva; a particular divine power of a deity in the divine hierarchy.

śakti-tattva. The second *tattva* of world creation; also the initial stage or plane of being, as the throb of creation begins to emerge out of Paramaśiva.

Śaktism. A type of philosophy held by those who worship Śakti or a form of the Goddess in India.

samādhi. State of meditative union with the *śūnya* aspect of Consciousness; absorption in a thought-free state of mind, considered in Kashmir Śaivism a superior state of *suṣupti*. See also *nirvikalpa* and *savikalpa*.

samāveśa. Sudden emergence into the amazing experience of one's Śivahood.

śāmbhava upāya. In Kashmir Śaivism, a means to Self-realisation whereby the seeker uses his will to maintain constant awareness of his unity with Paramaśiva; also called *icchā upāya*.

śāmbhava-yoga. The regular practice of keeping one's mind thought-free, while being fully awake. A blissful state in which the mind becomes lost inside the spiritual lustre of pure Consciousness. The practice of blissful awareness of I-Consciousness alone, free from all objectivity; *śāmbhava-upāya*.

Śambhunātha. A teacher of the Ardha-tryambhaka school during the time of Abhinavagupta.

Sāṃkhya. One of the six traditional Indian schools of philosophy, founded by the sage Kapila (sixth century B.C.E.). Sāṃkhya enumerates twenty-five stages of world creation and holds a dualist philosophical position (spirit vs. matter).

saṃsargābhāva. Principle of non-existence through lack of contact (*x* does not contain *y*). See also *anyonyābhāva.*

saṅkalpa. Imagination; generally used in the sense of intention or determination.

śāstra. A treatise discussing, through logical reasoning, the principles and doctrines of a subject such as religion, philosophy, law, politics, administration, grammar, prosody, literary criticism, dramaturgy, and medical science; thus it differs from a work of literary art, or a *kāvya.*

sat-kārya-vāda. A theory of world creation based on a principle of realism, including the idea that the effect exists in the cause.

sattva. See *guṇas.*

Sautrāntika. An early Buddhist school which explored the notion that the effects of one's deeds are transmitted as a series of 'seeds' until they ripen, and which accepts the real existence of matter outside mind.

savikalpa. Consisting of thought; a type of *samādhi* with thought. See also *nirvikalpa.*

Siddha. A perfected being.

siddhis. Supernatural powers.

Śiva-dṛṣṭi. The first philosophical treatise on Kashmir Śaivism, by Somānanda; considered one of the basic texts of Kashmir Śaivism.

śiva-tattva. The first *tattva* of universal creation in Kashmir Śaivism; the highest plane of existence.

Śiva-stotrāvalī. A collection of ecstatic devotional poems to Śiva by Utpaladeva.

Śiva Sūtras. A fundamental, seventy-seven-*sūtra* scripture of Kashmir Śaivism; said to have been revealed to the ninth-century sage Vasugupta.

smṛti. Remembered traditions, including the law books and books on the traditions and doctrines of Brahmanic Hinduism.

smṛti-śakti. The power of memory.

Somānanda. (c. 850-900 C.E.) An important Kashmiri Śaiva philosopher; author of the *Śiva-dṛṣṭi*.

spanda. The pulsating, vibratory activity of Divine Consciousness, leading to world manifestation.

sphurattā. The subtle throbbing of divine Consciousness.

stotra. A devotional hymn of praise.

sukha. Sweetness; happiness.

śūnya. A void or vacuum-like state, associated in Kashmir Śaivism with the causal, or deep-sleep, state of awareness. Also, the Buddhist concept of emptiness, Buddha nature, cosmic void, according to Śaiva traditions.

suṣupti. The state of deep, dreamless sleep, associated with the causal body and a vacuum-like state of awareness.

sūtras. Short and comprehensive aphorisms on the principles of a subject of study.

sva-lakṣaṇa. The basic character of an individual object, not related to anything.

sva-lakṣanābhāsam. Knowledge in which only the thing in itself becomes evident, without any name or form.

svapna. The state of dreaming sleep; associated with the subtle body and an active mentality.

svātantrya. The Lord's absolute independence, or supreme 'Self dependence'.

tamas. See *guṇas.*

Tantrāloka. A lengthy and outstanding work on Kashmiri Śaiva philosophy and practice by the philosopher Abhinavagupta (c. 993-1015 C.E.).

Tattva-saṃgrahādhikāra. Book IV of the *Īśvara-pratyabhijñā-kārikā*; mostly a summary of Books I-III, but containing some additional principles.

tattva. A category, class, or principle of world creation. There are thirty-six *tattvas* in Kashmir Śaivism, but only twenty-five in Sāṃkhya philosophy. See also *śakti-tattva,* etc.

Trika. Another name for Kashmir Śaivism, so called because it deals with the three-fold (*tri*) principles: God, His divine power, and His phenomena, including souls. This system is monistic since the three principles—and all creation—emerge from the being of God.

turīya or *turya.* The fourth, self-revelatory state of awareness; beyond waking, dream, and deep sleep.

turyatīta. A transcendental state of awareness which is sometimes said to surpass *turīya* or *turya.*

udāna. One of the five vital airs; in the *Īśvara-pratyabhijñā-kārikā* it is presented as a highly charged spiritual energy moving upwards through the subtle central spinal channel and leading to the *sahasrāra* centre in the crown of the head. Like a burning fire, it devours all conceptual ideas, and one feels it as a wonderful sensation moving upwards through the spinal cord, resembling descriptions of *kuṇḍalinī* in some other systems.

unmeṣa. The unfolding of the universe of form. See also *nimeṣa.*

Utpaladeva. (ninth century C.E.) Kashmiri Śaiva philosopher and devotional poet; author of the *Īśvara-pratyabhijña-kārikā.*

Varāhagupta. An ancestor of Abhinavagupta.

vāsanās. Impressions of past experiences that constitute one's karma.

Vedas. The four most ancient Hindu sacred scriptures, considered authoritative and divinely revealed. The *Ṛg-veda, Sāma-veda, Yajur-veda*, and *Atharva-veda saṃhitās.*

vidyā. Knowledge, limited or unlimited; the second plane or stage of creation; the fifth *tattva* or principle of creation, called *sad-vidyā* or *śuddha-vidyā.*

vidyā-kañcuka. The limitations of divine knowledge experienced by beings under the influence of *māyā.*

vidyeśvaras. Beings on the *vidyā* plane of existence; also called *mantras.*

vijñāna. Mental consciousness; higher conscious awareness.

Vijñānavāda Buddhism. A philosophical school of 'conscious mental awareness' or 'mind only', which first developed in Buddhism around 300 C.E. Its adherents were in Kashmir during the time of Utpaladeva's writing of the *Īśvara-pratyabhijñā-kārikā,* and many of his scriptural arguments are clearly written as refutations of the Vijñānavāda claim of the non-existence of *Ātman,* the conscious soul, or Self.

vikalpa. A definite idea, a thought.

Vimalakalā. The mother of Abhinavagupta.

vimarśa. The aspect of divine Consciousness by which the phenomenon becomes evident; the Self-awareness of Paramaśiva, full of knowledge and action, which brings about the world process. See also *prakāśa.*

Viṣṇu. One of the three supergods at the level of *māyā,* according to the *Īśvara-pratyabhijñā-kārikā,* along with Rudra and Brahmā; in general, the preserver/sustainer god of Hinduism.

Vivṛti. A philosophical commentary written in detail.

Vṛtti. A simple philosophical paraphrase.

Vyākaraṇa. The science of grammar.

vyāna. One of the five vital airs; in the *Īśvara-pratyabhijñā-kārikā,* the most pure and all-pervading type of the life-force. Experiencing it, one tastes the state of eternal and blissful I-Consciousness, or Paramaśiva. Only *akala* beings, or those in the highest spiritual state, experience *vyāna* in its fullness.

vyāvahārika-satya. Worldly truth; lesser truth applicable only to this world of forms and causation.

BIBLIOGRAPHY

Primary Texts

Ajaḍa-pramātṛ-siddhi of Utpaladeva, included in his *Siddhitrayī.* M. S. Kaul, ed. Srinagar: KSTS no. XXXIV, 1921.

Amṛtānubhāva: The Nectar of Divine Experience of Jñāneśvara. In English translation. Madhava ed., and trans. Pune: Ajay Prakashan, 1981.

Ānubhāva-nivedana ascribed to Abhinavagupta. In *Abhinavagupta: An Historical and Philosophical Study.* K. C. Pandey, 2nd ed. Varanasi: Chowkhamba Sanskrit Series, 1963.

Anuttara-prakāśa-pañcāśikā of Ādyanātha. J. R. Shastri, ed. Srinagar: KSTS no. XIII, 1918.

Anuttarāṣṭikā of Abhinavagupta. In *Abhinavagupta: An Historical and Philosophical Study,* K. C. Pandey, 2nd ed. Varanasi: Chowkhamba Sanskrit Series, 1963.

Ātmavilāsa of Amṛtāvāgbhava with his own commentary *Sundarı.* B. N. Pandit, ed. Jammu: Shree Peeth Shodha Sansthana, 1981.

Bhairavastotra of Abhinavagupta. In *Abhinavagupta: An Historical and Philosophical Study.* K. C. Pandey, 2nd ed. Varanasi: Chowkhamba Sanskrit Series, 1963.

Bhāskarī. 3 vols. Sarasvati Bhavana Texts, nos. 70 (1938), 83 (1950), and 84 (1954). The first two volumes consist of the commentary of Bhāskarakaṇṭha on the IPV of Abhinavagupta. The third volume is an English translation of the IPV by K. C. Pandey.

Cidvilāsa of Amṛtānanda. Appended to *Nityāṣodaśikārṇava,* Vārāṇaseya Sanskrit University, 1968.

Gaṇakārikā by Bhāsarvajña. C. D. Dalal, ed. Baroda: Gaekwad's Oriental Series, no. 15. 1920.

Gauḍapādīyakārikā of Gauḍapāda in *Māṇḍūkyopaniṣad.* Gorakhpur: Gita Press, 1936-37.

Īśvara-pratyabhijñā-vṛtti of Utpaladeva *(Īśvara-pratyabhijñā-kārikā* of Utpaladeva with author's own *vṛtti).* M. S. Kaul, ed. Srinagar: KSTS no. XXXIV, 1921.

Īśvara-pratyabhijñā-vimarśinī of Abhinavagupta. 2 vols. M. R. Shastri and M. S. Kaul, eds. Srinagar: KSTS nos. XXII, 1918 and XXXIII, 1921.

Īśvara-pratyabhijñā-vivṛti-vimarśinī of Abhinavagupta. 3 vols. M. S. Kaul, ed. Srinagar: KSTS no. LX, 1938; no. LXII, 1941, no. LXV, 1943. Commentary on Utpaladeva's own *vivṛti* (now lost) on his *Īśvara-pratyabhijñā-kārikā.*

Īśvara-siddhi of Utpaladeva. Included in his *Siddhitrayī,* M. S. Kaul, ed. Srinagar: KSTS no. XXXIV, 1921.

Kalikāstotram of Śivānandanātha. Jammu: Īśvara Ashram Trust.

Kāmakalāvilāsa of Puṇyānandanātha. M. R. Shastri, ed. Srinagar: KSTS no. XII, 1918.

Kāmakalāvilāsa of Puṇyānandanātha with commentary by Naṭānandanātha. Arthur Avalon, ed. and trans. Madras: Ganesh & Co., 1961.

Kramastotra of Siddhanātha. Jammu: Īśvara Ashram Trust.

Kramastotra of Abhinavagupta. In *Abhinavagupta: An Historical and Philosophical Study,* K. C. Pandey, 2nd ed. Varanasi: Chowkhamba Sanskrit Series, 1963.

Lalitā-stava-ratnam of Sage Durvāsas. Jammu: Ranvīr Vidyā-Peeṭh, 1987.

Lalitā-stava-ratnam-ṭīkā of B. N. Pandit. Jammu: Ranvīr Vidyā-Peeṭh.

Mahārtha-mañjarī of Maheśvarānanda with his Parimala. V. V. Dvivedi, ed. Varanasi: Yogatantra-Ratnamālā vol. 5.

Madhyānta-vibhāga-sūtra of Maitreya including the *bhāṣya* of Vasubandhu. Th. Stcherbatsky, ed. and transl. Delhi: Sri Satguru Publications, 1992 (reprint).

Mahāyāna-vimśaka of Nāgārjuna. V. Bhattachary, ed. and trans. Calcutta: Viśvabhāratī Bookshop, 1931.

Mātṛkā-cakra-viveka of Svatantrānandanātha. Datiyā: Pitāmbara Saṃskṛt Pariṣad, 1977.

Pancastavi of Dharmācārya. Jankinath Kaul, ed. and trans. Srinagar: Sri Ramakrishna Ashrama, 1996.

Paramārthasāra of Ādiṣesa *(The Essence of Supreme Truth)*. Henry Danielson, ed. and trans. Leiden: Brill, 1980.

Paramārthasāra of Abhinavagupta with *vivṛti* by Yogarāja. J. C. Chatterji, ed. Srinagar: KSTS no. VII, 1916.

Paraśambhu-mahimna-stava of Sage Durvāsas. Published in Grantha script, *Parameśvara-stotra-kadamba*. Chittoor: Vidyavinoda Press, 1886.

Parātriṁśikā with *vivaraṇa* of Abhinavagupta. Srinagar: KSTS no. XVIII, 1918.

Pāśupatasūtra with Kauṇḍinya's commentary. R. Ananthakrishna Shastri, ed. Trivandrum Sanskrit Series, no. 143. Trivandrum: Travancore University Publication, 1940.

Sambandha-siddhi of Utpaladeva. Included in his *Siddhitrayī.* M. S. Kaul, ed. Srinagar: KSTS no. XXXIV, 1921.

Saundarya-laharī of Śankarācārya. W. Norman Brown, ed. and trans. Cambridge, Mass.: Harvard Oriental Series, no. 43, 1958.

Siddhitrayī of Utpaladeva. M. S. Kaul, ed. Srinagar: KSTS no. XXXIV, 1921.

Subhagodaya-stuti of Gauṛapāda. Prithvi K. Agrawala and Rama Adhar Pathak, eds. Varanasi: Prithivi Prakashan, 1984.

Svātantrya-darpana (or *The Mirror of Self-Supremacy*) of B. N. Pandit. Sanskrit text with English edition. New Delhi: Munshiram Manoharlal, 1993.

Tantrāloka of Abhinavagupta with *Tantrāloka-viveka* of Jayaratha. 12 vols. Vol. I edited by M. R. Shastri and vols. II-XII edited by M. S. Kaul. Srinagar: KSTS nos. XXIII (1918), XXVIII (1921), XXX (1921), XXXVI (1922), XXXV (1922), XXIX (1921), XLI (1924), XLVII (1926), LIX (1938), LII (1933), LVII (1936), LVIII (1938).

Tantrasāra of Abhinavagupta. M. R. Shastri, ed. Srinagar: KSTS no. XVII, 1918.

Tantra-vaṭa-dhānikā of Abhinavagupta. M. R. Shastri, ed. Srinagar: KSTS no. XXIV, 1918.

Tattva-garbha-stotra of Bhaṭṭa Pradyumna. Quoted in *Spanda-vivṛti* and *Spanda pradīpikā* included in *The Stanzas on Vibration.* M. Dyczkowski, ed. and trans. Albany: SUNY Press, 1992.

Tripurā-mahimna-stotra of Sage Durvāsas. Kavyamāla Gucchakas Series no. XI. Bombay: Nirnaya Sagar Press, 1895.

Vimśatika-śāstram of Amṛta-vāgbhava. Bharatpur: Swādhyāya-sadan.

Vimśatika-śāstram-vimarśinī of B. N. Pandit. Bharatpur: Swādhyāya-sadan.

Virūpākṣa-pañcāsikā of Virūpākṣanātha. Ganapati Shastri, ed. Trivandrum Sanskrit Series, no. IX, 1910.

Secondary Texts and References

Anuradha, R. P., *Introduction to Lamaism, the Mystical Buddhism of Tibet*. Hoshiarpur: Vishveshvaranand Vedic Research Institute, 1975.

Briggs, George W., *Gorakhnāth and the Kānphaṭā Yogīs*. Delhi: Motilal Banarsidass, 1938.

Dasgupta, S. N., *A History of Indian Philosophy*, vol. 5. Delhi: Motilal Banarsidass, 1962.

Helmut Hoffmann/translated by Edward Fitzgerald, *Religions of Tibet*. Westport, Conn.: Greenwood Press, 1979.

Nandimath, S. C., *A Handbook of Vīraśaivism*. Dharwar: E. E. Association, 1942.

Pandit, B. N., *Aspects of Kashmir Śaivism*. Srinagar: Utpala Publishers, 1977.

Pandit, B. N., *History of Kashmir Śaivism*. Srinagar: Utpala Publishers, 1989.

Pandit, B. N., *Specific Principles of Kashmir Śaivism*. New Delhi: Munshiram Manoharlal, 1997.

Pillai, S., *Collected Lectures on Śaiva-siddhānta*. Tamilnadu: Annamalai Nagar, 1965.

INDEX

ābhāsa, 79
ābhāsa-vāda, 51, 59, 69, 215
abhilāpa, 14
Abhinava-bhāratī, xxxv
Abhinavagupta, xxv, xxix, xxx, xxxiii, xxxiii-xxxvii, xxxviii, xlvii, lii, liii, 6, 36, 105, 136
  date of, xxiii, xxxiii
  family and ancestors of, xxx, xxxiii
  works of.
    see Abhinava-bhāratī;
      Anuttarāṣṭikā;
      Bodha-pañcadaśikā;
      Dhvanyāloka-locana;
      Īśvara-pratyabhijñā-vimarśinī;
      Īśvara-pratyabhijñā-vivṛti-vimarśinī;
      Mālinī-vijaya-vārtika;
      Paramārthasāra;
      Parātrīśikā-vivaraṇa;
      Śiva-dṛṣṭy-ālocana;
      Tantrāloka;
      Tantrasāra
action, 115, 119, 139, 146-147, 155
  see also kriyā
  power of 21-22, 113, 149, 176. *see also kriyā-śākti*
adhyavasāya, 67
Āgamas, xvii-xviii, xxv, xxvii-xxviii, lii, lv, 160, 164, 173
agents of action, 119, 146-147.
  see also kārakās
aiśvarya, xliii, 62
Ajaḍa-pramatṛ-siddhi. see Siddhitrayī
akalas, 178, 188
Anandavardhana, xxxv, xxxvi
āṇava-mala, lv, lvi, 173-176, 179
āṇava-upāya, 202
aṇu, 168
anubhava.
  see nirvikalpānubhava;
    savikalpānubhava
Anuttarāṣṭikā, xxxv
anumāna, xi, 216
anyonyābhāva, 86-89, 212
apana, lvii, 186
apoha, xliv
apohana, 71, 74
apohana-śakti, 35-36, 71
Ardha-tryambaka, xxxiv, xxxv
asatya, 116
āśrayā-siddhi.
  see logic, defective arguments in
atheism, xxiii, xxxi, 8, 36, 38
Ātman, xxiv, xxxviii, xli-lii, 8, 165
  arguments against existence of.
    see under Vijñānavāda;
      Sautrāntika
  arguments for in IPK
    externality of reality an illusion, 94-99
    freedom of the knower, 38
    knowing inseparable from knower, 46
    matter not different from perception of it, 58
    memory, xl-xli, 16-17, 27-33, 37-47, 78, 85
    orderliness of world, 31-36
    powers of knowing and doing xxxix, 113
    relation between objects, 82-84

Ātman
arguments for in IPK *(cont'd.)*
relation between subjects and objects, xlviii, 112-113
relation of cause and effect, xlv, 84-85
refutation of incorrect cognitions, 85-86
unity of action, xlvii
unity of experience, 40
unity of external reality, xlvi
unity of knowledge, xlvi
unity of psychic activities, 46-47, 85, 100
unity of subject and object, 47
as I-Consciousness, 41-42
avidyā, li, 56, 135, 137, 150
Bhagavad-gītā, 120, 152
Bhairava, xxxvii
bhakti, xxxii
Bhartṛhari, xxix, 62
Bhaṭṭa Kallaṭa, xxviii, xxxvi
works of. *see Spanda-kārikā*
Bhaṭṭa Pradyumna, xxix
bhedābheda. see unity in diversity
bhoga, 193
Bodha-pañcadaśikā, xxxv
Brahmā, lv, 6, 101, 141, 165, 171-172, 200
Brahman, 150
Brahma-sūtra, xxiii
buddhi, 21, 72, 74, 112, 192
Buddhism, xxiii, xxv, xxxvi, xl, xli, 8, 106, 127, 183
logicians of.
see Dharmakīrti;
Dharmottara
schools and views of.
see Sautrāntika;
Śūnyavāda;
Vijñānavāda
Cāṇakya, xxxiii
cakra, 187, 188
citi, xliii, 66. *see also* Consciousness
citta, 15, 54
Consciousness
divine powers of, xliii, 33-36, 47, 56, 68. *see also apohana-śakti;*
jñāna-śakti;
kriyā-śakti;
smṛti-śakti
names for, xliii, 59, 65-66
as mirror, 47, 52
as pulsation, 63. *see also spanda*
as the Self, 7-9
self-awareness of, xliii, 60, 62, 100-101. *see also vimarśa*
self shining of, 49-51.
see also prakāśa
states of.
see dreamless sleep state;
see dream state;
see waking state
as Subject, 81
creation, xlvi, xlvii, li-liv, 32, 33, 40, 51, 56, 59, 60, 62, 65, 66, 79, 80, 101, 109, 110, 112, 132, 135, 136, 137, 138-143, 150-152, 156-157, 162, 165, 169, 172, 174, 176, 183, 184, 191, 192, 195, 197-200, 205-206, 215
deha, 75, 112
delusion, xxxix, xlix, 9, 32, 120, 133, 158, 162, 172-173, 182.
see also māyā;
moha
deśa-krama, 112
Dharmakīrti, xxiii, xxix
works of. *see Pramāṇa-vārtika*
dharmin. see dharmya-siddhi
Dharmottara, xxiii
dharmya-siddhi, 91
Dhvanyāloka-locana, xxxv
diversity, xlvii, xlix, liv, lv, lvi, 35, 54, 65, 66, 69, 76, 96, 109, 115-120, 129, 131, 149, 158, 162, 163, 166, 175, 178, 179, 194
diversity in unity, liv.
see also unity in diversity

divine powers, xliii, 5, 6, 9, 13, 34-36, 38, 59, 61, 64, 68, 71, 78, 80, 92, 100, 107, 133, 135, 136, 137, 149, 151, 152, 156, 165, 192, 194, 199, 204, 205.
see also causation, power of;
consciousness, divine powers of;
delusion, power of;
doing, power of;
knowing, power of;
potency;
restriction, power of;
sentience, power of;
time sequence, power of;
will, power of
doing, power of, xxxix, 7, 10-11, 79-80, *see also kriyā-śakti*
dream state, 9, 166, 168, 182-186
dreamless sleep state, lvi, 9, 111, 166, 182, 186, 187
duality, 71, 158
emanation, theory of. *see ābhāsa-vāda*
five divine activities, 60, 101, 132, 151-152, 156
God, xxxi, xxxvii, xlvii, li, lii, liii, lx, 5, 6, 7, 8, 10, 13, 16, 34, 35, 36, 61, 62, 64, 65, 77, 79, 80, 95, 100-101, 132, 133, 137, 140-141, 152, 157, 165, 191, 192, 193, 200, 201, 207
as each subject, xlv, 81
Buddhist views on, 8
Nyāya-Vaiśeṣika views on, 8
Sāṃkhya views on, 8
Godhead, lx, 7, 133, 135, 152, 165, 201-202
gods. *see* Brahmā;
Indra;
Īśvara;
Rudra;
Sadāśiva;
Varuṇa;
Viṣṇu;
Yama
guṇas, lviii, 148, 193-196.
see also rajo-guṇa;
sattva-guṇa;
tamo-guṇa
icchā-śakti, li. *see also* will, power of
I-Consciousness, xxxix, xlii, xlvii, xlviii, liii, lx, 8, 41, 50, 59, 64-66, 75, 85, 90, 92, 95, 97-100, 112, 127, 132-133, 136-137, 150, 152, 156, 161-163, 166-169, 174, 183, 186-188, 191-192, 201, 213
ignorance, li, lix, 23, 56, 91, 95, 133, 135, 150, 164, 176. *see also avidyā*
imagination, lx, 23-26, 30, 31, 33, 41, 46, 47, 66, 76, 79-80, 83-84, 99, 110, 116, 138, 144, 198, 199
inference, xi, xlii, xlv, 26, 53, 56-58, 84, 90, 127, 144.
see also anumāna
IPK. *see Īśvara-pratyabhijñā-kārikā*
IPV. *see Īśvara-pratyabhijñā-vimarśinī*
IPVV. *see Īśvara-pratyabhijñā-vivṛti-vimarśinī*
Īśavasya-upaniṣad, 120
Īśvara, xi, 6, 64, 66, 158, 159, 203
īśvara-bhaṭṭāraka, 157-158
Īśvara-pratyabhijñā-kārikā
aim of, xxiii, liii, 133
and all-powerful nature of consciousness, 93 101
arguments for *Ātman.*
see under Ātman, arguments for
author of, xxiii
and Buddhism, xi, xxv.
see also Sautrāntika;
Śūnyavāda, refutation of views of in IPK;
Vijñānavāda, refutation of views of in IPK;
and causation, 135-152
commentaries on, xxxii, 6.
see also Īśvara-pratyabhijñā-kārikā-vṛtti;
Īśvara-pratyabhijñā-vimarśinī;

Īśvara-pratyabhijñā-kārikā
commentaries on.
see also (cont'd)
Īśvara-pratyabhijñā-vivṛti-vimarśinī
compared to *Brahma-sūtra,* xxiii
compared to *Śiva-dṛṣṭi,* xxiv
date of composition, xxiii
and discrimination, power of, 71-80
epistemology of, 121-133
and God as the basis of all sentient activities, 81-92
historicial context of, xxiii-xxvi
and *jñāna,* xxvi, 5-101
and *kriyā,* xxvi, 105-152
and memory, power of, 37-47
summary of *Āgamādhikara,* lii-lviii
summary of *Jnānādhikāra,* xxxviii-xlvii
summary of *Kriyādhikāra,* xlvii-lii
summary of *Tattva-saṃgrahādhikāra,* lviii-lxi
and Trika, xxiv
Īśvara-pratyabhijñā-kārikā-vṛtti, xxxviii
Īśvara-pratyabhijñā-vimarśinī, xxxiv, xxxviii, xlvii, lii, 36
Īśvara-pratyabhijñā-vivṛti-vimarśinī xxv, xxx, xxxii, xxxiv, xxxviii, 208
Īśvara-siddhi. see Siddhitrayī
īśvara-tattva, liv, 157-158, 160, 163, 197
jāgrat, lvi, 182
jīva, 65, 168, 193
jīvan-mukti, 181, 204
jñāna, 66-67, 156
jñāna-śakti, xlii, 35-36, 50, 106
kalā, 168, 178, 180
kāla, 168
Kaḷḷaṭa. *see* Bhaṭṭa Kaḷḷaṭa
kañcukas, liv, 160, 165, 167, 168, 180.
see also *kalā;*
kāla;
niyati;
rāga;
vidyā
kārakās, 119
kārma-mala, lv, lvi, 174-175, 180
Kashmir Śaivism, xxiii-xxix, xxxii, xxxiv-xxxvi, xlii-liii.
see also Pratyabhijñā
and action, 139
and categories of beings, lii, liv-lvi, 171-188.
see also Brahmā;
mantra being;
mantra-maheśvara;
mantreśvara;
pati;
paśu;
pralayākala;
Rudra;
vidyeśvara;
vijñānākala;
Viṣṇu
cosmogony of, xliii, xliv-xlvi, li, 49, 61, 64, 136
cosmology of, lii-lv, lviii
and delusion, xlviii-xlix
epistemology of, xlix, 121-133
fundamental principal of, 47
masters of, xxiii.
see Abhinavagupta;
Bhaṭṭa Kallaṭa;
Somānanda;
Utpaladeva;
Vasugupta
metaphysics of, xxxviii
ontology of, xxviii, 151
opposing views.
see atheism,
Buddhism,
Mīmāmsā,
Nyāya-Vaiśeṣika,
Vyākaraṇa,
Vedānta
works of.
see Īśvara-pratyabhijñā-kārikā;
Īśvara-pratyabhijñā-vivṛti-vimarśinī;
Īśvara-pratyabhijñā-vimarśinī;
Śiva-dṛṣṭi;
Śiva Sūtra;
Spanda-kārikā

Kaula, xxxv
knowing, power of, 7, 10-11, 79-80, 101. *see also jñāna-śakti*
knowledge, xxviii, xliv, xlix, liv, 19, 20, 30, 87, 129, 155-156, 172, 181, 184, 203. *see also jñāna*
  awakened, 164
  conceptual, 14, 30, 32-33, 46, 47, 68
  correct, l, 31, 85-87, 121, 122, 132. *see also pramiti*
  correct means of, xlix-li, 121, 132. *see also pramāṇa*
  determinative, 15-16. *see also savikalpa*
  experiential, xxxix, xli, 27-29, 42, 44, 45, 46, 78
  ideational, 32, 73
  imperfect, liv
  incorrect, 30, 31, 32, 85, 86, 90, 161
  limitation of. *see vidyā-kañcuka*
  organs of, 170
  of a *pati,* 194. *see also jñāna-śakti*
  pure, liv, 68, 101, 120, 160-162. *see also śuddha-vidyā*
  relative, 120
  thought free, 14-16, 31. *see also nirvikalpa*
  verbal, 123. *see also śabda*
  of a *yogin,* 43-44, 201
krama, 108
Krama school, xii
kriyā, xxvi, xlvii-lii, 22-23, 101, 105-152, 195. *see also kriyā-śakti*
kriyā-śakti, xlvii, lii, 105, 149, 151, 152. *see also* doing, power of
Kumarila Bhaṭṭa, xlix
Locana on *Dhvanyāloka. see Dhvanyāloka-locana*
logic, 56, 58, 143
  defective arguments in, 52, 91-92
Mādhavācārya, xxiv
Mahābhāṣya of Pātañjali, xxxiv
mahāmāyā, 179
mahāsattā, xliii
Maheśvara, xlvii, 5-6, 66, 93, 101, 165
mala, lv-lvii, 173-180. *see also āṇava-mala; kārma-mala; māyīya-mala*
mālinī, xxxv
Mālinī-vijaya-vārtika, xxxv
Mālinī-vijayottara-tantra, xxvii, xxviii, xxxv
Mammaṭa, xxxvi
manas, 72
mantra being, lvi, 162, 179, 188
mantra-maheśvara, liv, lv, lvii, 157, 162-163, 187-188
mantreśvara, liv, lv, lvii, 157, 162, 187-188
Manu, 205
Mātṛkā-cakra-viveka, 155
māyā, xlvi, li, liii, lix, 9, 66-67, 68, 75, 77, 83, 95, 97, 100, 108, 135, 137, 150, 158, 160, 162, 163, 165-168, 172-173, 175-177, 179, 183, 194, 195
māyā plane, 158, 162, 168, 171
māyā-śakti, 66, 163-164, 165, 166, 195
māyā-tattva, liv, 112, 165, 166, 171, 197
māyīya-mala, lv, 174-175, 178
Mīmāṃsā, xxv, xxxiv, 121
mind, xliv, 7, 10, 13, 15, 74, 84, 92, 128, 205, 212. *see also manas; buddhi*
  Buddhist views on, xxxix-xl, 15-16, 18, 26, 32, 41, 52
  and external manifestation, xlvi, 15, 98-99, 140
  and I-Consciousness, 183, 188
  and ideation, 72, 140
  momentary states of, 15, 26, 33, 91, 100
  and objective entities, 128
  one of the organs of knowledge, 170
  and *prāṇa,* lvii, 183, 186
  Self as master of, xxxix, xlv,
  and transactional reality 116
moha. see delusion
mūla-prakṛti, xxxi, 109, 169, 183

Nāmaka-tantra, xxvii
name and form, xliv, 30, 40, 67-68, 72
Nāṭya-śāstra, xxxv
Netra-tantra, xxviii
nimeṣa, 159
nirvikalpa, 14-15, 31, 67, 117
nirvikalpa-anubhava, xlviii
niyati, 8, 168
Nyāya-Vaiśeṣika, xxv, xlviii, xlix, lvii, 8, 64, 86-89, 108, 115, 144, 183
organs of knowledge, 170
pakṣā-siddhi.
see logic, defective arguments in
Paramārthasāra, xxxv
Paramārthika-satya, 115
Paramaśiva, liii, lv, lvii, 59, 65, 132, 155, 156, 157, 203
Paramātman, 16, 65, 66
Pārameśvara, 157
Parātrīṃśikā. see Parātrīśikā
Parātrīśikā, xxxv
Parātrīśikā-vivaraṇa, xxxv
parāvāk, xliii, 62
paśu, lv, lviii, lix, lx, 160, 168, 172-173, 182
Pātañjali, xxxiv
pati, lv, lviii, lix, 172-173, 181, 194, 196
Philosophy of Self Recognition, xxiv. *see Pratyabhijñā*
planes of existence, 209.
see also śakti plane;
māyā plane;
vidyā plane
potency, divine, 33, 47, 56, 59, 60, 62, 77, 78, 148, 149, 172, 200
pradhāna, 169
pradhāna-tattva. see prakṛti-tattva
Pradyumna. *see* Bhaṭṭa Pradyumna
prakāśa, liii, 51-52, 53, 60, 71-75, 100, 156, 176
prakṛti, liii, liv, lv, lvi, 109, 135, 137, 148, 177, 194
prakṛti-tattva, 165, 169
pralaya, lvi, 178
pralayākala, lvi, 177-178
pralaya-kevalin, 178,
pramā, 122-123, 125. *see also pramiti*
pramāṇa, xlix-l, 35, 121-123, 126-128
Pramāṇa-vārtika, xxix
pramātā, 101
pramātṛ, 35, 100, 147.
see also pramātā
prameya, 35
pramiti, l, 122
prāṇa, lvii, 75, 112, 166, 167, 183, 185, 186
prāṇas, lvii.
see also apāna;
prāṇa;
samāna;
udāna;
vyāna
prāṇa-suṣupti, 183
pratyabhijñā, lx, 6, 133
Pratyabhijñā-darśanam, xxiv
puruṣa, liii, liv, 21, 165, 167, 177, 193, 195
puruṣa-tattva, 165, 167, 168, 169
rāga, 168
rajas, lix
rajo-guṇa, lix, 193, 194, 196
realism, xlii, xliv, xlvi, 49, 58, 96, 115, 138-139.
see also sat-kārya-vāda
recognition. *see pratyabhijñā*
relationship, 82-83, 115, 118
Ṛg Veda, 152
Rudra, lv, 6, 171, 172
Śābara-bhāṣya, xxxiv
śabda, 216
sābhilāpa. see savikalpa
Śabda-brahman, xxix
sādākhya-tattva, 157.
see also sadāśiva-tattva
Sadāśiva, 6, 158, 159
sadāśiva-tattva, liv, lv, 65, 157-163, 171, 197
sad-vidyā, liv, 158-162
sad-vidyā-tattva, liv, 158-160, 162, 165
Śaiva Āgama. see Āgama

Śaiva-siddhānta, liii
Śaivism, xxvii, xxviii, xxix, xxxv, xxxvi, lv, lvii, 8, 28, 31, 33, 44, 47, 52, 54, 100, 117, 120, 127, 135, 150, 155, 161, 163, 175, 183, 188, 206, 213.
  schools of.
    see Ardha-tryambakā;
      Kaula;
      Pratyabhijñā;
      Śaiva-siddhānta;
      Trika;
      Tryambaka;
      Vira-śaivism
śākta-upāya, 201-202
Śakti-bhaṭṭāraka, 158
śakti plane, 158, 162, 171
Śaktis, 195
Śaktism, xxix
śakti-tattva, liii, 156-157
samāna, lvii, 187. *see also prāṇas*
samāveśa, lvi, lviii, lx, 180-181, 205-206
Sambandha-siddhi. see Siddhitrayī
śambhava-upāya, 200, 202
Śambhunātha, xxxiv, xxxv
Sāṃkhya, xxv, xxxi, liii, liv-lv, lviii, 8, 20-21, 147-148, 169, 177, 183, 194
saṃsargābhāva, 88-89
saṃkara, 51-52
saṅkalpa, 66-67
Śaṅkara-bhāṣya, xxxiv
Śaṅkaracarya, xxiii
Sāṅkhya. *see* Sāṃkhya
sat-kārya-vāda, 59, 138
sattva-guṇa, lix, 21, 193, 194, 196
Sautrāntika, xlii
  refutation of views of in IPK, 55
  views of, 52-53
savikalpa, 15
savikalpa-anubhava, xlviii
Self-recognition, xxiv, xxxix, liv, lx, lxi, 6, 9-10, 76, 133, 207.
  see also pratyabhijñā
sheaths of limitation. *see kañcukas*
Siddha (enlightened being), xxiii, 155, 187, 205
Siddhanātha. *see* Śambhunathā
siddhi, 206
Siddhitrayī, xxxi-xxxii, xxxiv, 111
Śiva, xxxviii, lv, lx-lxi, 47, 86, 126, 164, 165, 171, 194, 203, 206, 207
Śiva-bhaṭṭāraka, 66, 158
Śiva-dṛṣṭi, 205-206, 208
  Abhinavaguptas lost commentary on.
    see Śiva-dṛṣṭy-ālocana
  and IPK, xxxii
  date of composition, xxiv
  description of, xxix
  Śiva-dṛṣṭy-ālocana, xxix
śiva-liṅga, 39, 126
Śiva-stotrāvalī, xxxii, lx, 208
Śiva Sūtra, xxviii, xxxiii, 61
śiva-tattva, liii, 155, 156, 158
smṛti-śakti, 35. *see also* memory
Somānanda, xxiv, xxviii-xxix, xxx, xxxiv, 205
  date of, xxiii
  lineage of, xxviii, xxx
  works of. *see Śiva-dṛṣṭi*
spanda, xliii, 63
Spanda-kārikā, xxviii
Spanda-tattva-vivikti, xxviii
speech, Supreme. *see* parāvāk
sphurattā, xliii
Śrīkaṇṭhanātha, 183
śuddha-vidyā, liv, 159-161
śuddha-vidyā-tattva, liv, 162, 171
śūnya, liv, 75, 112, 150, 152, 166, 167, 178, 180, 182, 185
Śūnyavāda, 183
suṣupti, lvi, 166, 182-183
Svacchanda-tantra, xxviii
sva-lakṣaṇa, 14, 15, 127
sva-lakṣaṇābhāsam, 14
svapna, lvi, 182, 188
svātantrya, xliii
Svatantrānandanātha, 155
tamo-guṇa, 194, 196

Tantra, xxvii.
see also Mālini-vijayottara-tantra;
Nāmaka-tantra;
Netra-tantra;
Tantrāloka
Tantrāloka, xxx, xxxiv-xxxv, xxxvii, liii, 136,
Jayaratha's commentary on.
see Tantrāloka-viveka
Tantrāloka-viveka, xxvii
Tantrasāra, xxxv
tattvas, liii-liv, 65, 112, 148-149, 155-170, 183, 195.
see also māyā-tattva;
sadāśiva-tattva;
sad-vidya-tattva;
śakti-tattva;
śiva-tattva;
śuddha-vidyā-tattva
three Siddhis. *see Siddhitrayī*
Ṭikā. see Vivṛti on *Īśvara-pratyabhijnā*
Trika, lvi, xxiv, xxvii, xxxiv, xxxv, xlviii, lii, 76, 78, 97, 135, 188, 200-201, 206
Tryambaka, xxix, xxxiv, 204
turīya, lvii, 151, 152, 181, 185, 188.
see also turyā
turyā, lvii, 181-182, 187-188
turyātīta, 151, 152, 181-182
udāna, lvii, lviii, 187
unity, xlvi, xlviii, l, lxii, 40, 41, 46, 76, 81-113, 151, 158, 160, 162, 186
unity in diversity, xlviii, liv, 115-134, 149, 158, 160-162.
see also bhedābheda
unmeṣa, 159
upādhi, 152
Upaniṣads, 120, 150
Utpaladeva, xxiii, xxvi, xxix-xxxiii, xxxiv, xxxv, xxxix, xl, xli, xlix, li, lviii, lx-lxi, 207-208
Utpaladeva *(cont'd)*
works of.
see Īśvara-pratyabhijñā-kārikā;
Siddhitrayī;
Śiva-stotrāvalī;
Vivṛti on Īśvara-pratyabhijnā by Utpaladeva;
Vṛtti on Īśvara-pratyabhijñā;
Vṛtti on *Śiva-dṛṣṭi*
Vāmaka-tantra, xxvii
Vasugupta, xxviii, xxxiii,
works of. *see Śiva Sūtra*
Vedānta, xxiii, 8, 119, 120, 150, 166, 176. *see also* Śankarācārya
differences with Kashmir Śaivism, li
liberated beings of, lv
works of.
see Brahma-sutrā;
Śaṅkara-bhāṣya
Vedic philosophy, 120
vibhakti, 147
vidyā, 161-164, 169, 172.
see also sad-vidyā;
śuddha-vidyā
different uses of term, 162
vidyā-kañcuka, 162
vidyā plane, 158, 162, 171
vidyā-śakti, 163-164. *see also vidyā*
vidyā stage. *see vidyā* plane
vidyeśvaras, liv, lvi, 163, 178-179, 188
vijñānākala, lv, lvii, 175-177, 187, 188
Vijñāna, 15, 40-41
Vijñāna-kevalin, 177.
see also Vijñānākala
Vijñānavāda, xxiv, xxv, xxix, xxxi, xxxix-xliv, xl, 152, 183
masters of.
see Dharmakīrti;
Dharmottara
refutation of views by IPK, 27-36, 54-55, 106
views of
on *Ātman,* xxxix-xl, 13-26
on cause and effect, 24
on consciousness as momentary, 15

Vijñānavāda,
views of *(cont'd)*
on doer, 25-26
on knowledge, 14, 19-20, 31
on *kriyā,* 22-23, 105
on memory, 17-19, 29-32
on mind, 16
on momentariness, 40
on relation, 24-26
on Sāṃkhya, 20-21
vikalpa, 14-15, 71-72, 73, 75-76, 188
vikalpātmā, 15
Vimarśa, liii, 60, 156, 176
Vimarśinī. see Īśvara-pratyabhijñā-vimarśinī
Vira-śaivism, liii
Viṣṇu, lv, 6, 165, 171-172, 200
Vivaraṇa. see Parātrīśikā-vivaraṇa
Vivṛti on *Īśvara-pratyabhijnā* by Utpaladeva, xxxii, xxxiv, xxxviii
Vivṛti of Utpaladeva. *see Vivṛti* on *Īśvara-pratyabhijnā* by Utpaladeva
Vivṛti-vimarśinī of Abhinavagupta. *see Īśvara-pratyabhijñā-vivṛti-vimarśinī*
the void, xliv, 7, 111, 112, 150, 152, 166, 172-173, 178, 180, 181, 182, 183, 185. *see also śunya*
Vṛtti on *Śiva-dṛṣṭi* by *Utpaladeva,* xxx
Vyākaraṇa, xxv
vyāna, lvii, lviii, 187-188
vyāvahārika-satya, 116
waking state, 9, 166, 182, 184-186
will, xli, xliii, l, li, 140, 142-143, 150, 151
power of, 80, 113.
see also icchā-śakti
divine, xliii, l, li, 6, 55-56, 59, 65, 77, 80, 82, 99, 111, 129, 135, 136, 141, 142, 150, 152, 177, 185, 198
Yoga-bhāṣya, 61
Yoga Sūtras of Patañjali, 31, 205
yogin, xxv, xxvii, xlviii, lii, liv, 43-44, 55-56, 97, 106, 141-143, 152, 163, 164, 168, 181, 187, 188, 200, 201, 204, 206

Muktabodha Indological Research Institute

The Muktabodha Indological Research Institute is a public charitable trust established in India and dedicated to the study, preservation, and dissemination of India's scriptural wisdom. It was founded under the inspiration of Gurumayi Chidvilasananda, the spiritual head of Siddha Yoga meditation.

The Institute recognises and honours the diverse scholarly perspectives that contribute to our understanding of South Asian texts. In addition to fostering its vision through publishing, the Institute supports a variety of archival, research, and educational projects and serves as an academic resource assisting students and scholars in their study of India's many religious and philosophical traditions.

The Muktabodha Indological Research Institute is also incorporated in the U.S.A. as a not-for-profit educational organisation.

www.muktabodha.org